INV

LEADERSHIP

INVITATION-BASED CHANGE™
IN THE NEW WORLD OF WORK

Daniel Mezick
Mark Sheffield

Inviting Leadership: Invitation-Based Change™ in the New World of Work

Ordering: Available from Amazon.com and other online stores

Quantity sales: Special discounts are available on quantity purchases by corporations, associations, and others. For details, contact the "Special Sales Department" at www.invitingleadership.com/contact.

For errata see www.invitingleadership.com/book/errata.

Inviting Leadership: Invitation-Based Change™ in the New World of Work / Daniel Mezick, Mark Sheffield.

ISBN (978-0-9848753-5-1) (print)
ISBN (978-0-9848753-6-8) (Kindle)

1.01

To Roberta:
For encouraging, and for helping,
and for making this book possible.

To Gail:
For your constant love, respect, support, and encouragement.

"Transformations can't be accomplished without others helping voluntarily, and people don't help unless you engage them first."
– Geoffrey Moore, author, Zone to Win

"Transformations occur through choice, not mandate. Invitation is the call to create an alternative future."
– Peter Block, author, Community: The Structure of Belonging

—

Contents

This book is organized into nine major sections:

1. Authority
2. Boundary
3. Invitation
4. Self-Management
5. Leadership
6. Leadership Invitations
7. Toolkit
8. Guidance
9. Appendices

PART I - ESSENTIAL CONCEPTS

Chapter 1 – Authority   45

Here we introduce the key aspects of authority and authorization that are essential to Inviting Leadership. We also discuss and explore Decision-making authority.

Effective boundary design, boundary implementation and boundary management are absolutely essential aspects of the Inviting Leadership style.

Inviting and delegating have several important differences and some similarities. In this chapter we explore invitation in depth and introduce the 4-part invitation structure.

PART II - ADVANCED CONCEPTS
Chapter 4 – Self-Management   133

Self-managed teams are high-performing
teams. For a team to be self-managed they

must be making enough decisions to keep
them engaged in the process.

Chapter 5 – Leadership   149

The act of leading always involves being
party to decisions that affect the whole
group. Leadership invitations are a primary
way to sense and decisively respond quickly
to challenges and opportunities.

PART III- APPLICATION
Chapter 6 – Leadership Invitations 197

This chapter provides a template for applying the Inviting Leadership approach to organizational change. We also introduce and explore the essential subjects of leadership signaling and leadership storytelling.

Inviting Leadership is about the design of
experiences that engage and enlist the entire
workforce. In this chapter we offer tools
for architecting and implementing your
experience designs.

Organizational change occurs in context. This
context often includes common patterns. In
this chapter we list some of these patterns
and offer guidance on how to address them
with the Inviting Leadership approach.

APPENDICES

Appendix A – "Ready for Agile" Checklist   265

Figures

Tables

Stories

Foreword by Mike Burrows

Daniel, Mark, and I are colleagues in an informal network that spans a diverse "community-of-communities." It is devoted to improving the way that organizations adopt Agile and continue their journey with it. It's an area of real need, which means that it's also an area ripe for innovation. So it's entirely unsurprising that these communities have developed a range of approaches that, on the surface at least, seem quite different.

Happily, not only do these communities inform each other's work and spur each other on, but we are seeing a convergence in how their respective approaches are understood and explained.

We're finding that we agree on many things, and on these perhaps most of all:

1. *Invitation beats imposition*: When people are invited, those that choose to respond come ready to help and find ways to address their organization's challenges

2. *Why beats how*: With clear agreement on needs and outcomes, the opportunity to discover acceptable and effective solutions remains open; to start by advocating a solution means that this vital opportunity is lost

3. *Leadership is needed at every level*: Until people decide that things can and should be better and then go on to do something about it, nothing really changes

Through this book, Daniel and Mark make a new innovation: bringing "invitation" and "leadership" so close together that exciting things happen. They delve deep into what these concepts mean, both separately and (most of all) together. If you're a leader yourself – of any kind, at any level – you will find the implications of this book surprisingly far-reaching, and surprisingly relevant to the 21st century workplace.

I'm reminded of a book of 40 years ago, Robert K. Greenleaf's *Servant Leadership*. With remarkable prescience, Greenleaf anticipated some of the societal shifts that would change the relationship between organisations and their workers, and between leaders and those they would lead.

Today's organizations can't afford to be led like it's 1978, and their leaders would do very well to read this book.

Mike Burrows
November 2, 2018
Chesterfield, England

Founder, Agendashift (agendashift.com)
Author, Agendashift: Outcome-oriented change and continuous transformation (2018, New Century Press, agendashift.com/book) and Kanban from the Inside (2014, Blue Hole Press, agendashift.com/kfti)

Foreword by Doug Kirkpatrick

Daniel Mezick is a force of nature, an imposingly tall and striking figure with strong opinions that just happen to be fully supported by decades of experience and research. I met Daniel in 2012 at a self-management symposium, where we became friends and occasional collaborators. A master of the art of invitation, he invited me to speak at a pair of Agile events that year in Boston and Philadelphia while riding in a sort of "future of work" party bus between the two venues. We periodically crossed paths over the years, often in conjunction with sudsy beverages, talking about how to create better workplaces. I wrote a review of his first book, "The Culture Game: Tools for the Agile Manager," and incorporate its themes into my own consulting work. I know Mark Sheffield by his sterling reputation, as the co-author (with Daniel Mezick, Deborah Pontes, Harold Shinsato, and Louise Kold-Taylor) of "The OpenSpace Agility Handbook," a highly-rated guide for successful Agile adoptions and a valiant forerunner to this volume.

Technology matters greatly as a source of innovation—as the authors note, your competition is only one click away. Technological change is accelerating, and is often disorienting: blockchain, artificial intelligence, virtual reality, nanotechnology, robotics, genetic engineering, 4D printing and many more are forcing leaders and the organizations they lead to react at a dizzying pace. The Millennials, and Generations Y and Z, are in no mood for traditional slow-moving career escalators. Bureaucracy is exacting a financial and moral toll on organizations and the people who work inside them. The organizational status quo (or as the authors might say, the liminality between present and future of work) seems almost unsustainable. Daniel and Mark write that: "Regardless of what business your company is in, if it does not have a strategy for keeping pace with ongoing changes in technology, then competing in the markets you serve becomes more and more difficult and may ultimately lead to a crisis: an urgent need to radically change." Would anyone disagree?

Leaping into this chaotic vortex, Daniel and Mark display an exquisite sense of timing. Their new book "Inviting Leadership: Invitation-Based Change™ in the New World of Work" is a splendidly accessible work that emphatically turns the traditional view of organizational change on its head at a pivotal moment in history. In the authors' ideal world, leaders would never invoke their formal position power to impose a risky, top-down organizational transformation. Instead, leveraging the power of involvement, they would *invite* employees to discuss change initiatives and give them the choice of opting into the conversation or not. Such a simple paradigm shift, yet one with enormous potential consequences, facilitates employee engagement (and ultimately, success). As the authors note, the freedom to choose demonstrably doubles the chances that a person will agree to a request.

Since brittle, weak Command-and-Control (or C2) is a proven loser when it comes to engaging people in change initiatives, how do the authors propose to transcend its flawed logic? By shifting power to the invitee, who is free to respond to an invitation in a manner of his or her choosing. The authors note an additional benefit: if someone accepts an invitation, it's a pretty sure bet they're deeply engaged in the subject matter at hand—a good place to start. Daniel and Mark call this the shift from Command-and-Control (C2) to Invitation-Based Change (IBC) (and its enabler, Inviting Leadership). The anxiety-provoking rumblings in the background are from the unstable tectonic plates of rapidly shifting paradigms.

Daniel and Mark pack an enormous amount of actionable content into a few hundred pages. I learned a lot of useful stuff that I can put into practice for interested clients right away. The tables, diagrams, definitions and appendices alone are worth the price of admission. The authors have a canny knack for zooming out into space for a panoramic view of the territory and then zeroing in on targets for comparative analysis. I was happy to see an old friend, John Boyd's OODA loop (one of my favorite models) play well with the Agile Manifesto. It's all about being empirical and iterative, as the authors conclusively demonstrate time and time again.

Daniel and Mark extensively explore multiple polarities: self-management vs. self-organization, invitation vs. delegation, power vs. authority, leadership vs. management, engagement vs. disengagement, formal vs. informal, Sense-and-Respond vs. Command-and-Control. Engagement and Engagement Models are big deals, of the make-or-break variety—and decisive for effectively Inviting Leadership. Kudos to the authors for adroitly weaving the crucial threads of decision-making, people, boundaries, culture, constraints, signaling, storytelling, Agile, Scrum, leadership and self-management into a durable tapestry of supremely valuable application. Their decades of hard-won experience shines in the quality of every thread and the elegance of the whole.

For leaders with any interest in organizational change, this book is Inviting Leadership of the most sustainable kind. Bring on the stigmergy!

Doug Kirkpatrick, November, 2018

Preface

This book is the third in a progression of management books on teamwork, leadership and organizational change, dating back to 2012. Understanding the progression can help you get the most of this book, and help to frame for you the context in which this book was written.

The Culture Game book was published in 2012. That book described 16 patterns of team behavior that can help make your team smarter, and much more adaptive. The content from that book was gleaned from several years of management consulting, which included coaching corporate software teams in the fundamentals of "Agile software development." The 16 patterns in *The Culture Game* are patterns of group and team learning behavior. Chapter 21, entitled "Open The Space," explained the value of an open meeting format called Open Space Technology. The use of this meeting format inside some of our client companies proved to be very effective in creating the fertile conditions that are essential for real and lasting enterprise-wide improvement.

After publishing *The Culture Game* we began experimenting with using Open Space in a very specific and very iterative way, at the enterprise level, to facilitate genuine and lasting culture change. By using invitation, iteration, and the frequent feedback generated by the Open Space events at the enterprise level, we were able to achieve impressive results with our clients during this period. Our clients during this interval included Intuit, Capital One bank and the American Society of Composers, Authors and Publishers (ASCAP.com).

During this time of experimentation, we were creating enterprise-wide Open Space events, sponsored, and authorized by the executive leaders. Getting this done effectively required that we coach the leaders on the concept of invitation, and how it supports higher levels of employee engagement and overall

xxxii   Inviting Leadership

Key Performance Indicator (KPI) improvement. Preceding an enterprise-wide Open Space event, the executives broadly circulate an invitation well in advance of the meeting date. It also included the ability for invitees to decline the meeting or "opt out" without any negative consequences whatsoever.

This work led to publishing *The OpenSpace Agility Handbook* in 2015. That book elaborated Chapter 21 of *The Culture Game* book, entitled "Open The Space," in much greater detail. *The OpenSpace Agility Handbook* defined and described what we call an Engagement Model. An Engagement Model provides a foundational basis for your Engagement Plan. Gallup[1] and other organizations have clearly established the causal link between higher levels of employee engagement and higher levels of business performance.

As we gained experience with the OpenSpace Agility Engagement Model, we began to notice how the invitation, with its "opt-in / opt-out" feature, was a big reason for the many successes we were having. We noticed how opt-in participation was substantially raising the levels of employee engagement as people decided independently for themselves whether and how to participate, and how engagement was absolutely essential to any genuine and lasting change. We also noticed that executives who integrated these invitation concepts into their wider leadership practice were getting *great* results – with or without the use of Open Space meetings. We observed substantially higher levels of self-management in the groups that were led by these types of leaders. These leaders knew how to present an attractive story about the future, and knew how to invite their people into participation, in helping to shape that future.

As a result of these experiences and insights we gleaned from working with leaders in client companies, the more we began to realize that what we were doing was significant – and that the

---

[1]   See www.invitingleadership.com/book/links/#gallup for detailed data on the relationship between higher levels of employee engagement and improved business outcomes.

subject was in fact a book in itself. Invitation and delegation are important, and differ in several important ways. These and other essential topics are covered in detail in this book.

For leaders, the effective use of invitation also requires some know-how with respect to leadership storytelling, boundary management, authority, and authorization. We have included substantial tutorials on these topics in Part 1, so you are well prepared to begin confidently using invitation in your own leadership work.

Daniel Mezick
Guilford, CT
USA
www.invitingleadership.com/book/links/#daniel-mezick

Mark Sheffield
High Point, NC
USA
www.invitingleadership.com/book/links/#mark-sheffield

December, 2018

Acknowledgments

Reviewers

We express our gratitude to these amazing people who accepted our invitation to review the manuscript and help get it ready for publication. This book would not be what it is without their participation: Michelle Holliday, Doug Marteinson, Salah Elliethy, Deb Pontes, Jon Jorgensen, Marai Kiele, Kert Peterson, Nicole Coyle, Todd Kromann, Diana Williams, Joe DeAngelis, Greg Wright, Niels Pflaeging, Miriam Sasse, Stacia Heimgartner, Deirdre Gruendler, Janet Sheffield, Caitlin Walker, Andrea Chiou, Astrid Claessen, Harold Shinsato, and Yannick Grenzinger.

Others

We also thank some equally amazing people who have contributed in other ways.

Mike Burrows and Darren Terrell, for encouraging employee engagement in organizations and for encouraging Inviting Leaders worldwide.

Bob Galen, for inviting us into conference events, and actively promoting the Inviting Leadership ideas inside the Agile industry.

Doug Kirkpatrick, for his pioneering work with the Self Management Institute and his pioneering books and writings on the topic of self-management.

Michael Sahota, for being first with "Leaders Go First."[1]

Our wives, Roberta Mezick and Gail Sheffield, for allowing the book to happen.

---

[1] For more information about Michael Sahota being first with "Leaders Go First," and how important this is, see
www.invitingleadership.com/book/links/#agile.

Authorizing Contributors

These three authors graciously granted permission for us to include their essays in the Appendices. We are grateful for their willingness to do so.

Zachary Gabriel Green and René J Molenkamp - *"The BART System of Group and Organizational Analysis: Boundary, Authority, Role and Task"*

Jo Freeman - *"The Tyranny of Structurelessness"*

Harrison Owen - *"A Brief User's Guide to Open Space Technology"*

Influences

Every author is influenced by thinkers and writers who have previously shared their ideas with the world. These are the key people who have strongly influenced our thinking and the content of this book.

Zachary Gabriel Green and René J. Molenkamp

Zachary Gabriel Green and René J Molenkamp are influential members of the Group Relations community, which conducts experiential conferences for exploring leadership and authority in the here-and-now. Our experience studying Group Relations and attending the conference events continues to be a major influence in our own thinking and work. Group Relations work has the potential to transform your leadership practice and your own practice of the Inviting Leadership methods.

Link: www.invitingleadership.com/book/links/#green-molenkamp

Ed Seykota

Ed Seykota is a highly accomplished and world famous commodities trader who pioneered quantitative trading in the 1960s. He later began publishing his ideas on personal and group psychology around 2003. A lot of this writing made reference to something called "the willingness test," a component of what he called the "Intimacy-centric" model. He often contrasted this model with what he called "the Control-centric model." What he was actually writing about was invitation, although we did not make that connection at the time. We are grateful for the pioneering work of Ed Seykota in the domains of individual and group psychology.

Link: www.invitingleadership.com/book/links/#ed-seykota

Harrison Owen

Harrison discovered and formulated Open Space, a scalable design for inspired events. This is an invitational meeting design; no one who attends an Open Space event is compelled to do so. Through our direct experience with these events, we have come to appreciate the power of invitation. To Harrison, we are grateful. Harrison is the author of 8 or more books, depending on how you count. Some of his many titles are listed in the Bibliography.

Link: www.invitingleadership.com/book/links/#harrison-owen

Michael Herman

Michael Herman is a management consultant, Open Space facilitator, and writer. His work and writing on invitation dating back to the 1990s was pioneering, and served to help define the domain as it applies to leadership and group process. His writing on these subjects greatly influenced our thinking on leadership invitations, and continues to do so.

Link: www.invitingleadership.com/book/links/#michael-herman

Mark McKergow and Helen Bailey

Mark McKergow and his co-author Helen Bailey wrote the book *Host* in 2014. This amazing book is required reading for those leaders who are pivoting away from delegations and towards invitations. This book successfully decomposes the inviting style of leadership into 6 roles and 4 positions. The concepts in this book have influenced our own thinking and it continues to do so.

Link: www.invitingleadership.com/book/links/#mckergow-bailey

Mark Burgess

Mark Burgess is the formulator of Promise Theory and the author of the book *Thinking in Promises*. He is a data scientist and theoretical physicist who worked for a time as a professor at the Oslo University College of Norway. Promise theory was introduced as a model of voluntary co-operation between agents in 2004. The theory holds that only the agent responsible for delivering on a promise can commit to that promise and that further, no external entity can force or otherwise compel any other agent to make a promise or commit to one. The central premises of Promise Theory continue to influence our thinking.

Link: www.invitingleadership.com/book/links/#mark-burgess

Michele McCarthy and Jim McCarthy

Michele and Jim McCarthy worked at Microsoft in the 1990's and were responsible for leading the C++ programming language team. After their work at Microsoft they began doing applied research on teams and teamwork. Their work on voluntary participation and consent-based decision-making continue to have a substantial influence on our thinking.

Link: www.invitingleadership.com/book/links/#the-mccarthys

Introduction

You're probably an organizational leader of some kind if you are investigating this book. And you are leading in a period of unprecedented change. The changes facing you and your company represent a need for a fundamental shift in leadership style. There is a shift required of you and your company. You must now be more flexible, more adaptable, and more innovative.

Just to keep pace.

Understanding the art and science of genuine invitation may be the most important and valuable business leadership skill of the 21st century. Here is why: invitations from leaders create the fertile conditions for higher levels of employee engagement and employee morale. It is this greater level of "employee energy" and employee awareness that makes your enterprise more competitive, and better equipped to effectively respond to all kinds of change.

Changes that affect businesses are growing and accelerating like never before. To be effective in this new world, businesses must continuously "sense and respond."

And gaining that capability, in a genuine and lasting way, for the organization you help lead, is what this book is all about.

Why Read This Book

Your competition is now just one click away.

Societal trends are now largely driven by software technology. And technology moves fast. Regardless of what business your company is in, if it does not have a strategy for keeping pace with ongoing changes in technology, then competing in the markets you serve becomes more and more difficult and may ultimately lead to a crisis: an urgent need to radically change.

This is the reality of business today. Technology matters. What we call I.T. used to be considered a "cost center," a kind of tactical expense to be *minimized*. But the companies that are winning in this new game realize that I.T. has the potential to be a center of *innovation*, a big part of *strategy*: a capacity to be *maximized*.

Agile and Digital Transformation

So-called "Agile transformation" and "digital transformation" are actually responses to the need to better respond to the business impact of technology. "Agile transformation" is about implementing radically more efficient ways of producing software. This includes software for sale to customers and software to support ongoing business operations. "Digital transformation" is about integrating digital technology into *every aspect of the business,* in service to better business outcomes.

Your competition is now just one click away. That is the reason you want to be reading this book.

Pivoting as a Leader - from Commanding toward Inviting

The traditional way of managing—through the exercise of formal authority—simply cannot keep pace. Indeed, it is only when individuals and teams are deeply engaged and self-managing that the entire enterprise can sense and respond to change in a timely, efficient, and effective fashion. Business opportunities are now more frequent and of shorter duration. Addressing these opportunities requires real agility. Self-management helps everyone to pay attention to and manage change. It is self-management that creates a more engaged and therefore responsive organization.

And it is invitations from leaders that create the conditions for self-management.

The Start of Something New

We are witnessing the end of one era of business management and the beginning of another. At the center of this transition are the core concepts of Invitation-Based Change™ (IBC) and Inviting Leadership. IBC enables a higher level of enterprise performance by engaging the entire workforce. Inviting Leadership enables and supports IBC. Both require formally authorized leaders to deeply understand the concepts and facilities of invitation, informed consent, and opt-in participation.

Make no mistake—some incumbent authority figures in many organizations will be losers in this epic transition from Command and Control (C2) to Invitation-Based Change (IBC). The good news is that those who study, understand and then implement IBC and support it with Inviting Leadership are sure to prosper and thrive in this new world.

And so; let this book serve as your tutorial and reference guide, as you pivot into the exciting world of Inviting Leadership and IBC.

The Core Principles of Inviting Leadership

These principles inform the policies and practices of the Inviting Leadership approach:

Feedback Is Essential: Gathering and responding to continuous feedback is essential to leading effectively

Leaders are Designers: Leadership has a very substantial design aspect, including the design and definition of clear goals, clear rules, and very clear ways for the workforce to measure and experience progress.

Invitation Is An Ask: Invitation triggers decision-making and substantial employee engagement. Invitation is often superior to delegation, especially during periods of change.

Engagement Wins: A focus on engaging the workforce results in positive business outcomes.

Systems Are Complex: Business enterprises are complex adaptive systems that respond dynamically to change.

Each chapter develops each of these principles in much more detail.

Who Should Read This Book

Readers in the following roles will benefit most from examining this book:

- **Formally Authorized Leaders:** Those who get their authority from the organization's formal hierarchy. This includes company leaders, CEOs, CFOs, CIOs and others with a "C" in their title. Also included in this group is anyone who is a mid-level executive, such as a Director or Manager.

- **Informally Authorized Leaders:** Those who get their authority from peers, co-workers and others with whom they work. Such leaders may or may not have a big title, a big salary, or lots of people reporting to them.
- **Internal Facilitators, Scrum Masters, and Team Leads:** Employees in organizations who serve teams by facilitating meetings, designing meetings, and delivering organizational-change initiatives such as the adoption of Agile software development.
- **Executive Coaches, Management Consultants and Agile Coaches:** Those who serve organizations by providing guidance, teaching and mentoring in pursuit of continuous improvement.

How to Read This Book

This book is best if you first completely examine Part 1. It is a kind of tutorial on the essentials. Later chapters build on that essential foundation.

This book is a comprehensive tutorial and reference guide on what we call Inviting Leadership and Invitation-Based Change™. It introduces invitation as a leadership art, explains how this style of leadership operates, and provides tools and resources for your learning journey.

We introduce over 40 new terms in this book. Most of these terms are introduced in in Part 1. As we introduce new concepts, we employ the language previously introduced. Because Part 1 introduces much of this language, we advise that you completely digest that part first.

We hope you find this book valuable, immediately useful and fun.

We hope you enjoy reading it.

PART I - ESSENTIAL CONCEPTS

Chapter 1 – Authority

Here we introduce the key aspects of authority and authorization that are essential to Inviting Leadership. We also discuss and explore Decision-making authority.

Chapter 2 – Boundary

Effective boundary design, boundary implementation and boundary management are absolutely essential aspects of the Inviting Leadership style.

Chapter 3 – Invitation

Inviting and delegating have several important differences and some similarities. In this chapter we explore invitation in depth and introduce the 4-part invitation structure.

Chapter 1 – Authority

Here we introduce the key aspects of authority and authorization that are essential to Inviting Leadership. We also discuss and explore Decision-making authority.

Overview

Accelerating advances in technology are forcing all business organizations to adapt to the new world of work. Effective leadership is essential. Your success as a leader depends heavily on how well you understand and exercise your authority.

Most people are keenly sensitive to and vaguely aware of authority and authority dynamics. We all use terms like "top-down," "bottom-up," and "higher-ups" in organizations while discussing people, procedures, decisions, and the exercise of authority We also use ambiguous terms like "empowerment" to describe authorization, and "structure" to describe how authority is distributed. And so on. But what do these terms really mean?

Many colleges and universities offer degree programs in Leadership Studies, yet the essential topics of authorization and authority are not taught as a distinct domain discipline.

Leadership is all about acquiring and then exercising authority effectively. To be successful, leaders need more than basic knowledge of authorization, authority, and authority distribution. We need a deeper understanding based on more precise language.

This book introduces the emerging discipline of Authority Studies. In this chapter we introduce precise terms and provide explicit definitions as we address the mechanics of authority and leadership in organizations. We begin deconstructing the mechanics of authority and authorization by defining leadership, authority, and authorization.

Leadership

Leadership has many dimensions including guiding, directing, being charismatic, and acquiring followers. In this book we focus on the most fundamental dimension – the work of making decisions. A well-led group understands how decisions are made, especially decisions that affect the group. When a group has trouble making decisions or does not understand how those decisions are made, that usually indicates trouble with the leadership function.

> **leadership** *n.*
> 1. Direct participation in making any decision that affects all of the members of a group.
> 2. An individual or set of individuals who participate directly in making any decision that affects all of the members of a group.
> 3. Exercising authority with respect to making decisions that affect all of the members of a group.

Decision-Making That Affects the Whole Group

The most important kind of authorized work is the work of making decisions that affect the whole group. This kind of work has the potential for creating productivity or problems. For now, recognize that "deciding for the group" is the most important work that is done inside any team, department, division, or enterprise. In nation-states, national and regional elections are hotly contested for this very reason. Who decides and how they find themselves in these roles is a major theme of this chapter.

Authority

authority *n.*
> 1. The right or permission to do a specific kind of work.
> 2. Status within a social system that confers one's right to do work. See also: power, right to do work.

This work typically includes decision-making that affects other people in the group or organization. Authority always comes from something or someone. The "something" might be the Board of

Directors. The "someone" might be the CEO, the CFO, or another person in a high-ranking role defined by the organization.

Authorization is the process of sending and receiving "specific (decision-making) rights." For leadership to be effective, it must first be authorized. Authorization manifests in two basic forms: the *formal* and the *informal.*

"Structure"

People commonly use the word "structure" to refer to the way authority is distributed within a group. In other words, it is the group's authority distribution schema.

> **authority distribution schema** *n.*
> The map of authority and authorization relationships in a social system. Dimensions include formal/ informal and networked/hierarchical.

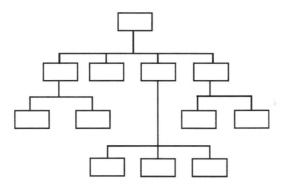

Figure 1.1: Organizational Chart

In most groups authority is distributed formally and informally. Formal authority is mapped by an organizational chart similar to the one shown in Figure 1.1. There is another, mostly undocumented web of friendships and relationships that influence decision-making. People tend to call this informal, less-obvious web the "politics" of the group. The formal authority distribution schema (organizational chart) tends to be public. The informal one does not.

Formal authority is managed from the top and flows downward. The distribution schema is rigid and fixed ... at least until the next formal reorganization.

Informal authority is self-managed. It originates from many sources. It is always moving as it dynamically responds to change.

Authority Information Is Key

In the book *Systems Thinking*,[1] Jamshid Gharajedaghi, describes social systems as being "information bonded." What specific information is the actual bonding agent?

The information about how authority is distributed provides the structure, and bonds the group together Without the information about authority, it is nearly impossible to function well as a member of a social system such as a team, a department, a division, or an enterprise.

That is one of the central premises of this book: understanding authority and having a language to describe authority dynamics, is essential to understanding and exercising leadership.

Inviting Leadership is a method and style of leadership that incorporates this knowledge and adds invitation as a powerful leadership technique.

Orientation to Authority

The worldwide Group Relations community of practice is dedicated to studying leadership and authority in groups.[2] They suggest that each person has a basic tendency or "valence" about responding to authority. It is an innate and natural part of your personality.

There are three types of authority valence:

Authority Seeking: Often characterized as "Type A" personalities, Seekers want to be in

---

[1] For more about Systems Thinking, see
www.invitingleadership.com/book/links/#systems-thinking-book.

[2] The Group Relations community offers conferences annually throughout the world. For more about the community, see
www.invitingleadership.com/book/links/#group-relations.

charge. Often these people contend with others to gain the right to make decisions that affect the group.

Authority Helping: The Helpers want to assist and support the people who are in charge. They are very good at identifying who has authority, and then doing their best to help that leader succeed.

Authority Opposing: Some people resist whenever someone else makes a decision. Opposers resist authority even when they agree with the decisions. They just don't like to be told what to do. They do not seek to lead and they do not seek to help those who are leading.

Now we can dive into the concepts of authority and authorization and explore a new set of terms and words that support deeper discussion of both.

Responsibility and Authority

Responsibility is being committed to deliver on an event or an outcome. Authority is the right to do work. If you are properly authorized, you have permission to make decisions as needed to complete the task. You have permission to access any resources (space to meet, enough time, and so on) needed to execute on your responsibility.

Formal Authority Distribution

The chart in Figure 1.1 shows an organizational hierarchy. The roles near the top have the most authority; those near the bottom of the diagram have the least.

Hierarchy is always present in one form or another whenever people gather. Hierarchy is always present in some form in work groups, because authority distribution is necessary for a social system to function.[3] The organizational chart shows the roles that are formally authorized such as CEO, CFO, COO, and so on down the line to SVPs, VP, Directors and Managers. It is commonly said that hierarchy causes many problems in organizations. In reality it is the flow of information and ambiguous decision-making rights through formal and informal structures that cause problems in organizations. It could be that formally authorized leaders not taking the informal structure into account is the core of the issue. Inviting Leadership gives the necessary tools to not only leverage the informal structure but to exploit it for the betterment of the organization.

The org-chart shows the *formal* authority distribution schema. It depicts how formal authority flows through a "chain of command."

The formal schema always has a counterpart, the informal authority distribution schema.

Everybody knows that the organizational chart does not really depict how work gets done. For work to get done, people have to figure out how to work together and informally support each other. They seek guidance from some people and not from others. They work together well or they don't. They follow one another's lead or they don't. People in some organizations refer to the informal network with a derogatory term like "shadow organization" or "shadow hierarchy."[4] Whatever it is called, the informal authority system is always present. It is the way work actually gets done because the informal system can respond to change much faster than the formal system can. It includes and excludes people quickly and dynamically, without any need to coordinate with HR or ask any kind of permission from anyone. The informal authority distribution system just IS.

---

[3] For more about hierarchy in social systems, see Appendix C or
www.invitingleadership.com/book/links/#the-tyranny-of-structurelessness.

[4] Informal authority systems are healthy manifestations of self-organization in action. When the formal system is functioning well, the overlap between the formal and informal systems is nearly 100%.

Characteristics of Informal Authority Networks

To understand the informal system, you have to work as a member of the organization for a while or have someone pass their tacit knowledge to you.[5] The currency of the informal system is respect, credibility and reputation. We sometimes call it "street credibility."

The informal system of authority distribution is how people normally operate. We naturally find people we want to associate with and we associate with them if they are willing. We demonstrate respect and deference towards people we prefer to work with and to follow. We often authorize these people to lead us and to lead the group as a whole. We may encourage them to offer proposals and guidance, to make suggestions, and to make decisions for the group

What is really going on is that we informally authorize specific people to be *leaders*. Problems that arise are dealt with quickly. For example, if someone suddenly acts like a "control freak" they may suddenly lose or be unable to get the level of informal authority they need to make decisions for the group. They are no longer being authorized by the group, regardless of what anybody else says or does.

Alternatively, a person might not be seeking a leadership role and find that others respect their judgment and are encouraging them to offer guidance and make decisions. This is the informal system at play. It is powered by opt-in participation and "human agency" as people decide independently for themselves whether and how to participate. The authority comes from the affected individuals, not from the formal organization.

Some people neither seek informal authority nor receive it from the group. They are part of the informal network too. Everyone in the organization participates in the informal network, either actively or inactively.

Because the self-managed, self-organizing, reputation-based system of authority distribution adjusts and adapts so quickly, it is well-suited

---

[5] For more about tacit knowledge, see
www.invitingleadership.com/book/links/#knowledge.

for very complex, high-change scenarios where frequent pivots are necessary for survival. In the world we live in today, the overall pace of business and societal change is rapidly accelerating. This reality is putting pressure on organizations to find ways to respond quickly. Why not leverage the power of informal authority distribution?

Meeting formats such as Open Space Technology[6] do this quite naturally, by helping create the conditions for self-organization and for taking responsibility for one's own behavior. These formats also provide a lightweight structure of essential rules and boundaries to make sure that the explicitly stated goals for the meeting are being met.

Legitimate and Illegitimate Authority

Authority is legitimate (or authentic) when those affected by the decisions actually support (or authorize) someone to participate in making decisions for the group.

Authority is illegitimate (or inauthentic) when the people affected by those decisions do not support (and therefore do not authorize) that person to make decisions for the group.

Recall that most important work in any group or organization is the work of making decisions that affect the group as a whole. This is the work of leadership. The formal system of authority distribution must heed and respond to the signaling from the informal system. If the explicit and formal system is not sensitive to the signals from the implicit and informal system, eventually the informal system of authority distribution will work to undermine the formal one. When the implicit and informal system makes decisions, we call that self-organization. We explore self-organization later in this chapter.

The Tyranny of Structurelessness

Without explicit rules, constraints, and boundaries, a completely informal schema of authority distribution will be ineffective and

---

[6] For more about Open Space Technology, see Appendix E or www.invitingleadership.com/book/links/#open-space-technology.

even dysfunctional. This can and will happen when rules are not easily accessible or are known only to a few people.

The feminist author Jo Freeman enumerates these problems brilliantly in her essay, *The Tyranny of Structurelessness.*[7] The essay provides a valuable lesson in how to balance the need to adapt by using self-management with the need to make sure everyone is playing by the same clear and formal "rules of the game."

She points out that every group has a structure regardless of whether that structure is described formally.

> *"Contrary to what we would like to believe, there is no such thing as a structureless group. Any group of people of whatever nature that comes together for any length of time for any purpose will inevitably structure itself in some fashion. The structure may be flexible; it may vary over time; it may evenly or unevenly distribute tasks, power and resources over the members of the group. But it will be formed regardless of the abilities, personalities, or intentions of the people involved.*

Power rests in the people who know the structure of how authority is distributed within the system.

> *"As long as the structure of the group is informal, the rules of how decisions are made are known only to a few and awareness of power is limited to those who know the rules. Those who do not know the rules and are not chosen for initiation must remain in confusion, or suffer from paranoid delusions that something is happening of which they are not quite aware.*

In the healthiest groups the formal authority distribution schema and the informal one overlap nearly 100%.

---

[7] For more information about The Tyranny of Structurelessness, see Appendix C or www.invitingleadership.com/book/links/#the-tyranny-of-structurelessness.

"For everyone to have the opportunity to be involved in a given group and to participate in its activities the structure must be explicit, not implicit."

A key focus of Inviting Leadership is designing and implementing explicit boundaries, rules and constraints that clearly define what is and is not being authorized. We explore boundaries in greater detail in Chapter 2.

Power – Exercising Authority

The dictionary definition of authority refers to power, and the dictionary definition of power refers to authority. Are they really the same thing?

No. Authority is the right to do something, while power is exercising that right.

power *n.*
> The exercise of authority.

For example, in America, citizens have the right to vote. The act of voting is the exercise of that right.

When you are a member of a group and are authorized to make decisions that affect that entire group, leading means demonstrating your power by making those decisions.

Personal Authority

personal authority *n.*
> The way a person in a formally authorized role takes
> up that role. See also: formal authorization.

Personal authority is how a person exercises the authority of that role.[8] In the workplace we like to believe that formal roles are well described by formal job descriptions. The problem is that these job

---

[8] For more information about personal authority, see "Appendix D – The BART System" or
www.invitingleadership.com/book/links/#BART.

descriptions get out of date and need periodic amending. In truth, most job descriptions are actually full of gaps. How far can I go when occupying this role? What are the limits of my authority around the authorized tasks? And so on. Your personal approach to the role comes into play. Personal authority informs your overall style of how you occupy that role.

Here is an example. A policeman pulls you over and then lets you go with a warning. That policeman makes a judgment call (a decision) about how to handle his formal role in a given situation. That's personal authority at play.

Here is another example. A policeman knocks on your door and tries to persuade you let him into your home, implying that you must, when he knows for a fact that he can't force you to let him in unless he has a search warrant (USA law.) He is overstepping his formal authority.

Under-stepping is another way of misusing personal authority. Under-stepping occurs by *not* exercising your full level of authority when the situation calls for it. This is a bigger and far less understood problem!

In the Scrum framework[9] for delivering products and services, the Product Owner plays the very important role of representing the needs of the stakeholders, including the organization as a whole and the people who use and benefit from what the Development Team produces. A good Product Owner understands those needs, balances them with what the Development Team can provide, and prioritizes the work to maximize the value of the work that is done. If the Product Owner only fills part of the role, the well-meaning Development Team may make decisions that lead them to do work that results in little or no value. Likewise, if executive leadership fails to exercise their authority well, unauthorized people may make uninformed decisions that harm the entire organization.

---

[9] The Scrum framework is described in *The Scrum Guide™ - The Definitive Guide to Scrum: The Rules of the Game.* For more information, see www.invitingleadership.com/book/links/#scrum.

When your sense of personal authority prevents you from fully occupying your formal role, serious dysfunction results. If you leave scraps of authority lying around, someone else will pick them up quickly and begin using them. When you cede or abandon authority in this way, others can and will take it up, and begin exercising it. What's actually happening is that authority is being exercised outside of the role that defines it. Not understanding the boundary of your formal role authority can cause serious problems in your organization.

Mapping Authority

Authority Maps™ provide a convenient way to depict visually how well an individual is exercising the formal authority of their role, based on the tasks authorized by the formal job description.

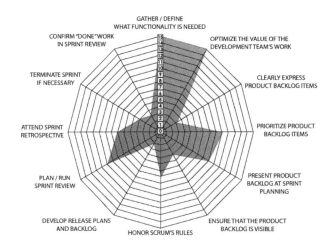

Figure 1.2: Authority Map of How Person A fills the Product Owner Role

Figure 1.2 shows an example of twelve authorized tasks of the Product Owner role. The colored portion represents how completely the individual is doing the work of the role. This work includes making decisions that affect the Development Team. The white part represents the portion of each task that is not being addressed. The Product Owner depicted in that diagram is only filling the "Gather / Define What Functionality is Needed" and "Optimize the Value of the Development Team's Work" tasks. The low coverage on all other tasks indicates an authority vacuum. People who are unauthorized and possibly incapable will begin making those decisions, to fill the gap. In addition to less valuable work being done as a result of poor decisions, team morale can be destroyed. As the ancient philosopher Aristotle observed, "nature abhors a vacuum."

In Figure 1.3: Authority Map of How Person B fills the Product Owner Role, the colored area almost covers the entire graph. For the most part, Product Owner B is fully executing on all of the authorized tasks associated with the role.

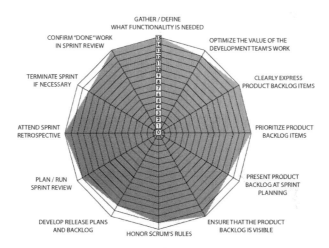

Figure 1.3: Authority Map of How Person B fills the Product Owner Role

Authority maps depict the degree to which an individual in a role is taking up authority to execute on specific tasks and decisions.

Authorization

authorization *n.*
The process of sending and receiving authority.

Authorization involves a sender and a receiver. The sender conveys or grants authority to the receiver. For example, when a team member acquires and demonstrates proficiency with a certain skill, her boss or leader might offer her a promotion. This is *formal authorization* from boss to employee. Or her teammates might ask her to make decisions for the team based on that skill. This is the sending of informal authority from the team to that individual. In this example, the manager and the teammates are acting as senders.

Figure 1.4: Authorization Always Involves a Send and a Receive

The authorization game also involves a receiver. Authority sent by a person in a formally authorized role is called a *delegation*. There is no opting out. When authority comes from peers, opting out is possible. It is up to the receiver to decide whether to accept the authority that is being sent. The receiver can either opt in and accept the authority or opt out and decline. In both cases, authorization is complete only when it has been sent and it has been received.

Being offered more authority can be very flattering, or the receiver may fear negative consequences for declining, so the receiver may feel compelled to accept unwanted authority. Receiving authority is one thing; consciously consenting to it is quite another.

Formal Authorization

formal authorization *n.*
Authorization that is conferred from the formal

organization to someone in a role defined and duly authorized by that organization.

We are all familiar with the situation where a person is being hired to serve in a top leadership position such as CEO. The organization determines the duties and responsibilities, and a suitable person is found to fill the role. The person who accepts the job offer has permission to do the work (the duties and responsibilities) described by the role. It involves an official role and a title. This is formal authorization. It applies to all levels in the organization. Authorization is sent by the official organization and received by the person who accepts the job offer and becomes a formally authorized leader.

Formal authorization requires a significant amount of effort and negotiation. For this reason, it usually takes a long time to enact and a long time to reverse. This tends to impede the speed at which the formal system can respond to change.

Self-Authorization

self-authorization *n.*
> The act of sending authority to yourself instead of receiving it from elsewhere.

"Ask forgiveness not permission" is a familiar saying that speaks to the concept of self-authorization. Self-authorization is the act of taking authority or doing something on one's own, without permission from anyone else.

Self-authorization may also arise from natural authority, the set of rights and permissions that one receives as a result of being in the world and interacting with it on one's own terms.

Self-authorization is not necessarily good or bad. The results from it can be either good or bad, depending on what happens. We regularly engage in self-authorization as we make our way through daily life.

Daniel tells a story that he calls Lot Full.

Lot Full

I was once driving in a car with a colleague to catch a train to New York City from New Haven, Connecticut. We were potentially late for this train. As I approached the train station, I immediately sought a parking space for our automobile. As I approached the parking garage, a large and imposing sign, in red letters, was displayed in front of the entrance: "LOT FULL."

I noticed however that this sign did not prevent me from pulling up next to the ticket machine. So I started to do that. "What the heck are you doing?" said my colleague. "I'm doing an experiment," I replied. "But the sign says LOT FULL," said my colleague. "Well, let's just see about that," I replied.

As we pulled around the sign and up to the big green button, I looked at my friend and said, "this is the moment of truth." I punched the big green button. It worked. The machine chattered, I grabbed the coupon, I tucked it under the driver-side visor, and proceeded to park the car. There were several spaces on the topmost level of the garage.

And so I chose to ignore the imaginary boundary created by the imposing "LOT FULL" sign. I self-authorized.

Informal Authorization

informal authorization *n.*

> Receiving authority from peers and colleagues rather than formally from the organization.

Informal authority is the "respect" or "street credibility" that you accumulated over time as a result of your explicit interactions and signaling with everyone in your organization, especially your team.

An enormous amount of work gets done by people who are not in any formally recognized role within the group. These folks seem indispensable to how the team or organization functions. How can that be?

Informal authorization occurs when the people around you become willing to allow you to do some specific work, like advising, explaining or even deciding for the group. It is based on your reputation, and your willingness to serve. It is offered to you. You can accept it or not. It can be sent very quickly, and it can be declined (or revoked) just as quickly.

In an ideal world, the officials – the formally authorized leaders – are the very people whom everyone respects, enjoys, and is willing to follow. The result is a group of highly engaged, productive, and innovative people. A formal leader's ineffectiveness in a role has the opposite effect. It is an impediment to the people doing the work. In that case, the informal authorization system will exert much more influence over how work actually gets done. The informal system will create informal workarounds to accomplish the work. This can result in all kinds of distortions and what is often referred to as organizational dysfunction.

Drafting or Nominating Someone Into a Role

If you are perceived as someone who gets things done, people may attempt to draft, nominate, or invite you to accept an informal leadership role. If you accept this invitation, you are consenting to it. You are opting-in.

Table 1.1: Steps involved in drafting or inviting someone to occupy an informal leadership role

Step	Things to Consider
1: Drafter (a team member) suggests that Draftee (also a team member) could lead. This suggestion may be public, or private.	The Draftee might prefer and appreciate being asked privately first. If the Draftee tends to seek authority and enjoys leadership, they may prefer a public approach.
2: The Draftee considers the offer and might observe how others are signaling that they like or dislike the idea.	If the Draftee does not seek leadership, they might decline. Otherwise they may accept, depending on what they observe in the group.
3: Draftee responds to the suggestion that they lead some aspect of the group's work	The Draftee may decline or accept. Declining or accepting the offer can be passive or active since the entire process is informal, ad hoc, and emergent. Suggestions to lead are often played out in front of other team members in face-to-face meetings and exchanges

When we "volunteer" others into roles without their explicit consent, without asking, we don't even acknowledge that our method of "encouraging" them to accept might feel imposing. Persuasion is a mild form of coercion and is in fact a kind of manipulation. When people feel that they have been manipulated, trust disappears, they disengage, and the entire team suffers.[10]

---

[10] For highly detailed applied research into the dynamics and mechanics of persuasion, see the work of B. J. Fogg of Stanford University at www.invitingleadership.com/book/links/#persuasion.

In high-functioning, self-managed, self-organizing teams, these offers tend to be made as genuine invitations. Inside these teams, manipulation attempts are rare, and cultural tolerance for coercion is typically very low or non-existent.

If you are a member of a group and you see something that needs doing, you might draft or nominate someone into a role to do that specific and important work. In effect you would support and sponsor them in that role. For example if you are on a software development team, the work is about databases, and you think Jonathan has that expertise and is qualified to lead, you might suggest to Jonathan and the group that he provide direction, make some key decisions, and lead the group's effort for some period of time. If Jonathan makes bad decisions or otherwise behaves in ways that offend the group, his informal authority can and will be revoked just as quickly.

Dynamic Authorization and De-authorization

By definition, self-organizing teams are informal authority systems. They routinely authorize one or more individuals to inform decisions, influence decisions, and make decisions as needed. As you think about this, you may notice these dynamics in your own working life, inside the teams and groups where you have membership. High-functioning teams exhibit extremely flexible and fluid authority-distribution behaviors.

When seen in this light, we can safely say that self-organization is actually the dynamic sending and receiving of authority, and supporting information related to it. This allocation of authority tends to be responsive, highly adaptable, ... and highly *efficient*. It is the informal authorization system. The formal authorization system (the one represented by the org chart) is no match in a test of adaptability with a self-organizing system. It's not even close.

The informal system of dynamic authority distribution changes moment by moment as needed to respond to conditions. The formal system does not do this, and might be up to 1000 times slower than the informal authorization system which is dynamically and continuously adjusting to changing conditions.

High-performing teams authorize and de-authorize their members to do specific kinds of work and make specific decisions depending on the current needs of the team. Authority moves around from one team member to another, sometimes with lightning speed, while the team members tend to be highly engaged and innovative.

Authority can be granted, and it can be rescinded. Hiring is a form of authorization. Firing is a form of de-authorization. Formal authorization takes much longer to send and much longer to receive. It is in your best interest as a formal leader to make the most of the leverage that the informal authorization system provides.

Responding to Change

Consider the situation where a person in a formal leadership role is not being effective. The formal process to remove them must comply with employment law and be followed carefully. This takes time. Lots of time. Compare that to what happens in the informal system of authority distribution, the "self organizing" system. If a person previously held in high esteem suddenly demonstrates a complete lack of judgment, the informal system can de-authorize (effectively "demote") them almost immediately.

The formal system simply cannot move this fast.

Leaders who want to increase their organization's capacity to sense and respond to change must first recognize the power of this informal system of authorization.

The informal system has several advantages:
- It is self-managing and therefore cheaper to operate
- It moves and adjusts to change very quickly
- It taps the collective intelligence of the group
- It rapidly identifies and authorizes effective leadership

In any organization, "who is authorized to do what" has both formal and informal dimensions. The work of making decisions that affect the whole group is the most important work that can be done in that group. The authorization to do this work originates formally from the organization and informally from those who are affected by these decisions.

The future of work is about better understanding and leveraging the "always-on" system of informal authority distribution. The differences between formal and informal authority are profound. These differences include:

- **Speed of authorization and de-authorization:** Formal authority takes time to send and receive. It also takes time to rescind. We are all familiar with the "progressive discipline" process of formally de-authorizing a person and potentially removing them from their role in the organization. On the other hand, informal authorization is very fluid and dynamic. It is several hundred times faster than the process of formal authorization. *This fact has profound implications on efficiency and productivity in your organizations.*

- **Acceptance by the group:** Since informal authorization originates with the group, there is agreement from the beginning that the person is the right one for the role. The group chooses the leaders they would like to follow.

Table 1.2: Formal vs Informal Authority Distribution

Leadership Attribute or Task:	With Formal Authorization	With Informal Authorization	Notes
Source of Authority	The business entity	Peers and colleagues	Great things can happen when the leader has both kinds of authority

Leadership Attribute or Task:	With Formal Authorization	With Informal Authorization	Notes
Delegating Tasks	Directive and non-negotiable	Requires discernment and willing individuals	Delegation applies to sending responsibility and/or authority
Inviting Participation	Optional	The way things typically get done	Informal leaders are invited to influence or make decisions that affect the group
Accountability	To formally authorized higher-ups in the organization	To peers and colleagues who authorized the informal leadership	
Leadership Style	Can be purely directive or "command and control"	Can never be purely "command and control"	
Relationship with co-workers	Based largely on position in formal hierarchy	Based largely on respect and reputation	

Leadership Attribute or Task:	With Formal Authorization	With Informal Authorization	Notes
Amount of time it takes to be removed from the leadership role	At least as long as it takes to comply with all employment and labor laws	Immediate	An informal leader can be de-authorized immediately
Capacity to respond to changing conditions	Largely constrained by bureaucracy	Constrained only by the willingness of leaders to lead and others to follow	Informal authority systems are much more responsive to change

Delegation and Invitation

delegation *v.*

> The formal assignment of responsibility and/or authority to someone in a lower-authority role.

Delegating is assigning. The sender expects the receiver to accept the assignment; there is seldom any opportunity to opt out. This means the receiver is under compulsion and must receive the delegation, regardless of what it is, what it includes, or how it is structured. A delegation is an order.

Organizations are under pressure to be more adaptive. One of the biggest problems facing organizations today is delegating responsibility without providing the authority needed to actually execute. This pattern is a signature aspect of low-engagement, low-performance cultures ... and of failed change initiatives.

Ideally, delegation includes responsibility for getting work done and the authority to access the essential supporting resources that are needed to achieve success. These resources can include access to a budget, physical space, the help of a wider supporting team, etc. The key point here is that where delegation is concerned, responsibility and authority are distinct. Both can be delegated individually, or together. The BART System in Appendix D provides an excellent backgrounder on this topic.[11]

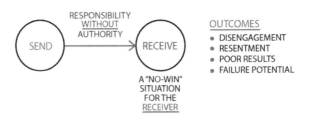

Figure 1.5: Malformed Delegation

Figure 1.5 shows a no-win situation where the receiver does not have the authority needed for executing the work. In this type of environment, you can expect disengagement, resentment, poor results, and possibly failure.

Figure 1.6: Well-Formed Delegation

In Figure 1.6 the delegation includes responsibility and authority. This well-formed delegation has a high potential for

---

[11] Chapter 3 also has a detailed comparison of delegation and invitation.

employee engagement and great results, a win-win situation for the sender and the receiver.

Invitation

Delegation is distinct from invitation in this way: with invitation, there is no compulsion. The receiver of the invitation is in charge of deciding whether to engage or not. The receiver decides whether to accept or decline the invitation. With invitation, the receiver can opt-out of any "responsibility without authority" situations. With delegation, they cannot.

Most organizational change initiatives are compulsory in nature. Everyone must participate, regardless of what they think. And as you might suspect, in these change initiatives there is usually delegation of responsibility without the authority needed to actually do the job.

Typical Scrum implementations offer a great example of this. Scrum is often implemented during digital and Agile transformation initiatives. In the Scrum framework, the person in the Product Owner role makes decisions about prioritizing the work.

The Scrum Guide says:

"For the Product Owner to be successful, everyone in the organization must respect his or her decisions."

Since it is seldom the case that everyone in the organization respects the decisions of the Product Owner, the person in that role cannot actually do the job. When the Product Owner has all of the responsibility and little if any of the decision-making authority needed to actually execute, Scrum cannot work.

The "responsibility without authority" pattern virtually guarantees failure. If this pattern is occurring in your "transformation" initiative, what is really happening is that the way decisions are being made is *not* changing, so nothing is actually being transformed at all.

Invitation prevents the "responsibility without authority" pattern from occurring. Why?

With invitation, the receiver is not compelled and will rationally avoid any "no-win" situations. Leadership invitation is often superior to leadership delegation, because the receiver will accept an invitation to be responsible "if and only if" the requisite authority is also part of the deal.

Think about this deeply as you consider the change initiative inside your own organization. Do you want to engage people, in service to better results through more self-management? If so, consider favoring invitation over delegation, because invitation forces more rigor on the sender, and sidesteps the risk of disengaging the receiver.

Authorizing Emergent Leadership

emergent leadership *n.*
> Informal authorization that arises as a person takes initiative and leads something they are passionate about. Informal authorization arises from colleagues, peers, and communities over time as the informal leader develops engagement, progress, accountability, and authorization within the organization.

Meeting formats such as Open Space[12] help to create the fertile conditions necessary for leaders to emerge. They get their authorization from those around them, who encourage them to lead by supporting what they say and do.

Here is what happens:

1. One or more persons attempt to draft someone into an informal leadership role
2. That specific person accepts the opportunity to lead by signaling acceptance with their behavior.[13]

---

[12] The Open Space meeting format is an essential aspect of Inviting Leadership and Invitation-Based Change™.

[13] Signaling, an essential leadership task, is covered in detail in Chapter 5 and at www.invitingleadership.com/book/links/#semiotics.

Those who are invited to occupy an informal leadership role may not actually want to take up or occupy that leadership role. If there is any kind of demand that they agree, then the person invited is not being invited at all but rather, imposed upon and coerced. The person being drafted and those doing the drafting both need to agree voluntarily to proceed. This is self-organization in action.

Self-Organization in Teams and Groups

Now that we have defined and discussed leadership, authority, power, and formal, informal and personal authorization, we can address self-organization as it pertains to groups of people.

Self-organization occurs primarily inside the dynamically self-adjusting informal system of authority distribution.

> **self-organization** *n.*
> A process by which order arises in a social
> organization as a result of interactions between
> members of the group without being initiated or
> managed by a formal authority.

That's it. In other words, "self-organization" is actually the act of dynamically establishing, at the group level, who has the right to do what work.

Figuring out who has the right to do what work is a dynamic process. It responds to the situation at hand. Without the dynamic sending and receiving of authority by and between individuals and the group, there is no "self organization." There is no order. There is the absence of order. There is no "structure."

Therefore: A major and essential aspect of social system organization is the dynamic sending and receiving of the authority to make decisions. Self-management is focused on managing decision-making.

> **self-management** *n.*
> Taking responsibility for decisions that affect oneself
> and others. Self-management can be applied at
> the individual, team, and enterprise levels. A self-

managed team makes most of the decisions that
affect the work of that team as a whole.

As a leader in an organization, it is your job to create the
conditions for self-management while also creating the explicit
rules under which that self-management will play out.[14]

Some of the most important work in a group is the work of
deciding. People who make decisions that affect the others must
have higher informal authority than others in that group if the
decision is to be honored.

Authority and Authorization as the "Connective Tissue" of an Organization

Groups have many properties. The most important of these concern
authority and authorization. Decision-making that affects the
group as a whole is the most important kind of work that is done
inside a group. By definition, it is the leaders who do this work of
deciding. To do this work, they must be authorized formally and
also (in most cases) informally as well. Those who are authorized
to participate in decision-making are the people who actually do
that work. The key question is: who decides? How are decisions
that affect the whole group actually made?

The authorization information about decision-making actually
holds the group together. Information about where decision-
making authority is coming from and who is receiving and/or
holding it is the key information that helps participants make
sense of group membership. Without this key information, group
members have a difficult time understanding their roles. Without
this information, most group members will experience worries
and anxieties about their role and membership in the group. The
energy consumed by these worries is not available for the actual
work.

If you want to increase the level of anxiety and worry in a group,
all you have to do is make it completely unclear how decisions are

---

[14] See "Chapter 2 – Boundary" for more about enabling constraints,
boundaries, and boundary management.

actually made. To quickly reduce anxieties and greatly increase the amount of energy available for the work, simply make it clear how the group makes decisions that affect all the members.

The work of deciding for the group is the most important kind of "authorized work." This is the work of leadership.

Agreements

Chris Rufer, the CEO of MorningStarCo, says that "an organization is nothing more than a set of agreements between people."[15] Almost every one of these agreements has an essential "authority and authorization" dimension. People routinely authorize and de-authorize the various proposals, policies, decisions and procedures of others. This authorization can be formal or informal. This authorization can also be passive ("silence as consent") or active ("explicit agreement").

With this as background, we can now detail the three structures that manifest and generate flows of authority and authorization in organizations.

Organizational Physics: The Three Fundamental Ways In Which Authority is Manifested in Groups

Every organization has three distinct authority distribution patterns. There is no decision to make about whether to have all three of these structures. None of the three are optional or merely "nice to have." Silke Hermann and Niels Pflaeging, authors of the book *OpenSpace Beta*,[16] call these patterns "organizational physics." According to Hermann and Pflaeging, organizational physics is the set of universal laws that apply to every organization, large or small, old or new, for profit or not, everywhere in the world.

---

[15] MORNINGSTARCO is a company that has done significant experiments and made significant advances in operationalizing self-management. See www.invitingleadership.com/book/links/#morningstarco.

[16] For more information about authority distribution patterns, see www.invitingleadership.com/book/links/#openspacebeta.

Under this system, these three authority distribution schemes (or "structures") are in fact the source for three kinds of authority, and how it is exercised.

The Formal Authority Schema

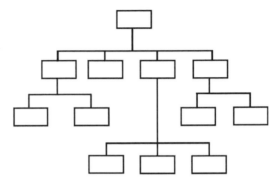

Figure 1.7: The Formal Authority Schema

The Formal Schema is the domain of *compliance*. The authority held in this structure is referred to as hierarchy. This is the authority structure commonly referred as "the org chart." Sadly, it is often wrongly assumed that work or value creation can be organized or improved through formal authorization and hierarchy. This structure is useful mostly for compliance or "operating within the boundaries of the law," instead of organizing or improving the creation of value. We refer to the leadership here as formally authorized leadership.

The Informal Authority Schema

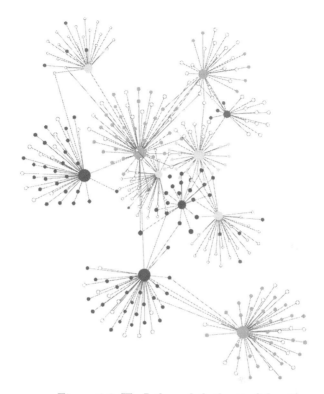

Figure 1.8: The Informal Authority Schema

The Informal Schema is the domain of the social organization of the organization. The authority held in this structure is commonly referred to as *influence*. It is a system of informal authorization, arising from social relationships inside the organization. The Informal schema is neither good not bad; it just "is." We refer to the leadership here as *informally authorized leadership*. This leadership has nothing to do with the Formal Schema.

The Participatory and Semi-Formal Value Creation Schema

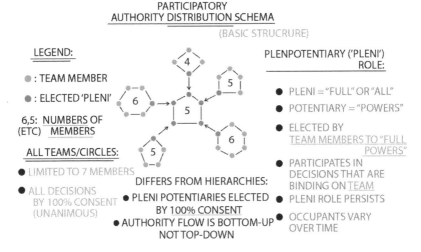

Figure 1.9: A Participatory and Semi-Formal Value Creation Schema with Roles and Related Rules About Making Decisions

The Value Creation Schema is essential. It is the domain of work, performance, and innovation. Authority held in this structure is referred to as *reputation*. It is achieved by having mastery. Organizational performance can only emerge from this structure. This is a structure of federated teams and groups. This is where "the flow of value" actually happens and where value creation can be strengthened and various forms of waste can be reduced. We refer to the leadership here as authorized value creation leadership. We say "authorized" because the Value Creation Schema's authority to make high-impact, wide-scope decisions comes from the Formal Schema. Under ideal conditions, the Value Creation Schema combines the best of both the Formal and the Informal structures.

These three authority structures are interdependent. With few exceptions, every member of an organization has membership in all three structures. In the Formal structure, each person typically operates in one formally authorized role. In the Informal structure, that person operates inside a personal web of social relationships. In the Value Creation structure, that very same person may occupy several roles within one or more team or "cell" constellations. You can increase the effectiveness of interventions within an organization's system by examining in advance the structure in which these interventions are planned. You can also increase effectiveness by examining what reactions are likely to occur within these three structures. It is also useful to determine who from one or more of these structures is essential to achieving success in realizing the intended outcome of the intervention.

Federation is Essential in the Value Creation Schema

Complex organizations must be arranged in a decentralized yet federated manner. In a federated system, representatives are elected to receive and exercise "full powers" at the next level of scale. This is a scale-free approach that can work regardless of how large the structure gets.

When outside markets reign, the organization's periphery necessarily earns the money, learns from the market, and adapts quickly and intelligently to external market forces. During periods of high change, the Formal structure in the center is isolated and insulated from the market by the periphery. Under these conditions, it can rarely give useful orders. Its ability to steer decays exponentially. The linkage between center and periphery must be designed accordingly, so that the center becomes able to sense and respond to market dynamics. For that to happen, the periphery must steer the center through internal pull and demand-supply relationships.

In "decentralized mode," the need for having a middle management disappears entirely. Here, self-management of decision-making from the bottom up and from the outside in becomes possible. The principle of decentralization of decision-making and the exercise of authority at the periphery or edge goes on and on. It is "scale free." The decentralization of decision-making, or what we call self-management – has no upper limit.

The following table summarizes the three fundamental authority distribution structures:

Table 1.3: Fundamental Authority Distribution Structures

Structure Name	Domain	Source of Authority
Formal	Compliance	Org Hierarchy
Informal	Social	Social Influence
Value Creation	Value Delivery	Work reputation

Recap

This chapter introduced several important concepts and definitions about authority and authorization. A solid understanding of authorization types is essential to understanding Inviting Leadership, so it is a good idea to confirm your clear understanding of the definitions and terms introduced in this section before reading further.

The Glossary also lists each of these terms:

- Agreement
- Authority
- Authority Distribution Schema
- Authority Helping
- Authority Map™
- Authority Opposing
- Authority Seeking
- Authorization
- Delegation
- Drafting
- Dynamic Sending and Receiving of Authorization
- Emergent Leaders
- Formal Authorization
- Informal Authorization
- Informal De-authorization Leadership
- Legitimate and Illegitimate Authority
- Personal Authority
- Power

- Responsibility
- Self-Authorization
- Tyranny of Structurelessness
- Under-Step

Chapter 2 – Boundary

Effective boundary design, boundary implementation and boundary management are absolutely essential aspects of the Inviting Leadership style.

Overview

Invitations from leaders require careful and thoughtful design. The constraints, rules and boundary settings are an absolutely essential element of any well-designed invitation. The boundaries make the invitation clear and actionable.

For this reason you need to understand the topic of boundaries and constraints.

Topics:

- Boundaries and Bounded Containment: General Concepts
- Boundaries in Living Systems: Biological Boundaries
- Boundaries in Social Systems: Sociological Boundaries
- Boundaries in Organizations: Sociological and Psychological Boundaries

Fundamentally, all boundaries are lines of demarcation. Boundary lines define the limits of an area. In this chapter we quickly cover boundaries generally and then focus on how boundaries apply to membership and leadership in organizations. Later on in "Part III- Application" we provide guidance on how to apply these universal boundary concepts within the context of leading with invitation.

A boundary line that is connected end-to-end forms a container. The closed perimeter defines what is in and what is out. Some boundaries serve to define a transactional area or zone.

A doctor's office with a reception area is a good example. The reception space forms a transitional zone. All of those who are authorized may enter the inner office; others do not get past the reception space.

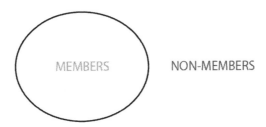

Figure 2.1: Simple Thin-Line Boundary

Figure 2.1 shows a sharp boundary. A thicker, wider boundary is shown in Figure 2.2 This boundary has no transitional zone.

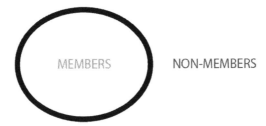

Figure 2.2: A Wide Boundary Line Forming a Perimeter

A very wide boundary line can form a transitional area around the container as shown in Figure 2.3:

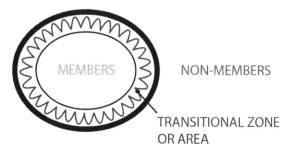

NON-MEMBERS

TRANSITIONAL ZONE
OR AREA

Figure 2.3: A Boundary Line Wide Enough to Form a Transitional Area

The content of the container can vary considerably. Job descriptions contain authorized tasks and duties. Time boundaries can contain events. Ceilings, windows, doors and walls can contain workplaces. Boundaries can be categorized according to what they contain, and what they recognize, allow, and respond to at the perimeter.

Rules: Boundaries and Constraints

Let's assume you have a clear set of goals and know how to articulate them clearly. The people who receive your leadership invitations are not required to say yes to the invitation, so you'll need to be careful about designing it. Pay very close attention to defining the rules, boundaries and constraints in your invitation.

In a business setting, invitations from leaders are intended to advance business goals and objectives directly or indirectly. Usually, achieving those goals means engaging employees in a process or set of tasks. The Rules portion of an invitation should make it easy for employees to engage quickly.

The rules can pertain to wide range of items. Here are some of them:

Authority Boundaries

If you are inviting people to execute specific tasks, you must be clear about who has authority (permission) to do what. The classic pattern of "responsibility without authority" will not be well received. You must be sure to define clearly the level of authority you are inviting people into.

Regarding Decision-Making Authority

The most important kind of authority is the authority to participate in decision-making that effects entire groups. Making decisions is fundamentally engaging. If you are inviting people into decision-making, and we hope you are, then you must be very clear about the scope and limits of that decision-making.

Task and Responsibility Boundaries

Tasks must be defined clearly and have solid "Definition of Done" measurement criteria that makes it easy for the person doing the task to experience progress. Responsibility for a task must be accompanied by the *requisite authority* needed to accomplish the task.

Time Boundaries

Tasks, responsibilities, and authority can be bounded by time. A particular role can start and end on a specific date. Events can begin and end at specific times. The "RSVP" of an invitation establishes a time boundary. Deadlines are important boundaries, expressed in units of time.

Territory Boundaries

Territory includes authorized access to meeting spaces, work spaces and other physical things such as tools and supplies. What territory is authorized for use or not is an important boundary definition in your leadership invitations

Budget Boundaries

Money is a scarce resource. It is important to use clear and unambiguous terms to express who has decision-making and spending authority, and to what level, event, and limit.

Leadership Invitations Have Limits and Constraints

Leadership invitations can be used to test the ability of the organization to change, to test the willingness of employees to engage, or to generate feedback about the workforce.

Daniel provides a concrete example in a story about testing willingness by running a relatively inexpensive experiment.

$400 Book Benefit

In the 1990's, Daniel ran a technical consulting organization with over 50 consultants. These consultants were spread across three offices in 3 states. "As part of the process of managing talent, I created a 'book benefit. Any employee could spend up to $400 per year on books which "pertained to your work in some way." After the calendar year was up, the balance was reloaded to $400 and employees could continue buying new books. All that was needed to get reimbursed was a receipt showing the book title, the date, and the cost."

The rules:

1. *Spend up to $400/yr on books that you can keep as a gift from the company*
2. *Any book purchased must pertain to your work "in some way"*
3. *To be reimbursed, simply submit receipts for all books purchased*

The goals:

1. *Keep consultants current on important emerging technologies*
2. *Define an important new benefit for all employees*
3. *Find out who wants to learn new things, and find who is interested in what*

The invitation went out in plain English to all technical employees and engineers. The goals and rules were clearly stated, and the progress-tracking was clear: by budget ($400 annually) and by the books purchased. No one was required to participate.

"The results were very interesting. I found out a lot about the employees. I learned that some people learned much and that some were not actually engaged in learning new things. They did not buy many books. I found out that some employees were looking to work in technologies that they were not currently working in. And I found out who the ambitious people were. Since some of these folks were highly introverted, it was not obvious at first who the ambitious ones actually were. I had many great conversations with some of these folks after seeing the titles of the books. I took a strong interest in developing the careers of several engineers. Some of them signaled a strong interest in leading and managing engineering teams. Some of those folks ended up on the management team. None of these outcomes were possible without getting the big data that resulted from the $400/yr book benefit policy."

So, this is the idea with leadership invitations. Those invitations generate a lot of actionable feedback. They can be used for learning all kinds of things, for identifying willing participants, and for identifying new leaders.

In "Part III- Application" we delve deeper into these boundary types and how they apply to designing the invitations you will send to the wider workforce.

Organizations are social systems and social systems are living systems populated by people. For this reason it is useful to take a look at how boundaries play in the natural world and particularly in cell biology.

Boundary Testing and Boundary Management

Boundary management is the directing and controlling of one or more boundaries. The goal of boundary management is to maintain overall boundary integrity. Most healthy individuals and healthy groups exhibit good boundary management.

Those who desire membership in a healthy group may have to pass a series of tests or answer certain questions in an acceptable manner before achieving Member status. The tests and questions are a form of boundary management. Boundaries like membership boundaries invite testing and probing. Unmanaged boundaries are quickly breached. Breaches and the troubles that come with them are natural consequences of boundary management that is weak or entirely absent.

To issue a genuine invitation is to acknowledge and respect the boundaries of the receiver. "Invitations" that are not respectful of boundaries are not invitations at all. Respectful invitations are delivered near but outside of the boundary. Disrespectful invitations that do not honor the boundary are actually experienced as *impositions*. They may even be experienced as directives or commands. These points are important to keep in mind if you are planning to use invitations to increase your leadership effectiveness. Your invitations must be respectful and not appear to be imposing. Effective organizations display high levels of respect for the defined boundaries of individuals and groups.

A major overall theme of this book is the focus on good boundary design and good boundary management. This focus includes the intentional design and management of role-based decision-making authority boundaries. You the leader need to pay particular attention to this, as you re-architect the way authority is being distributed. The decision-making scheme or map (the so-called "structure") influences communication flows and ultimately, culture itself. The design of the boundaries on decision-making by role is therefore essential to define in explicit terms.

When the decision-making authority of two roles is unclear or overlaps, there is high probability that a lot of waste will be generated as the two "agents" (two individuals or two teams for example) figure out where one decision-making boundary ends and the other one begins. You want total clarity on decision-making boundaries for each role you define, and make sure there is nothing ambiguous in the definition of who has decision-making rights. This is achieved through good boundary design.

As you'll see in the next section, microbiological systems run on well-defined boundaries and the active and ongoing management of communication and signaling along these perimeters. In cell biology, there is nothing random about communication protocols at the boundary, and the communication is highly efficient. Responsive organizations can be designed to have these same characteristics.

Boundaries in Living Systems

Boundaries form perimeters. Consider the boundaries of a cell, the basic building block of all life. Every cell has a cell wall; the interior of the cell contains cytoplasm. This intra-cellular cytoplasm is bounded by the cell wall or membrane, which forms a closed perimeter defining the cell boundary and the cell itself.

Cell walls contain receptors which "listen" for "signals" in the form of molecules. When certain kinds of molecules interact with the receptors, this interaction can trigger processes and actions on the other side of the cell wall boundary, inside the cell.

This same dynamic plays out in the social world. People, teams, and organizations are sensitive to signaling that occurs along their boundaries. Living systems use signaling to regulate the sequencing and flow of essential processes needed for survival. Processing at the boundaries enables the signaling function. Anything that impedes the flow and processing of signals can reduce overall living system health and functioning.[1]

The bounded perimeter of a cell processes signaling that originates outside of the cell. The boundary also plays an essential role in maintaining the health of the cell by forming an enclosure.

---

[1] The relationship between signal processing and system health has important implications for leaders in organizations; we discuss these implications in "Chapter 5 – Leadership".

Organizations include teams, departments, divisions, and business units. Each of these is in part defined by various boundaries such as authority and responsibility limits. We go deeper on this concept of boundaries on authority and responsibility for teams, departments, divisions, and business units in the "Part III-Application" section.

Boundary and Boundary Integrity at the Cellular Level

Almost every living cell has a nucleus. The nucleus regulates cell functioning and contains the replication information – the DNA.

It is a little-known fact that a cell can and will continue to survive for some time even if the nucleus has been removed. Without the nucleus the cell does not function but it is still very much alive. If the membrane that encloses the cell is breached, the entire cell quickly dies. A breach at the cell boundary threatens the very life of the cell. The lesson here is that boundaries play an essential role in maintaining the health of living systems.

Social systems are living systems and businesses are social systems. We cover this idea and others in more depth in the "Leadership Invitations" and "Guidance" chapters.

Action and Protocol at the Boundary

Life at the cellular level implements very intricate procedures at the boundary. The boundary of a cell contains receptors that "listen" for certain molecules as they pass by. These "signaling molecules" are recognized by some cell types and ignored by others. The cells that recognize a specific kind of signaling molecule do not all respond to it in the same way. The responses vary according to cell function and other factors. Receptors built into the cell wall "listen" for signaling molecules. Then these signal are received as the receptor "binds to" a signal molecule. From there, the cell is triggered and responds according to its design and function. "Secondary" messenger molecules inside the cell may become active and generate a substantial response-process inside the cell. Sometimes the received signals actually influence the expression of DNA in the nucleus of the cell.

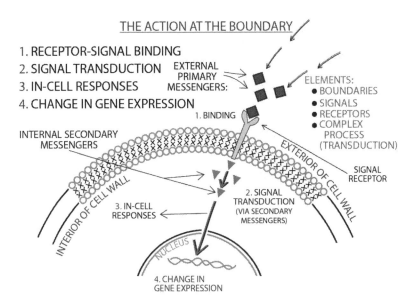

Figure 2.4: Action at The Boundary: Communication Protocols and Signal Processes Trigger a State Change

Why does this matter for business leaders reading this book? Because cells are bounded entities, just like teams, departments and enterprises.

These bounded entities interact via signaling and signaling protocols.

Apparently, for cellular life to function well, highly detailed process and protocols are required at the boundary. That's an important concept to keep in mind as you work to improve your organization's ability to adapt. Leadership invitations are signal, and those under the authority of the leader are highly receptive to those signals.

Boundaries, signaling at the boundary, protocols for communication, and action. These elements are present in cellular processes and also team and enterprise process. We will return to signaling and develop this concept further as we apply it to Inviting Leadership in the Leadership chapter.

Attracted and Repelled

Cells are attracted to nutrients and repelled by toxins. Social systems respond similarly. This has implications for how you issue your leadership invitations. Those invitations must be sent with respect for the boundaries of the receiver. Disrespect for the boundary will be perceived as disrespect for the person or group.

For example, if your organization is using the Kanban Method to organize work, the rules for Kanban apply.[2] One of these rules is that an item of work cannot be placed into the workflow until and unless it is characterized by Work Item Type, which has properties such as Cycle Time, the estimated wait for work completion. If you ignore this rule by using your high authority to force an item into the work flow, you are violating a rule of the Kanban Method and in fact violating a key boundary of the team that is using that Kanban board to visualize and manage work. Healthy teams must engage in good boundary management to stay healthy. For this reason, breaching the agreed-upon decision-making boundaries of teams, departments, and cultural divisions is a terrible idea. Breaching behavior by authority figures is interpreted as *signal*.

People are sensitive to signaling about respect, in much the same way that cells are sensitive to signals at the cell wall or membrane.

These facts about microbiology can be used to inform how you think about boundaries of individuals, and the actions and reactions that are created by your invitations.

We cover this idea in fuller detail in "Chapter 6 – Leadership Invitations" and in "Chapter 8 – Guidance".

Transitional Zones In Social Systems: The Ecotone

When two living communities are adjacent to each other, a transitional area is often created that blurs or merges the boundaries. This transitional area is called an *ecotone*. Figure 2.5 illustrates the concept.

---

[2] Kanban helps organize work and work flow. For more information, see www.invitingleadership.com/book/links/#kanban.

ecotone *n.*

> A narrow or wide, local or regional transition area between two communities where members of those communities meet and integrate. The boundary between the two communities may be blurred and fuzzy, containing some members from both communities or it might begin at a distinct, sharp boundary.

AN "ECOTONE" OR TRANSITIONAL AREA
FORMED BY THE BOUNDARY OF TWO
(ADJACENT) COMMUNITIES - STEP 1

Figure 2.5: An Ecotone

Example of ecotones are plentiful in nature. Estuaries are formed where rivers meet the ocean. Marshes form where ocean tides advance and recede. The banks of rivers form a transitional zone between "terra firma" and flowing water. In nature, the richness of these transitional zones creates the potential for rich interactions between various forms of life that live in the two intersecting and overlapping communities. In organizations, the intersecting and overlapping of decision-making rights can also generate some rich interactions as both communities negotiate the decision-making ecotone.

Within organizations and with individuals, the boundaries are often blurry. Transitional regions form and rich interactions begin to take place there. Negotiations are a good example of the kind of interactions that take place within organizational ecotones.

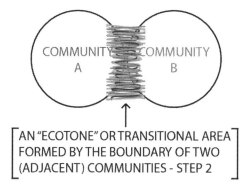

Figure 2.6: Closely Adjacent Boundaries Are Obscured at the Ecotone – Forming a Purely Transitional Area

As a leader in an organization, understanding the basic biology of boundaries helps to make sense of what is really going on inside your own organization. Every complete invitation from a leader includes boundaries and constraints that help define exactly what is (and is not) being invited. In "Chapter 3 – Invitation" we cover this in more detail.

Figure 2.7: When Boundaries Overlap, Communities Fuse Together At the Ecotone

The most important ecotones that exist in your organization are those that are formed when the boundaries of the decision-making rights of two distinct entities overlap in any way whatsoever. As much as possible, for any specific decision to be made, you must design the decision-making rights such that there is no ambiguity about which person or group (which role) is authorized to make that decision. The design of decision-making rights determines the level of efficiency you can achieve in day-to-day operations.

Boundaries in Social Systems: Groups of People

Social systems are groups of two or more persons. Social systems are living systems that are populated by human beings. Families, soccer teams, and circles of friends are all social systems. Each group has a boundary that defines who is a member and who is not. Groups process signaling and messaging at the perimeter just like cells do. Groups contain members, some of whom are leaders. Leaders manage the process of making decisions that affect the whole group. The leaders' signals to other members inside the group are the most important signals in the entire system. Inside social systems, the signals contain sociological rather than biological meaning.

Groups respond to internal ("inside the group") and external ("outside of group") signals. If you signal well, those who are listening for your signals can respond quickly and in the way you intended. If you signal poorly, you can expect the response to be muted as the recipients of your signals try to figure out what the signals mean.

Organizations that are adaptive are highly sensitive to signals from the environment and external sources. Less adaptive organizations are not at all sensitive to these signals.

Clear understandings and related protocols for communication inside the group open group awareness to the wider environment. How sensitive the group is to these external signals is a function of leadership effectiveness. If the leadership is effective, the group will be high-functioning. This includes a sensitivity to the external environment and the signals from those sources.

Signaling well means paying attention to the boundaries of the receiver when you are sending. This concept is developed in more detail in the "Leadership" chapter in "Part I - Essential Concepts" and the "Leadership Invitations"and "Guidance" chapters in "Part III- Application". For now, understand that invitations are a form of *leadership signaling* and that these signals are most effective when they are sensitive to (and respectful of) the boundaries and perimeters of the receiver.

Recap

Leaders who use invitations need to understand the basics of good boundary design, boundary types, leadership signaling, and boundary management.

Chapter 3 – Invitation

Inviting and delegating have several important differences and some similarities. In this chapter we explore invitation in depth and introduce the 4-part invitation structure.

Overview

This part of the book introduces invitation as a leadership art. Invitation triggers decision-making, human agency, and action, which affect self-management, self-organization, authority, and company culture.

In this chapter we assume that you have digested Chapter 1 and Chapter 2 before proceeding.

Although this book is written for those holding formal authority in organizations, anyone can apply these concepts to just about every interaction and every aspect of life.

Now let's investigate invitation as it applies to your role in the workplace.

Invitation in the Workplace

There's a crisis in most workplaces. The pace of change, driven by technology, is accelerating. Change is the new constant. And the impact of these changes is usually not small.

The typical response is to continue operating as we have been. Instead of being complacent, we need to modify one thing in our response to change — the way authority is distributed. Repeat: the way authority is distributed.

The composition of the workforce is also changing, and a new generation is changing it. They bring their distinct values, biases, and opinions. Nowhere are these distinctions more striking than in the way they view authority, authorization, and "management."

Executives, the highest of the "formally authorized leaders," are largely unprepared for these changes. Old-school management science and traditional leadership training do not provide many tools to address these challenges. The leadership solutions that actually work in this new world are deeply rooted in *complexity science*.[1] Instead of theory, today's executives, directors and managers need more (and better) actionable guidance.

This section of the book introduces the fundamental building blocks for understanding and then applying the dynamics of invitation in your leadership work.

There's a link to the topics of authority and authorization that we think you may find interesting: each invitation from executive leaders to members of the workforce causes a small, temporary, and very important change *in the way authority is distributed*. The mechanics of this change are super-efficient. Self-management is what actually scales, and invitation encourages it. This chapter introduces some underlying concepts (and a supporting language) for discussing and applying these ideas.

Invitation Defined

invitation *n.*
1. The act of offering someone the opportunity to go somewhere or do something.
2. A written or verbal offer for someone to go somewhere or to do something.
3. A situation or action that tempts someone to do something or that makes a particular outcome likely. Note: A genuine invitation may be declined without any sanctions or other implied or expressed negative consequences.

An invitation is a kind of test, a test of the receiver's willingness. An invitation tests the willingness of the receiver to go somewhere or do something. This test generates feedback.

---

[1] For a primer on complexity science, see
www.invitingleadership.com/book/links/#complexity.

It must be OK for the test to return negative results. It has to be OK for the receiver to decline (to not accept) the invitation. If the recipient of an invitation cannot opt-out, the so-called invitation is really a directive.

Promise Theory

Promise Theory is an approach to system design that focuses on maximizing throughput at scale. It originated in the discipline of computer science, as a way to efficiently scale computer networks with millions of nodes. Promise Theory describes a set of architectural principles.

In the book *Thinking In Promises: Designing Systems for Cooperation*, Mark Burgess challenges the reader to imagine:

> *"Imagine a set of principles for understanding how parts combine to become a whole, and how each part sees the whole from its own perspective. If these principles are any good, it shouldn't matter whether we are talking about humans on a team, birds in a flock, or computers in a data center. A theory of cooperation ought to be pretty universal, so we should be able to apply both to technology and the workplace."*

The central premise of Promise Theory is that the agent responsible for delivering on a promise is the only entity that can make that promise. Promise Theory further states that any attempt by an external entity to project a promise upon an agent is not a promise at all, but rather, an imposition.

Promise Theory has important implications for scaling enterprises and business operations with no loss in efficiency. According to Promise Theory, the most efficient pattern for scaling starts with placing authority to make promises with the agent who is responsible for delivering on it. Anything less is sub-optimal. Promise Theory offers a bottom-up constructionist view of the world.

With Promise Theory, Burgess differentiates between a promise and a guarantee. While a guarantee can be hard to come by, a promise is not. A promise in Promise Theory is a statement of intent. Because the world is full of uncertainty, an absolute guarantee can be difficult to deliver on. Promises on the other hand deliver a very clear statement of intent upon which plans can be constructed.

Here are some additional clarifying statements about Promise Theory, from page 2 and page 3 of the book *Thinking In Promises*:

> *"Promise Theory has nothing to do with being nice. It's not about being moral. It's not about democracy rather than dictatorship. It's simply about realism, and attaching responsibility for outcomes to the agencies that have the best chance to deliver. It does not tell you how to be immune to uncertainty, it just helps to clear away a veil of delusion, to see more clearly what kind of mess you are in.*

> *"Promise Theory turns out to be a pragmatic way of coming to terms with the complexities of a world where you are not certain of having your own way.*

> *"Why is a promise better than a command? Why a promise? Why not an obligation, command or requirement? In Promise Theory, these latter things are called impositions because they impose intentions onto others without an invitation.*

> *"Promises expose information that is relevant to an expected outcome more directly than impositions because they always focus on the point of causation: the agent that makes the promise is responsible for keeping it.*

> *"...Why is a promise better than a command? A promise expresses intent about the end point, or ultimate outcome, instead of indicating what to do at the starting point... promising the end point is independent of your current state of affairs."*

Promise Theory[2] tends to support the Inviting Leadership style and vice-versa. Inviting Leaders acknowledge that only an invitee can be responsible for responding to an invitation that addresses that invitee. Every invitation prompts a decision, and under the Inviting Leadership approach, the invitee is the only one who can form and deliver a decision regarding how to respond. Readers who want to deeply understand the bonuses and benefits of the Inviting Leadership style are wise to study Promise Theory in much more detail.

The Promising Linguistics of Invitation: "Speech Acts"

The Inviting Leadership approach requires leaders to engage in the sending of requests rather than the sending of commands or directives. It turns out that both commands and requests are 'speech acts.'[3] Speech acts are verbalizations (utterances) that serve a function, such as making a greeting, issuing a command, or making an offer or request. One type of speech act is the commissive: in a commissive speech act, the speaker is committing to some kind of future action; the speaker is making a promise or oath about the future. "You are invited to join the meeting on Tuesday" is a commissive speech act, because it is binding the speaker to a course of action, namely: the arranging and delivery of the meeting on Tuesday.

Your leadership depends in part on your behavior being predictable and reliable. The way you use speech is behavior and that behavior is being carefully scrutinized by listeners and followers who are under the formal authority of your role. For this reason, you want to be familiar with the linguistic concept of the "speech act." Doing so helps you to understand the nature

---

[2] Mark Burgess has written several books on Promise Theory. For more information about Promise Theory, including references to these books, the design principles of Promise Theory, and the mathematical proofs regarding the network and system efficiency of promises, see www.invitingleadership.com/book/links/#promise-theory.

[3] For more about speech acts and illocutionary acts, see www.invitingleadership.com/book/links/#speech-acts.

of leadership speech (in general) and the nature of invitational speech (in particular.)

In the next section, you'll learn more about how language can be used as a very effective tool to increase your leadership effectiveness.

Invitation and Games

People enjoy good games. Invitation is part of any good game. To some people, "game" is a loaded term associated with phrases like "gaming the system," or "corporate games." Or they think that all games must involve competition. However, some games (such as puzzle-making) are purely cooperative. Consider the "game inside the game" of being on a football team. The team is 100% competitive against their opponents. Yet inside that team, a mixture of collaboration, cooperation and competitive games are all being played.

Games have many dimensions. They can be competitive, cooperative or collaborative. A game might have a specific end point or it could continue indefinitely. Some games even have rules that dynamically change as the game is played.

Good games (the kind of games that are actually fun to play) have four essential properties, which were originally identified by Jane McGonigal in her book *Reality is Broken:*

- A very clear goal
- Very clear rules
- A way to track progress
- Opt-in participation

The opt-in aspect is essential. Every good game has optional participation. All potential players are *invited and not compelled* to participate.

For our purposes, it is important to study and commit to memory the four properties of a good game.

This connection between gaming and invitation is fundamental. We can use it to structure invitations so that they are easier for the receiver to understand and accept.

We have all been in situations where we were not sure what we were being invited into. Ambiguity can make it hard to accept an invitation. To avoid this problem, structure your invitation using the game properties: clearly described goals, rules, and progress tracking. And of course, make it clear that accepting the invitation is 100% optional.

Invitation Structure

Let's say you are having a dinner party and want to issue an excellent invitation that is easy for the receiver to understand and respond to. Here is one way to do it.

Well-Formed Dinner Invitation

I am inviting you to dinner for next Saturday night.

We are planning a group of 8 people. It's at my house and starts with beverages at about 630PM.

We'll sit down at about 7PM and enjoy a 5-course meal and 6 kinds of wine.

The intent is to enjoy fine food and finer conversation as we dine.

We plan to end at around 10PM. I hope you can make it.

Can you please let me know by this coming Wednesday?

Here are the elements and the structure:
1. Goals
   - Enjoy fine food
   - Enjoy finer company, and socialize
2. Rules
   - Who: 8 participants

- ○ Where: It's at my house
- ○ When: It's on Saturday, it starts at 630PM and ends around 10PM
- ○ Details: Can you please let me know by this coming Wednesday?

3. Progress Tracking
- ○ By time, from 630PM to 10PM
- ○ By the progression of food consumed: "a 5-course meal."
- ○ By the progression of wine consumed: "6 kinds of wine"
- ○ By the progression of conversation: "conversation as we dine."

4. Opt-in participation
- ○ No one is compelled to participate; participation is 100% voluntary.

Here we can observe how an invitation to an event (a dinner) can be structured in the 4-part format, with all of the key aspects of a good game included and clearly defined. This is a well-formed invitation. All the key elements are present, and are easy to identify. This dinner party invitation is in fact an invitation to play a kind of game.

Even though the 4-part invitation structure is precise, it easily translates to free-form, conversational language. Your highly structured invitations do not have to sound clinical.

When your invitation has these 4 elements, the receiver can quickly understand what the invitation means, and reply confidently because the receiver understands what they are being invited into.

You want to structure all of your invitations in this way. Note: Throughout the rest of the book we refer to the four-part game structure by the acronym FGS.

The Sequence of Invitation Events

The mechanics of invitation are simple and their implications are complex. Figure 3.1 shows the simple steps for the sender.

The receiver is doing most of the processing: receiving, studying, considering, checking schedules, perhaps speaking to others about the invitation.

But there is some processing going on at the sender side of things as well. Any genuine invitation has these two properties or characteristics:

- The sender does not hurry or rush the receiver to respond.

- If the receiver declines the invitation, the sender does not   demand any explanation from the receiver.

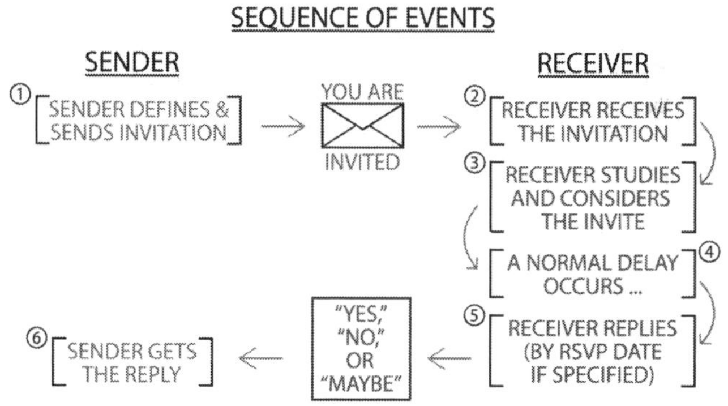

SEQUENCE OF EVENTS

Figure 3.1: The Invitation Sequence

While these aspects of a good and genuine invitation are not depicted in the figure, it is assumed that the sender is sending a genuine invitation, without demands or any sanctions for declining.

Let us now examine each step in the invitation process:

1. **Sender designs and sends the invitation:** The design is important. We recommend that you use the FGS structure described above.

2. **Receiver receives the invitation:** This is analogous to receiving and opening a letter in an envelope. The invitation may be delivered in the form of a letter, an email, during a conversation, or some other way.

3. **Receiver studies and considers the invitation:** This is where is gets complex. We have no knowledge of why a receiver declines an invitation, so we cannot attach too much meaning when someone declines. There may be multiple reasons for declining. The sender is responsible for making sure that the invitation is clear, and for waiting for the receiver to respond. For this reason, we want to make sure the invitation is "well formed" using the FGS structure of goals, rules, how progress is experienced, and opt-in participation.

4. **A normal delay occurs:** It's totally normal for people to wait before responding to an invitation. They will think about it. They may talk to others who are invited. They may instinctively "never commit early unless they know why."[4] Every invitation is a kind of *option*. Options have value and options expire. The delay is normal because until the option expires, there is little or no cost for delaying. But once the option expires, any perceived value evaporates instantly. Most people wait until they are at the threshold of this boundary before responding.

5. **Receiver replies to the invitation:** When the time for deciding has arrived, the receiver replies with a "yes," a "no," or a "maybe." The sender has no idea in advance about how the receiver might respond.

6. **Sender gets the reply:** When the sender gets the reply, it will be one of these types:
   ○ An active YES

---

[4] This axiom is from Olaf Maassen and Chris Matts. For an explanation of "real options" and making optimal decisions regarding them, see www.invitingleadership.com/book/links/#options.

o   An active NO
o   A passive NO (time expires), for example if
    someone says "Please leave it on my desk,
    I will look at it later," and then never does
o   A MAYBE (unless otherwise prohibited)

The main thing to take away from this discussion is the fact that, in a genuine invitational situation, after the invitation is received, the receiver is in charge of the timing of events. The sender is not.

Figure 3.2 shows the invitation sequence in detail. When the invitation is being sent from someone with higher authority to someone of lower authority in an organization, the result is a special kind of authorization that originates with the sender.

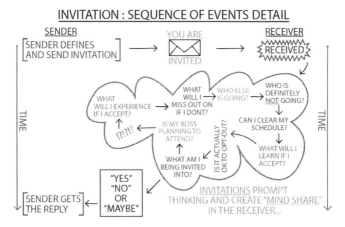

Figure 3.2: The Invitation Sequence in Detail

This is explained in the next section.

Authority and Leadership Invitations
There are some authority dimensions that come with an invitation; let's take a look at these now.

•   **The recipient cannot be compelled.** This
    means the receiver is in charge of what happens
    next. The sender of a genuine invitation is not
    authorized to direct the receiver's response in

any way except to define a response deadline or "RSVP." Except for this stipulation, the receiver is the only one who determines what happens next. The sender cannot compel the receiver to accept the invitation. So the receiver is the only person with the "right to accept" or "right to decline" the invite. All genuine invitations include this form of opt-in participation.

- **The invitation is for the receiver, not someone else.** We might say that the receiver is the only one authorized to use the invitation to participate in the event, because only the receiver has been invited. An invitation is a kind of authorization for a single person to optionally participate in "going somewhere or doing something."

- **How you handle authority in the new world of work.** This is the gating factor on how successful you are as a leader. When you issue invitations as a formally authorized leader in an organization, you are *changing the game.* You are moving from *delegation* to *invitation.* Instead of you telling them, <u>they</u> are telling <u>you</u> – they, the receivers of your invitations, are telling you what they are willing and not willing to do. Invitation creates a *micro-authorization* and causes a temporary restructuring of the normal top-down flow of authority. The receiver is in charge of the form, the timing and the content of the next step.

Invite with Curiosity

What can a manager/coach do to reduce the likelihood that a colleague will feel compelled, especially if that manager/coach has a strong desire for the colleague to accept a certain goal or adopt a certain way of thinking? The key is to invite from a position of genuine curiosity instead of expectation.

An effective way to express genuine curiosity and build genuine engagement is to use a technique called Clean Language, which was developed by Maori psychotherapist David Grove.[5]

"In asking a [clean] question we do not impose upon the client any value, construct or presupposition about what he should answer."
- David Grove and Basil Panzer

Caitlin Walker studied with David Grove, extended his work with individuals, and applied it to groups. She uses Clean Language to uncover differences in how group members are thinking and behaving and gets them curious about themselves and one another. She provides this guidance about inviting with curiosity:

According to her, there are at least three levels to inviting with curiosity:

- You need a process for putting your assumptions and your agenda to one side.
- You listen carefully to the words / watch the gestures of the other person before you apply your question. Repeat back if you have to, then you know you've heard.
- Ask a Clean question – Clean because while it asks for more information, it doesn't introduce your content or assumptions or agenda.

"These three things create an atmosphere of curiosity. These inquiry-filled micro interactions start to create the invitation-based space.

"Once you ask a Clean question, with genuine curiosity, you then take their answer, and no matter what it is, accept it, and extend what they've said.'

---

[5] For more information about Clean Language, see www.invitingleadership.com/book/links/#clean-language.

Curiosity and Clean Questions

In this example, a senior manager is trying to support a previously brilliant software engineer to hit deadlines on one specific project. The engineer was becoming disengaged and was struggling to stay focused and showed none of his earlier creativity. Caitlin Walker demonstrates how Clean Questions rather than 'trying hard to motivate him' can help invite him to greater engagement and effectiveness.

Caitlin: When you're creative that's like what?

Rupert: It's like a spark (snaps fingers in front of him)

Caitlin: What kind of spark?

Rupert: It's like I'm looking at other stuff and then suddenly, (snaps fingers again) I know exactly how to solve that problem and the whole thing is laid out in front of me.

Caitlin: You're looking at other stuff, then (snaps fingers), and where does the spark come from?

Rupert: Behind me, from the primordial soup of everything I know.

Caitlin: What happens just before that spark?

Rupert: I'll be reading about biology, or gaming, or chatting with colleagues and then (snaps fingers) one of the projects, in the back of my mind, is just solved.

As the interview progressed, Caitlin helped Rupert and his manager uncover how his creativity worked, how tight deadlines prevented him from being fully creative and how the way he was being managed and 'incentivized' was actually preventing him from working. His manager altered work conditions so that Rupert had more projects and looser deadlines and his productivity increased 300%. The invitation to think around the problem meant that something they'd grappled with for over a year was resolved in minutes.

Caitlin states that listening cleanly and accepting and extending answers, no matter what they are, is core to this approach. You can also use a Clean stance to set the stage for any important meeting.

Setting the Stage for Creativity

People typically enter meetings with low expectations about what will happen. If you want people being fully engaged in the meeting, first you have to find out how they are thinking. You can do this with a few Clean questions.

You: "If this meeting were to go just as you'd like, it will be like what?"

Bob: "It won't be death by PowerPoint."

(You don't laugh or challenge what they say, you just accept it and extend it)

You: "Is there anything else about death by PowerPoint?"

Bob: "It's a distraction and never gets us to the point.

You: "When death by PowerPoint is a distraction, what would you like instead?"

Bob: "I'd like it to be an honest discussion. I'd like us to be able to stop hiding the truth."

You: "An honest discussion. What kind of honest discussion would that be?"

Bob: "One where we feel safe to say what's happening."

These interactions are ways of saying, "Let's be present to what is, even if it isn't what we want." Your behavior will allow their system to settle because you're being present to how they are thinking, listening to them, and extending it.

Once the meeting participants know each person's expectations and concerns, the group knows what issues, if any, need to be resolved for the meeting to be most effective.

From here, individuals and groups can think with less resistance and therefore with more capacity for creativity and outcome focus.

Clean Language isn't just about creating a safe listening space. It isn't about going, "Oh, that sounds awful" or "I hear that things have been difficult here." You don't join in with them. You just accept their experience and use Clean questions to extend each person's understanding until you all know:

What is happening, what's working and not working, what you'd like to have happen and what action to take.

If it's a Clean conversation between peers about joint outcomes, then you need to pass the questioning back and forth between you so you each get a chance to find out what the other wants. If team members are doing this simultaneously, they begin to create a shared model of the system that they're in. This common understanding allows more of them to be working at their best, more of the time. Walker calls this process Systemic Modelling.[6]

Instead of coercion and compulsion with resistance, Clean Questions create a space for people to understand what's happening for them and what they'd truly like to have happen, under the current circumstances. From this position, genuine engagement is much more likely.

Interpreting Big Data Generated By Leadership Invitations

The ways that each person responds to an invitation is data about what the receivers (the members of the organization) are ready for. That big data is extremely useful to you the leader in many ways:

- **Identifying Support:** The responses are a signal to you regarding who is "in" and willing to support and participate in a new initiative. NOTE: Those who respond in the affirmative respond that way because they found the invitation appealing and attractive. People may decline an invitation for many reasons. They might have something else scheduled, or they might have another kind of obligation that prevents saying "yes," etc. You cannot attach too much meaning to a "no" or an invitation that is declined. But you can almost always assume that those who accept the invitation willingly do so because they find it attractive.

- **Identifying Organizational Readiness:** The responses to leadership invitations offer signals about what the organization is ready for. At any given time, the group has a kind of "adjacent

---

[6] For more information about Systemic Modelling, see www.invitingleadership.com/book/links/#clean-language.

possible"[7] into which they can grow and expand. Invitations are small leadership experiments that help the leader gauge the group's current state of willingness to move in a new direction.

- **Identifying New Leaders and Champions:** Some people may respond with an unambiguous "yes!" These people are potentially helpful. They may be new and emergent leaders who can assist you strongly in moving your plans forward.
- **Identifying Poor Bets:** If the majority of the invitees respond unenthusiastically or decline the invitation, you have just saved yourself potentially hundreds of thousands of dollars (or more) in budget by *not* attempting a change initiative that the organization clearly is not ready for... *yet*.

Invitations provide rich feedback. You send the invitation, some time passes, you receive feedback (in the form of a response) that provides rich data on who is willing to accept the invitation and do something (like attend a meeting) or go somewhere (for example moving from one team to another.) Since self-organizing, self-managed groups rely on feedback to sense and respond, invitation aligns with and strongly supports self-management, self-organization and the use of collective intelligence.

To engage in Inviting Leadership is to engage in leveraging all of these invitational concepts in service to a very large improvement in your overall leadership effectiveness.

Invitation versus Delegation

In general, as a manager or an executive you will continue to delegate. When you issue invitations to those who are subject to your authority, these invitations look like this:

---

[7] The term "adjacent possible" was coined by the complexity scientist Stuart Kauffman from the Santa Fe Institute. For more information, see www.invitingleadership.com/book/links/#adjacent-possible.

1. The sender designs the invitation using the FGS pattern and clearly describing the receiver's responsibility and authority
2. The invitation is sent and received
3. The sender waits for the receiver(s) to respond (by the RSVP date, if defined)
4. The receiver(s) experience a sense of perceived control as they ponder the invitation and how they will respond
5. If the receiver declines, there are no sanctions or negative consequences from the sender
6. If the invitation is an offer to participate in a multi-person event, then everyone who accepted it experiences a sense of belonging and membership with each other and in all of the FGS details related to the invitation

Compare that sequence to the normal sequence of events when delegating responsibility:

1. A superior (a formally authorized leader in a superior/subordinate relationship) formulates the plan for delegation.
2. The leader delegates the responsibility to the subordinate.
3. The subordinate accepts the delegation of this responsibility, typically without question, based on the existing "subordinate reports to superior" relationship.
4. The receiver likely experiences a low sense of perceived control
5. Regardless of what the subordinate thinks or feels about it, an order is an order and that is that. Except…
6. If the delegation includes responsibility without the appropriate level of authority and the tools to exercise it, the subordinate is in a no-win situation. The subordinate experiences a marked

decreased in the sense of control and the sense of overall engagement.

With the delegation-of-responsibility approach, a boss is telling an employee what to do. The potential for employee engagement is much lower. Furthermore, if that responsibility is delegated without the appropriate level of authority and the tools to exercise it, the potential for employee engagement actually might approach zero. Assigning responsibility without authority does not consider the level of interest or motivation of the receiver.

Decisions are Engaging

With the invitational approach, the receiver is in charge of the timing and content of the next interaction. That is the protocol of genuine invitation. There is at least the potential for the receiver to become more engaged because they truly get to decide whether to participate in something without fear of sanctions for opting out.

Being put on a decision is engaging.

Table 3.1 summarizes the differences between delegation and invitation.

Table 3.1: Comparing Delegation and Invitation

Dimension	When using delegation	When using invitation
Responsibility of the receiver	To accept 100% responsibility to complete the task	To consider the invitation carefully
Responsibility of the sender	To describe the task clearly and provide enough authority for completing it	To describe the invitation clearly, send it, and wait for a reply; Do not demand a reason or apply any sanctions if the receiver declines

Dimension	When using delegation	When using invitation
Authority of the receiver	It depends upon how much authority the sender includes with the delegated responsibility	The receiver determines when and how to respond
Authority of the sender	Always higher than the authority level of the receiver	Almost equivalent; the sender "waits on" the receiver, who is now in charge of what happens next
Motivation Level of the receiver to Engage	Is undefined and can vary	Is clearly motivated to engage when the answer is "yes." In addition, the receiver is clearly thinking about the invitation before responding, since each invitation asks for a decision
Engagement Level of the receiver	Is undefined and can vary	Is clearly at a high level based on the opt-in "yes" reply. Is clearly at a lower level in the case of a "no"

Dimension	When using delegation	When using invitation
Information available to the sender	Delegation amounts to an order that must be followed; the receiver is unlikely to express or otherwise offer much honest information if they do not like the task being delegated	Since the timing and the content and the choice of medium for responding are all under the control of the receiver, invitations generate a lot of information
Malicious Compliance	Definitely possible	Not possible. A well-formed invitation always includes responsibility and authority When the invitation is not attractive, the opt-out feature means the receiver need not "comply" at all

Volunteers and "Malicious Compliance"

One hypothesis of Inviting Leadership is that individuals do what they are willing to do. We tend to lack enthusiasm to do things that we are unwilling to do. This hypothesis has important implications for your leadership practice and the results you are getting. If the hypothesis is true, it means that as a leader, you are in fact dealing with a workforce full of what we might call *volunteers*.

Malicious compliance is the kind of compliance that is not really sincere. Under malicious compliance, the receiver of a command or directive follows the letter (but not the spirit) of the directive. Let's investigate this concept further.

malicious compliance *n.*

> Intentionally inflicting harm by strictly following the orders of a superior, knowing that compliance with the orders will not have the intended result. The term usually implies the following of an order in such a way that ignores the order's intent but follows its letter. (Source: Wikipedia)

Interestingly, the Wikipedia entry for this term also includes the following under "see also" related topics:

- Counterproductive work behavior
- Gaming the system
- Passive-aggressive behavior

Using invitation in leadership work sidesteps the issue of malicious compliance by using a test of willingness instead of a directive or a mandate to get things done.

Micro-Authorization

A special situation is created when the invitation is sent inside an organization. When the invitation is being sent from someone with substantial authority to someone of relatively lower authority, the result is a special kind of small and temporary authorization. We call this *micro-authorization*. The sender is putting the receiver in charge of ("in authority over") all aspects of the reply: the timing, the content, and the medium for communication. The receiver's perceived sense of control is much higher than what is experienced in a delegation. All three aspects of the reply (timing, content and the medium selected) have the potential to generate key and important data about the overall level of organizational readiness for change.

All of these aspects of invitation generate important data in a way that delegation does not, as summarized in Table 3.2: Micro-Authorization.

Table 3.2: Micro-Authorization

Authorized Aspect of The Reply	Details
Timing	The receiver chooses when to reply. If there is a deadline or "RSVP" then not responding at all is a passive form of declining the invitation.
Content	The receiver chooses to respond with a "Yes" or "No" or possibly a "Maybe" if the invitation does not prohibit a "Maybe" response. The receiver may choose to add information with the reply, for example a reason for declining, or comments about his or her level of enthusiasm, or a question.
Medium for Communicating the Reply	The receiver chooses how to reply - by phone, by text, by email, during a face-to-face interaction, or in any other way that suits them and their intentions, motivations, and style.

Accepting an Invitation Establishes an Agreement

Good invitation design includes the clear definition and description of any key constraints like event date, event time, dress code, what to bring, what to expect, and other important information about the event. When the invitation is to a multi-person event like a meeting, these two things are true:

- Each individual agrees to the constraints

- There is a sense of perceived belonging that is created between all of the individuals who consented to the terms, conditions and constraints (the "rules") of the event. Since they all agreed, they all have something in common via those individual agreements. Each person who accepted actually consented to and agreed to be bound by to the constraints described in the invitation.

Accepting an invitation is agreeing to something, and making a commitment.

Belonging and Community

When you invite someone to participate in something with others, you are building a small community.[8] Consider the fact that everyone who participates agreed to something. The *same* thing. They all said "yes" to an invitation and all of its stated goals, rules and progress tracking. Everyone who accepted the invitation agreed to play the same game.

Agreement creates potential for alignment. Alignment on leadership intent is essential if that leadership it to be effective. In an organization, followers need clear signals from leaders so they can align with the leaders' intent. Agreement creates the necessary alignment on the stated goals, rules and progress tracking. Invitation to a group-level event offers membership in a set of agreements. Invitation therefore has the potential to create real alignment among the participants who accept the invitation.

This fact has important implications for leadership in the new world of work.

---

[8] For more information about community and communitas, the "spirit of community," see
www.invitingleadership.com/book/links/#communitas.

Control, Progress, and Membership

The sense of perceived membership and perceived belonging that happens when an invitation is accepted is part of a wider set of perceptions. These perceptions tend to enable a sense of well-being.

Most people want a sense of *control*, a sense of *progress* and some sense of *belonging*. To confirm this idea, investigate your own experience. At various points in your life where you were feeling down, how strong was your perceived sense of control, progress and/or belonging?

Invitations deliver a perceived sense of control, a perceived sense of progress, and a perceived sense of belonging.

Let's take a look.

Control

When you receive an invitation, you are in charge of what happens next. You get to make the next move. You can respond "yes" or "no." Or you can simply let time run out if there is a deadline or "RSVP" date. You are in control of what happens next.

Progress

Most people have a psychological need to perceive progress. When people are depressed they often report a very low sense of progress. By clearly defining how progress is measured towards the goal, you are helping to make the invitation easy to follow, understand, and to accept. None of this has to be complicated. Something as simple as a dinner invitation can be structured as a good game (see the "Well-Formed Dinner Invitation" earlier in this chapter).

Membership and Belonging

Membership is determined externally, by the sender. Belonging is inferred and sensed internally, by the recipient. A sense of belonging feels good. If you and others are invited into something, everyone who accepts has membership. Membership is a kind of agreement. Consider the invitation to participate in a dinner party: if you accept, you agree to a set of understandings about date, start time, end time, RSVP (response) deadline, and so on. You have a shared understanding with not just the host, but also with everyone else who accepted the invitation. We all agree. That's where the membership (and sense of belonging) is generated.

Table 3.3: Good Games Generate Perceived Control, Progress, and Membership

Game Property	How it Delivers Perceived Control	How it Delivers Perceived Progress	How it Delivers Perceived Belonging
Clear defined goal(s)	If I understand the goals, I know how to succeed in the game.		Each player knows exactly what game we are playing. We all agree about how to play the game successfully.
Clearly defined rules	If I know the rules, I can agree to them or not. This adds to my sense of control. If rules are vague, my sense of control is diminished.		Every player knows exactly what they and all of the other players are agreeing to. All players have membership in that agreement.

Game Property	How it Delivers Perceived Control	How it Delivers Perceived Progress	How it Delivers Perceived Belonging
Clearly described methods of tracking progress & feedback	Participants can see progress toward the goal, and use that information to determine their next action.	Clear methods depict how much is complete and how much remains to be done.	Seeing one's own efforts contribute to progress toward the common goal increases the sense of belonging.
Opt-in participation	Potential participants decide (control) whether to participate.	Everyone can see who has decided to participate and who has not.	Agreeing with other individuals who are aligned around the goals, rules, progress-tracking, and voluntary participation.

Practical Applications of Invitation

Let's say you are the formally authorized leader and you are trying to figure out who in the organization might be willing to help lead an initiative that you have planned. You could simply choose a subordinate and delegate responsibility for completing that task. Or you could issue a well-formed invitation to a wider group, perhaps all of your direct reports and all of their direct reports. In the invitation you describe the goals, the constraints, how progress will be experienced, and the 100% opt-in nature of the request.

The people who respond will likely be the ones who are *passionate* and *responsible* about the task. These are the kind of people who are motivated enough to engage authentically in supporting and helping to lead your initiative.

This is the primary difference between delegation and invitation. With invitation there is a far greater likelihood you will find an aligned, motivated, and willing person (a "passionate and responsible" person) to fill the role you have in mind.

Invitations from leaders also have the advantage of sending important signals to the workforce about trust and respect. In "Chapter 5 – Leadership" we cover this positive signaling aspect in much greater detail.

Ideally, your leadership will produce great results. Great results come from an organizational ability to sense and respond to change. For this to happen, the people in the organization must be learning all the time. Fear reduces learning, so it is important to minimize fear. People need to feel safe enough to not be afraid of the boss, not be afraid of being fired, and so on. That safety comes from leaders who consistently signal respect and trust.

Figure 3.3: The Safety Stack

Leadership invitations indicate that you respect and trust the people to whom you send the invitations. Figure 3.3 shows how great results ultimately depend on respect and trust.

Psychological Safety and Respect

Invitation fundamentally respects the receiver's interpersonal boundaries. This is a major strength of this style of leadership.

Respect is holding and/or demonstrating esteem for a person. Any organization that has a healthy culture holds respect as an expressed or implied core value. That's because respect is necessary for people to feel psychologically safe and not be nervous. When respect is not present, nervousness, anxiety and fear reduce people's learning capacity and their ability to be adaptive.

Inviting Leadership is 100% aligned on the core value of respect. The opt-out feature, which any legitimate invitation has, operationalizes respect. The sender of an invitation must accept the "decline" or "no" if that invitation is to be genuine and authentic. A genuine invitation respects the boundaries of the receiver.

Invitation is fundamentally respectful of the receiver because the receiver is in charge of what happens next. Instead of forcing compliance or using coercion or persuasion to get agreement, an invitation makes an offer and then waits for a response.

Therefore, the act of issuing a genuine invitation is authentically respectful. This is perhaps the greatest strength of the Inviting Leadership method. Invitation is especially important in the new world of work, because invitation has the potential to greatly increase levels of demonstrated respect and employee engagement.

It's not easy to imagine a modern workplace without leaders who encourage and model respectful interactions. Not only do the leaders have to communicate and encourage respect as a core value, they must consistently model that behavior. When respect is not present in the culture, psychological safety is low. That leads to a disengaged, low-innovation culture. Lack of respect also greatly reduces the ability of the organization to respond to change. Invitation is the manifestation of respect from sender to receiver.

Figure 3.4 depicts the rise and fall of psychological safety. Growth in safety is linear and builds over time. Decay in psychological safety is exponential and nearly immediate. Layoffs and the firing of personnel without clear communication from leadership, for example, can obliterate in one day the safety that took months to build up. Point C depicts a low-safety event, decay to point D, and subsequent recovery to points E, F and G. Safety levels off periodically, as represented by points G, and H. Point I depicts another low-safety event like a change in leadership followed by sudden policy changes. In a spot like that, safety will plummet and will decay exponentially. Recovery can take months.

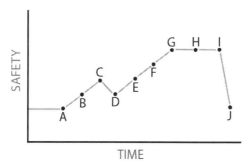

Figure 3.4: Exponential Decay in Psychological Safety

Inviting Leadership creates the conditions for psychological safety and helps to maintain it by consistently manifesting respect for people. A leadership style that takes an invitation-centric approach to change has the potential to create and then maintain an authentic culture of respect across the entire organization.

Identifying and Working With the Willing

In organizations, it is the willing people who power most all of the improvement and progress. The unwilling people power most all of the impediments. These improvements and impediments have great impact during change initiatives. This has serious implications for how you lead the change. You must identify and work with the willing. Leadership invitations are an excellent way to identify the people who are willing. Invitations generate a lot of data about who is enthusiastic and who is not. Each invitation is a small experiment that probes the environment. We know from complexity science that during a period of high complexity, the recommended approach is to experiment and to probe. Since organizational change is a complex endeavor, it is exactly the right context for favoring invitation over delegation.

Try This

Issue one invitation per day for 4 days
- o   To anyone
- o   Make sure it is well-formed

        o   Inspect the results

What If They Decline?

There is one more key technique in the Inviting Leadership style: *When they say no, reduce the ask by half.* This works in any situation where you are the one doing the inviting.

Sometimes you will design and send well-formed invitations that are not widely accepted. The thing to do after a brief delay is to ask for less.

The thing to do is ask for less. Here are the steps:

1. **Describe an experiment that is to be inspected later.** The experiment should be completely temporary in nature, with no long-term commitment. For example, ask management team to try doing a daily stand-up meeting.

2. **Define the exact time-duration of the experiment.** Be specific. So for example, you might suggest "I wonder if you all might be willing to try doing a daily stand-up meeting, as an experiment to be inspected, for *one month* or about four weeks. Do you think you might be willing to do that?"

3. **Watch. Observe.**

4. **If they say "no" reduce the ask by about half.** After a brief delay, ask again and define the exact duration of the proposed experiment as *two weeks* instead of one month.

5. **If they say no AGAIN, repeat that last step a couple more times, until they say 'yes' or just refuse to do any experiments at all.** Almost all of the time they will agree to try something for a limited amount of time.

This is a very simple way to encourage others to try new things and learn really, really fast.

Advantages:

- They get to choose (control) what happens next

- They are committing to try something small
- They are getting direct experience instead of long-winded lectures
- Big surprises often ensue (via direct experience) leading to "a convincing learning experience" without any "logical arguing" or convincing required
- By inviting them, you get to continuously gauge their current level of willingness to try new things
- You are not arguing "for or against" anything. Instead you are testing their willingness to try this or that, to get direct experience... to learn something

When you start using the Inviting Leadership style, you will encounter situations where your well-planned and well-designed invitations are not being accepted.

When that happens, reduce the ask by half.

Recap

We have covered a lot of ground here on the fundamental dynamics of invitation.

This is key information that sets you up to examine and understand the following chapters - Self-Management and Leadership.

PART II - ADVANCED CONCEPTS

Chapter 4 – Self-Management

Self-managed teams are high-performing teams. For a team to be self-managed they must be making enough decisions to keep them engaged in the process.

Chapter 5 – Leadership

The act of leading always involves being party to decisions that affect the whole group. Leadership invitations are a primary way to sense and decisively respond quickly to challenges and opportunities.

Chapter 4 – Self-Management

Self-managed teams are high-performing teams. For a team to be self-managed they must be making enough decisions to keep them engaged in the process.

Overview

Doug Kirkpatrick, author of the book *Beyond Empowerment*, helped form and found the Self-Management Institute[1] and is acknowledged as an expert in the field. Here is Doug's definition of self-management:

> *"Organizational self-management is the philosophy of individuals freely and autonomously performing the traditional functions of management (planning, organizing, coordinating, staffing, directing, controlling) guided by principles and without mechanistic hierarchy or arbitrary, unilateral command authority over others."*[2]

In this book we offer a complimentary and somewhat shorter definition. In addition, our definition boils it down to authorizing teams of employees to make truly impactful decisions. In the Inviting Leadership approach, we use this definition:

self-management *n.*
  Taking responsibility for decisions that affect oneself and others. Self-management can be applied at

---

[1] For more information about the Self Management Institute, see www.invitingleadership.com/book/links/#sminstitute.

[2] For more information about self-management, see www.invitingleadership.com/book/links/#self-management.

the individual, team, and enterprise levels. A self-managed team makes most of the decisions that affect the work of that team as a whole.

By "most decisions" we mean the set of all decisions that are not explicitly reserved by executive leadership. It is essential that these authority boundaries are very well defined. By "team," we mean from one to about fifteen members. For purposes of this definition and subsequent discussion, we are allowing that a team can have as little as one member. In the vast majority of cases teams will have multiple members. We view a total of 15 members as the extreme upper limit.[3]

Differentiating Self-Organization from Self-Management

Self-organization is a term that is rooted in complexity science. Self-management is a specialized subset of self-organization in our definition. Self-management applies to certain groups and individuals in a goal-seeking situation, while the wider concept of self-organization applies also to living systems and physical systems (such as weather systems) that occur in nature. Fish, for example, exhibit self-organization when they group into schools. Birds exhibit self-organization when groups of individuals form a flock. But only humans explicitly define and then agree upon a procedure for making a decision that affects all the members of a goal-seeking team. We call this process of managing decisions that affect the whole group the *self-management* process. Self-management in this context is the intentional design and implementation of a defined protocol or procedure for decision-making, by the group that is being affected by the consequences of that decision. These protocols and procedures become effective every time a decision that impacts the whole group is being made.

---

[3] Group size determines various options and dynamics. Teams of less than ten members can employ unanimous consent. Dunbar's number (150) is commonly used as the maximum number of stable relationships that the typical person can maintain. For more information, see www.invitingleadership.com/book/links/#group-size.

Importantly, our definition of self-management applies to a group or team that exists within the context of working toward realizing an objective or aim. Examples of such goal-seeking organizations include for-profit institutions, non-profit corporations, academic institutions, government institutions, and the military.

Creating the Conditions for Self-Organization and Self-Management

Inviting Leaders create the conditions for the self-management of "How"-level decisions by teams. Teams decide "How" a product is built, or a service is delivered. Formally authorized product and service leaders generally define "What" is to be built or delivered, and executive-level leaders define overall direction and strategy. They define and communicate the overall "Why."

Self-managed teams are responsible for almost all of the improvement that results from an agile approach to work. As a consequence, Inviting Leaders need to do everything they can to encourage teams to behave in this way.

To encourage self-management, certain core elements need to be in place. These include:

- Clear constraints- boundaries and limits that must be carefully designed and managed
- Maintenance of boundaries- leadership behavior that guarantees the structural integrity of those constraints
- Authorized decisions – The freedom to act autonomously within the container formed by the clearly defined constraints

These elements work together as shown in Table 4.1.

Table 4.1: Constraints, Boundaries, and Decisions

Element	How it Works	Notes
Clear Constraints	Complexity science confirms that the absence of constraints impedes self organization. Clear constraints define a container within which individuals in groups will get creative and self organize.	Design the boundary conditions of "dos and don'ts" with the right amount of tension. If too loose, progress with self-organization will often be slow. If too tight, little or no self-organization can happen.
Maintaining the integrity of the constraints	Constraints form boundaries. Boundaries form perimeters and containers. A successful challenge and breach of the constraint's integrity will compromise self-organization and self-management inside the container.	Leaders need to design the right level of tension or "tightness" into the constraints and boundaries, and then carefully adjust that tension if needed. When the boundary tests occur, they need to be managed carefully to maintain the boundary integrity.

Element	How it Works	Notes
Decisions inside the boundaries of the constraints.	The group of individuals subject to the container formed by the constraints must be allowed to make substantial decisions that affect their environment inside that container.	Self-management as we define it in this book is the management of significant decisions that affect the group. It is essential that these decisions are authorized and encouraged if any self-management is to take place.

Constraints alone cannot not encourage self-management. Even if they are designed with the right level of tension, if the group members subject to the constraint cannot make decisions that affect their work, they will not be able to self-manage because others outside of their "container" are effectively managing and making those decisions.

Meaningful decisions at the team level about "How" without clear constraints or very "loose" constraints will not encourage much self-management either. Any decision is allowed in the absence of clear constraints. This leads to decisions that are not aligned with the wider and intended goals and aims defined by the formally authorized leaders.

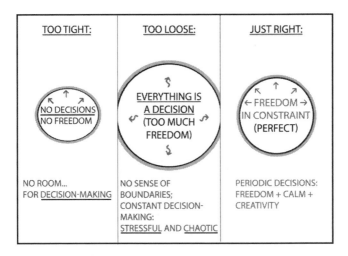

Figure 4.1: Boundaries in Three Sizes

Follow these rules to quickly encourage significant levels of self-management:

- Define clear constraints and boundaries on authority – *with the right level of tension*
- Maintain the integrity of those boundaries
- Authorize significant decision-making within those well-defined constraints.

Decisions and Leadership

Making decisions that affect the whole group is one of the authorized tasks of *leadership*. The leadership of a group can take many forms. The group may choose to authorize one person to make such decisions or create some other process that includes more people.

But: regardless of the form of leadership, we can safely assert that "decision-making that affects the whole group" is a fundamental task of the then-current leadership of that group.

Therefore: if self-management is "the management of most decisions that affect the whole group, by that group" then it is also true that self-management is actually active management of *the leadership function.*

Decisions That Affect the Whole Group or Team

To make a decision, you must consider many factors. A decision is not always complete with a binary "yes-no" or "go/ no-go" response. Indeed, there is often a nuanced range of possible responses at a decision point. Likewise, before a decision is made, there is a range of influences and inputs to consider. There is also the timing of the decision and an assessment of the likely long-run effects of the decision being made. Making a non-trivial decision requires focus and attention. For this reason, making decisions is engaging.

GREAT RESULTS START WITH GREAT INVITATIONS:
THE RESULTS STACK

GREAT RESULTS AND OUTCOMES
CAPACITY TO SENSE & RESPOND TO CHANGE
SELF-MANAGEMENT
EMPLOYEE ENGAGEMENT
DECISION-MAKING
RECEIVING INVITATIONS

Figure 4.2: The Results Stack

There is a very tight and correlated relationship between human engagement, decision-making, self-management, and positive business outcomes. Employee engagement is essential for success in introducing any kind of change.

engaged employees *n.*
> Employees who are involved in, enthusiastic about, and committed to their work and workplace. (Source: The Gallup Organization)

The Gallup Organization has produced a lot of data that illustrates and confirms the clear correlations between higher levels of employee engagement and higher scores for business outcomes, key performance indicators, and OKRs (Objectives and Key Results).[4]

Figure 4.1 shows how important it is for employees to make decisions. The goal of Inviting Leadership is great results. To obtain those results, there is a progression:

Great Results

Improvement in measurable outcomes is what we want. To get there, we need to increase the capacity of the group (any team, division or entire organization) to respond to change.

Capacity to Sense and Respond

The capacity to sense and respond to change is a function of how fast observers can make new observations, and make decisions based on these new observations.[5]

Self-Management

Self-managed employees (who are by implication deeply engaged) is where most of the improvement in response time actually comes from. When employees self-manage, decisions and responses happen faster. Those observations and responses are tailored and customized to address and solve the problems and opportunities that exist in the here-and-now.

Employee Engagement

There is no self-management without engagement. Have you ever seen a self-managed team that was not deeply engaged in their work? Engagement is essential for self-management; with few exceptions all self-managed employees and teams are engaged and focused on the work at hand. Some of the most important work

---

[4] For more information about the correlation between engagement and outcomes, see
www.invitingleadership.com/book/links/#self-management.

[5] For more information on sensing and responding, including readings from science and the military, see
www.invitingleadership.com/book/links/#sense-respond.

of a team is the work of making decisions. That work is inherently engaging. For teams and groups to self-manage decision-making, they must be engaged. Engagement sustains self-management and vice versa.

Decision-Making

A primary device for raising the level of employee engagement is raising the level of authorization to make decisions. This cannot be overstated. By raising the level of decision-making authorization while also defining and explaining a very short list of clear boundaries (rules) about limits to that decision-making, higher and higher levels of employee engagement can and will be achieved. Higher levels of decision-making authority are correlated with higher levels of engagement.[6]

Emergent Properties Improve in a Linear Fashion, But They Decay Exponentially

Emergent properties are characteristics that arise due to the environment. They are typically non-existent or exist at levels that are so small that they are difficult to measure. Emergent properties typically are slow to grow and quick to decay. Employee happiness is one example. Other examples include levels of organizational learning, levels of psychological safety, and levels of self-management. These are exactly the properties which, if cultivated and attended to in an ongoing way, can and will produce superior results in teams and enterprises.

As an Inviting Leader, it is vitally important that you understand the dynamics of emergent properties in the main. *The emergent properties are what you are after.* If you want consistently higher performance, if the goal for your group is to become world-class delivery organization, then you had better pay attention to these five emergent properties:

- Employee engagement

---

[6] For more information about decision-making and engagement, see www.invitingleadership.com/book/links/#deciding-and-engagement.

- Team and organizational learning
- Psychological safety
- Self-management
- Manifest (actual) Innovation

Figure 4.2 depicts levels of employee engagement and can just as easily be applied to the other four emergent properties you are after. Groups of people who gather together to seek agreed-upon goals are social systems in the truest sense of that term. All social systems are "complex adaptive systems."[7] In technical terms these complex adaptive systems are "first-order, non-linear feedback systems." What this means to you is simple: *very small changes in certain variables can and will have a very large impact on overall system performance.* One of these variables is the level of external/management involvement in decision-making that affects the day-to-day work of the team. If the frequency and magnitude of external management involvement in these decisions are above certain limits, *the result is exponential decay in the very emergent properties you are looking for.*

In the diagram below, management decision-making that affects the teams is depicted as a histogram. To simplify the diagram, the frequency of management decision-making is steady and constant (a total of 12 samples) while the magnitude of how those decisions affect the work of the teams varies. For the first seven periods or samples, the management decisions consistently stayed below the key limit represented by the horizontal line depicted in the histogram and entitled "Management Decisions That Affect the Work of Teams." During this time, employee engagement steadily ramped up in a linear fashion. But after that, the 6th, 7th, 8th, 9th and 10th samples each have a magnitude that is clearly above the line. When this happens, it can trigger immediate exponential decay from a falling inflection point. When

---

[7] This phrase borrows from the late Jay Forrester, a professor at the M.I. T. Sloan School of Management. Forrester had quite a bit to say about the design of social systems. For more information, see www.invitingleadership.com/book/links/#forrester.

this happens, it can take months to recover, because recovery of an emergent property from *exponential* (non linear) decay is a *linear* process.

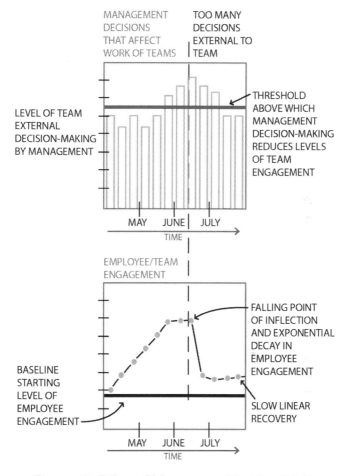

Figure 4.3: Effects of Management Decision-Making on Engagement

This two-part diagram applies not just to levels of employee engagement but also to levels of team learning, psychological safety, self-management and innovation. Keep this in mind as you begin your journey into the Inviting Leadership style. Leadership is in part about setting a clear direction and communicating the *why* of that. Leave the *what* to your product people and leave the *how* to your teams. Make sure the folks responsible for the *what* decisions also refrain from meddling in the *how* decisions that belong to the teams. If you end up making too many of the *what* and *how* decisions, you can expect exponential decay in the very emergent properties you are seeking to increase and maintain.

One last point on the subject of the desirable and emergent properties of engagement, psychological safety, self-management, innovation and group-level learning: they are very sensitive to the environment *beyond* the issue of decision-making. Here are some of the other events that can cause exponential decay on these desirable and emergent properties:

- Executive leadership changes: changes in who is occupying top leadership roles
- Layoffs: Fear is a natural consequence of layoffs and fear works against making progress in safety and learning
- Firings: In general, firings damage levels of psychological safety and increase fear levels
- Mergers, acquisitions, reorgs: Major changes to the organization cause a period of instability, concerns about job safety etc.

It is important to be aware of the fact that these events can severely impact hard-won gains and improvements that you and the organization have achieved over time. Each of these events has a psychological impact across the organization. If any of these events are occurring or about to occur, it is essential that there is a strong and consistent narrative designed to minimize the damage and help to cushion the impact of these kinds of events. Have a strong communication plan and a strong leadership narrative in place, well in advance of these kind of destabilizing events.

Receiving Invitations from Leaders

An understandable invitation automatically triggers a process of decision-making. All invitations are "an offer or a proposal to go somewhere, or do something."[8] Such offers and proposals (especially from executive leaders) will trigger a chain of positive-business-outcome events: deciding, engaging, self-managing, rapid sensing and responding to change, and ultimately, generation of great results in the form of positive and measurable business outcomes.

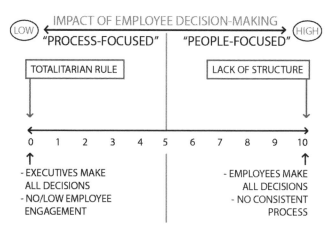

Figure 4.4: Impact of Employee Decision-Making

Figure 4.4 shows the range of impact from employee decision-making. In general, the more frequently changes are occurring, the more decision-making authority needs to be located at the edge (rather than the center) of the operation. There are a set of problems that executives need to address when making these adjustments. Too much decision-making authority for employees can result in a lack of consistent process and consistently good results. On the other hand, too much centrally-planned decision-making results in "totalitarian rule," and subsequently very low levels of employee engagement. A skew or bias towards "people focus" is the right approach if and when the level of ambient change is frequent and/ or increasing in velocity.

---

[8] For more information about invitation, see
www.invitingleadership.com/book/links/#invitation-defined.

Figure 4.5 shows how typical organizations are skewed toward the "process focus" and tend to be less responsive than what is required to thrive and grow. Decision-making is centralized and occurs very far away from where the environmental change was first observed. The bureaucracy associated with central planning and decision-making also causes delays. Previous plans have authors and sponsors. These individuals are invested in those plans, even when environmental change completely invalidates those plans. Meanwhile, employees begin to disengage as the few decisions they are allowed to make are frequently overridden and/ or are not of much consequence. The result is an organization with a very low capacity to respond to challenges and opportunities.

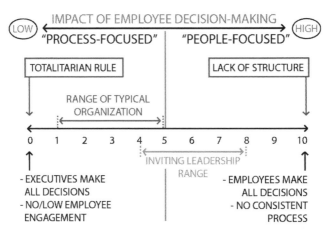

Figure 4.5: Inviting Leadership Range of Employee Decision-Making Impact

As depicted in Figure 4.5, the typical organization operates in the range of 1 to 4 on a scale of 1 to 10 in terms of the impact of employee-sourced decision-making. What needs to happen is a pronounced shift to the right, into the range of 4 to 8 on the depicted scale of 1 to 10.

When executives begin using structured invitations to motivate and engage the workforce, this shift can be achieved. The result is an organization with an elevated capacity to sense and respond.

It is important to focus on the fact that there is a range with a minimum and maximum boundary. If the impact of employee decisions is too low, then employee engagement levels will also be low. But if the organization-wide impact of those employee decisions is too high, then disorganization, "chaos" and wasteful lack of consistency in process and procedure will ensue and have a negative impact on business goals and outcomes. Each organization is unique and you will need to tailor and customize your implementation of Invitation-Based Change and Inviting Leadership to obtain the best results. The key takeaway here is that there is a range, and the results quickly decay at the boundaries of that range. The chapters on Boundary, Invitation and Leadership cover the mechanics of how to identify and implement the correct range for your situation and context.

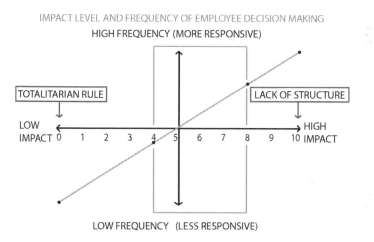

IMPACT LEVEL AND FREQUENCY OF EMPLOYEE DECISION MAKING

Figure 4.6: Impact and Frequency of Employee Decision-Making

An important aspect of self-managed employee decision-making is not just the impact of the decision on the performance of the organization. The *frequency* of these decisions is also important. If employees only make a few decisions a year, or otherwise are not engaging in decision-making frequently enough, the result will be on-again/off-again levels of employee engagement. The frequency of decision-making is an important factor in employee engagement. In fact, if you as a leader authorize lower-impact but higher-frequency decisions by employees and teams, you can raise employee engagement levels over the intermediate term and improve results that way. But the effects will be shallow and temporary instead of deep and lasting. As depicted in Figure 4.6, self-managed decision-making by employees and teams must be impactful enough to be meaningful and frequent enough to maintain optimal levels of employee engagement and the other related emergent properties.

Recap

Executive leaders who want better results can get those results by developing skills in defining and sending leadership invitations. Invitations invite decisions, and decisions are engaging. Each invitation must be properly structured with the goals, boundaries, feedback mechanisms and opt-in aspects all set up very clear and easy to understand. Inviting Leadership is the art of sending invitations out, into the organization, with the intent of generating the best possible results, as soon as possible, at the lowest possible cost. The key to this is the triggering of *decisions*, which creates a chain reaction leading to positive results in everything you are measuring.

Chapter 5 – Leadership

The act of leading always involves being party to decisions that affect the whole group. Leadership invitations are a primary way to sense and decisively respond quickly to challenges and opportunities.

Overview

The pace of change is constantly speeding up due to technological advances. You can address the resulting opportunities and dangers profitably only if you recognize them and respond faster than the competition in your industry.

We assume that if you are reading this chapter, you are a leader in an organization that is trying to make the most of rapid change. Responding to rapid change does not make everyone happy, and support for the necessary response can be hard to come by. Change is stressful. Fear of change makes it hard to learn. Organizations must learn if they are to adapt.

Our best idea for solving this problem is to bring invitation into your leadership toolkit and begin using it. This chapter addresses how the concepts of invitation and Inviting Leadership can help you safely and pragmatically bring more responsiveness to your organization, regardless of how big your organization might be. The techniques in this chapter are designed to be "scale-free";[1] that is, applicable at any level, from one team to a global enterprise with 50,000 people or more.

Here, we also assume that you are familiar with terminology and concepts from previous chapters. If you are not, you can still

---

[1] For more information about the origins and concept of scale-free architecture for organizations, see www.invitingleadership.com/book/links/#scale-free.

work with this chapter by reading the chapter overviews and referring to the Glossary for definitions of unfamiliar terms.

This chapter ties together many of the essential topics introduced in previous chapters. Table 5.1 briefly summarizes the topics of this chapter and how each of these topics applies to using the concepts and facilities of Inviting Leadership

Table 5.1: Essential Topics for Applying Inviting Leadership Successfully

Topic in This Chapter	Why it is Essential to Inviting Leadership	Notes
Agreements	Accepting an invitation is making an agreement. Organizations are held together by the agreements made by and between its members	Agreement and the potential for alignment is a major strength of the Inviting Leadership approach
Authority and Authority Distribution	Inviting means the sender is putting the receiver in authority over what happens next. Inviting therefore conveys a small amount of authorization	Invitations can help obtain the broadest possible support for aligning the decision-making process to maximize the flow of value in a value stream[2]

---

[2] For more information about value streams and value stream analysis, see www.invitingleadership.com/book/links/#value-stream.

Topic in This Chapter	Why it is Essential to Inviting Leadership	Notes
Leadership Semiotics & Signaling	An invitation from a leader initiates an interaction. Every invitation from a leader is a signal that conveys meaning	Signal-sending is a primary task of effective leadership. Participants are listening for clear signals from leaders, especially during times of change
Design	Leadership is in part a design task. This design aspect also applies to invitations and what you are inviting the workforce into	Inviting Leaders design enterprise change as a kind of emerging story (or "game") that others are invited into. The receivers are invited to complete the story of the change
Employee Engagement and Engagement Models	Employee engagement is essential for advancing a positive process of change. Invitations from leaders do prompt decision-making by the receivers. This decision-making tends to quickly elevate levels of engagement	Enterprise change is not really possible without engaged employees. "Business agility frameworks" are silent on this essential component of success

Topic in This Chapter	Why it is Essential to Inviting Leadership	Notes
Liminality	Change creates a stressful feeling of transition between an old story and a new story. Inviting Leaders can reduce this stress through invitations	The demand for a coherent and easy-to-follow story greatly increases during times of change. Inviting Leaders leverage this fact by designing, delivering and repeating an ongoing, coherent and clear narrative
Leadership and Management	Delegation provides far less feedback than invitation. Inviting Leaders use invitations to generate data and gauge what the organization is capable of doing next in terms of incremental, evolutionary change	

Topic in This Chapter	Why it is Essential to Inviting Leadership	Notes
Tools	Some very effective tools for group work and leadership of group work are based on consent, invitation and opt-in participation. We survey some of these tools in this chapter	

Agreements

An organization is nothing more than all the members, and the set of agreements by and between all of those members. Agreements can be expressed or implied.

When you issue invitations and those who receive it accept the invitation to engage, they are in fact agreeing to all the terms of your invitation. This link between invitations and agreements allows you the leader to work from a position of strength. Those who accepted are not resisting your plans, and those who declined the invitation are not participating against their will, which can create resistance and other related problems like higher employee turnover. Healthy organizations run on good agreements. Invitations from leaders automatically create agreements of this kind. Those who feel a sense of passion and responsibility about what the invitation is offering will tend to accept it, and those who do not will tend to decline it.

Agreements on Word Definitions

When you are trying to bring change, some new terminology and some new rules are usually introduced. Getting widespread agreement about terminology definitions and what they refer to, in advance, is very important. It is not a good idea to start a change program without these fundamental agreements about the language. You want everyone using the same language in the same way and with the same meaning. Change usually means changes in how authority is distributed and the last thing you need is confusion about what the change actually is. Clear definitions for the new *words* do help and may in fact be essential.

Another important task is making sure you get agreement on the new *rules* which that new terminology often refers to. For example, if you are implementing the Agile framework "Scrum At Scale,"[3] it is essential to clearly define this term, socialize the rules of Scrum At Scale, and then get agreement to honor those rules, from everyone who is affected by the change.

The best way to get a good agreement is to reduce what you are asking for. Invitation can be used to do this. Time is a boundary and can be used as an enabling constraint. You can gain support for the planned changes by asking for support that has an end date followed by an inspection of results. Invitation-based change leverages the power of invitation to encourage incremental change that occurs in stages. The stages include an inspection of results and an explicit review of the experience.

(NOTE: If you are planning or currently involved in an "Agile transformation," refer to "Appendix A – "Ready for Agile" Checklist". In this checklist, we enumerate the agreements that must first be established with teams, their stakeholders, management, and executive leadership. This checklist describes all of the agreements you must have in place to be ready to begin. These agreements are essential to success. You can use the template to create your own custom checklist for initiating any other kind of change that you are planning.)

Getting good agreements up front about terminology definitions and the new rules is an essential first step in preparing

---

[3] Scrum At Scale describes a lightweight, "scale free," authority distribution scheme for running a modern enterprise. For more information about Scrum and Scrum At Scale, see
www.invitingleadership.com/book/links/#scrum.

for change. Well-designed invitations from executive leadership can help to rapidly generate some of these essential agreements.

For example, if you are trying to build support and reduce resistance to change, try inviting everyone to a meeting to discuss some aspect of the change (such as essential word definitions and some of the new rules) and make it very clear that the meeting is 100% optional to attend. Then pay attention. Those that accept your invite are agreeing explicitly to all of the clearly stated goals for that meeting, and all of the other constraints that you outlined in your invitation.

Agreements on Rules

Agreeing on a set of common word definitions is an important first step. Often, these words will be names for a new framework or some kind of new structure for decision-making. "Scrum" is defined by *The Scrum Guide* and *The Scrum Guide* describes a set of *rules* about roles, the decisions those roles are authorized to make, and so on. Agreements about the rules are critically important.

As a leader you can try to force agreements on the new words and new rules, or simply mandate that everyone comply without further discussion. But since the most innovative and independent-minded people respond negatively to being pushed around, asking and inviting is a far better approach. We suggest that you begin by inviting participation in some meetings that can start the following processes:

1. Getting good agreements on essential terms and words
2. Getting good agreements on any new rules

You cannot force this and you need to create an "open space" for the dissenting opinions and objections. These objections must get a hearing and be addressed.

Of particular importance are the agreements on new rules or policies about decision-making. New rules will generally address the way decisions get made. These changes in decision-making authority are usually what most people are most concerned with. If they have objections to the change, it will usually be about any changes around who is authorized to make what decisions. These are legitimate concerns that need a hearing.

When you kick off this process, you want to make sure you structure your invitations in the four-part game structure format (FGS) described in Chapter 3 and that you refrain from chasing anyone who does not chose to participate. In general, the willing people are the people that can power any lasting change.

Invitations generate important feedback on who the willing and able people actually are.

Authority and Authority Distribution

Executive leaders are faced with change every single day.[4] In response to this, the terms "transformation," "Agile transformation," "digital transformation," and "business agility" have entered the business lexicon to help describe various kinds of responses and approaches to dealing with change.

"Agile transformation" is about improving the processes and the results related to the delivery of software. "Digital transformation" refers the act of aligning business processes to more rapidly respond to the digital aspects of being in business. These "digital transformation" adjustments include:

- Improving the ability of the organization to sense and respond to opportunities, challenges and threats
- Incorporating social media into overall marketing and customer relationship management (CRM) strategy
- Automation (digitization) of CRM
- Smoothly changing and reorganizing continuously, in response to a continuous flow of feedback from customers, markets, suppliers and employees

---

[4] For more information about the pace of change, see www.invitingleadership.com/book/links/#pace-of-change.

- Creating and sustaining a culture that supports all of the above
- Aligning the process of decision-making to the company's value streams, in service to maximizing the flow of value from the company to the customer

Decisions

Aligning decision-making to strongly support the company's value streams is by far the most important change, and also the change that is the most difficult to make. A *value stream*, as the name implies, is a set of business activities that produce a good or a service that flows from the business to stakeholders and/or customers.[5]

The basic problem to solve is not how to simply *increase* the flow of value, but rather how to actually continuously *maximize* that flow at any point in time. The solution usually involves identifying obstacles and impediments to the flow of value, and removing the largest obstacles first. This is the basic idea behind the Theory of Constraints as developed by the late author, Eliyahu M. Goldratt.[6]

Here is the reality: in most businesses, and probably your own organization, the biggest obstacle to the flow of value is *how decisions are being made* at every decision-point along the value stream, at every decision-point along the way towards achieving the delivery of value.

Decision-making procedures that are not strongly supporting the maximization of value-flow are usually the largest constraint and must be removed first. Those currently authorized to make certain decisions are not happy when the decision-making policies change the decision-making status quo. Those who make decisions today are typically those who resist any change in policies that

---

[5] For more information about value streams, see www.invitingleadership.com/book/links/#value-stream.

[6] For more information about the Theory of Constraints, see www.invitingleadership.com/book/links/#theory-of-constraints.

redefines who decides what. It is important to surface these objections in advance of implementing change.

The Way You Distribute Authority
Drives Communication Flows and Culture

The figure below depicts what is really going on at your company. And here is what is going on: attempts to improve communication and "culture" will fail, if you fail to address the "authority-to-make-decisions" aspect. This is because the "org chart diagram" is actually an "authority to make decisions" diagram. And how this authority *to decide* is distributed literally drives *everything* about communication and company culture. Therefore, to change culture, change the decision-making schema. Almost immediately, the way communications flow changes, and with that, some changes in key aspects of the culture immediately follow.

THE DOMINANT INFLUENCE ON YOUR COMPANY
CULTURE IS HOW AUTHORITY IS DISTRIBUTED:

Figure 5.1: The Culture Stack

The lower two foundational parts of this stack are what are commonly called "the structure" which is a very imprecise way of saying "the authority distribution schema." Authority may be distributed in a hierarchical scheme, or in some type of networked scheme, or in some other way. The topic of authority distribution design is a complex subject. For now, let's take a look at a predesigned scheme for effectively distributing authority in service to building great products: Scrum.

Example: The Scrum Framework

The Scrum Guide describes the Scrum[7] framework. The Guide's subtitle is *"The Definitive Guide to Scrum: The Rules of the Game."*

So. What is Scrum exactly? What we call "Scrum" is a set of roles, rules, artifacts and events that form a coherent system for rapidly developing and delivering complex products, such as software. Scrum originated in the software industry and has since been proven to be applicable anywhere that complex products are being designed, constructed and delivered.

So the real question is, if Scrum is a "framework," then what kind of framework is it exactly? Here is our conclusion: Scrum is a framework that defines how specific *decisions* are made. **Scrum is an "authority distribution framework."** The roles, artifacts, events and rules of Scrum describe, very clearly, *who has the authority* to decide what.

Each role in Scrum has a set of authorized tasks.

The quotes below are direct quotes from *The Scrum Guide* (Note: the "Product Backlog" is a to-do list of prioritized work...)

"The Product Owner is the sole person responsible for managing the Product Backlog.

"...those wanting to change the priority of a Product Backlog item must address the Product Owner."

"...For the Product Owner to be successful, everyone in the organization must respect his or her decisions."

The Scrum Guide is full of very specific statements like these, defining the "authorized decisions" for each Scrum role. In the quotes above, we can see that the Product Owner and *only* the Product Owner may make decisions about work prioritization. Others may influence the priorities, but only the Product Owner can decide. Implementing Scrum changes the way decisions get

---

[7] For more information about Scrum see Appendix F or www.invitingleadership.com/book/links/#scrum.

made and who makes them. This is why culture changes if you implement it well.

Example: The Kanban Method

The book *Kanban: Successful Evolutionary Change for Your Technology Business* by David J. Anderson defines the Kanban Method. The method is explained further by Mike Burrows in *Kanban from the Inside: Understand the Kanban Method, connect it to what you already know, introduce it with impact.*[8] Like the Scrum framework, Kanban describes artifacts, roles, rules and events that collectively work together to form a complete system. It is important to note that the Kanban Method describes some rules about decision-making. In other words, if you commit to Kanban, you are committing to implementing these new decision-making rules. For example, it is a rule in the Kanban Method that before a new work item enters the work queue, it must be characterized by Work Item Type. This characterization has implications for when the completed work is likely to be delivered.

If you are implementing Kanban, it is important to spend some time getting agreement about terms like Work Item Type and the related rules. Failure to do so results in almost immediate issues in implementation, as those who are accustomed to making decisions about work flow ignore the basic rules of Kanban since they never agreed to them in the first place. Before introducing change, it is imperative to surface objections to new decision-making rules and get agreement up front.

Value Streams and Decisions

Software development and in fact any product development is performed in service to a flow of value from the business to paying customers. In general terms, value streams are flows of business value that result in business revenue. Value stream mapping depicts the steps (the work) along the way to value delivery. Some value

---

[8] For more information about Kanban, see Appendix G or www.invitingleadership.com/book/links/#kanban.

streams are internal; the flow of value in this case tends to support others who are directly involved in revenue generation. In all cases, value streams are concerned with either delivering value to end-users or supporting that flow of value in some other way.

Aligning Decision-Making with the Value Stream

Real transformation involves changing decision-making such that the timing and content of those decisions maximize the flow through the value stream. When the flow of value in a value stream slows down or otherwise becomes clogged, it is always a good idea to inspect the alignment of decision-making with the flow of value. All too often, decision-making becomes decoupled from the flow of value, and actually impedes it. The decision-making becomes the bottleneck.

To "transform" the results, therefore, the following axiom applies:

No matter what kind of change you are seeking, and no matter what method you use to try to manifest that change,

Until and unless there is a change in the way decisions are made, there is no genuine "transformation" of anything at all.

In any "transformation," therefore, what is actually being transformed is the *decision-making*.

The Use of Scrum Transforms Decision-Making

Consider the use of Scrum[9] for improving the process and results of software development. When a team in an organization adopts Scrum, what actually happens is the following:

- The existing rules for decision-making are *discarded*.
- The rules of Scrum *replace* the existing rules for decision-making.

---

[9] For more information about Scrum, see www.invitingleadership.com/book/links/#scrum.

- If Scrum is implemented properly, all decisions are now made in alignment with rules of Scrum as defined in *The Scrum Guide*. These rules align decision-making with the flow of value.

If Scrum is not implemented properly, then the way decisions are made and who is making them does not actually change in any meaningful way. This means that decision-making continues to be out of alignment with the intent of improving value stream flow.

This is vitally important to understand. *There is no "transformation" unless and until the way decisions are made is aligned to support (and does not in any way impede) the flow of value.*

If we utilize the Theory of Constraints,[10] and do value stream analysis,[11] we will quickly notice that the way decisions are currently being made is often a very big impediment to the flow of value. That is, the decision-making as it stands has little if anything to do with maximizing value-flow. Indeed, if the way decisions are made could be *redesigned* to better support the *flow of value*, we could improve more quickly by satisfying more customers much faster. This is achieved by removing the primary block to the flow of value: the way decisions are being made.

Around the world, on a daily basis, thousands of software teams in hundreds of companies are achieving more value delivery and higher rates of value flow by replacing their current decision-making system with the Scrum system of decision-making. For them it is a new and better decision-making framework. The new method of making decisions improves the flow of value through the software development value stream. The use of the Kanban Method and the decision-making rules found in that system also produces improvement in the overall of flow of value.

The moral of this story: the way decisions are currently being made is often the primary obstacle to the flow of value. Align

---

[10] For more information about the Theory of Constraints, see www.invitingleadership.com/book/links/#theory-of-constraints.

[11] For more information about value stream analysis, see www.invitingleadership.com/book/links/#value-stream-analysis.

decision-making with improving flows of value through the value stream and you will experience immediate improvement in most of the flows (value, revenue, quality, etc.) that you are actually measuring.

There's Only One Problem

Changing the way decisions get made is not as easy as it looks. Let's consider the idea of introducing Scrum into a software development team in your organizations. Let's introduce it as the new decision-making schema (the plan) for how decisions get made. Let's assume that we simply introduce that team to Scrum, and assume that the team is willing to use it.

Here is what immediately happens:

- **Stakeholders and executives** continue to assert authority over most (or even all) important decisions that affect the Team.
- **Managers** of the Development Team members continue to direct the work of the individuals that report to them, in effect interfering with the implementation of Scrum.
- **Performance reviews** that are based on individual performance continue to influence the behavior of Team members. This behavior is at odds with the Scrum method (because the fundamental unit in Scrum is the team, not the individual.) The policy that guides performance reviews is now an impediment to the use of Scrum decision-making.
- **The Team itself** is not a problem, since we are assuming they are in. But, if the Team was never consulted about the change, and some of the individuals on the Team do not really agree to the rules of Scrum, then there is some resentment on the Team about the imposed and mandatory use of Scrum to guide their work.
- **Departments that were previously authorized to make certain decisions** are no longer making

those decisions. Now the people occupying the three Scrum roles are making these decisions. It is safe to say that the people previously making these decisions are not happy that Scrum is now being used for making those decisions.

As we can see, "transforming" a software development team is not quite as simple as it sounds. That's because changing the way decisions get made is not as simple as it sounds. There is a lot of preparation and pre-work that is needed. This work includes:

- **Preparing executives and stakeholders** and customers and anyone else who is affected by the Team. (The people in these roles need to understand what is expected of them to support the change, and agree to do what it takes to support the use of Scrum by the Team.)
- **Preparing the managers** of the individual employees who work on the Scrum team. (These managers need to understand Scrum, and agree to align their behavior to support the use of it by the Team.)
- **Preparing the Team** for Scrum. (This includes getting the agreement and "informed consent" of all the members of the Team before starting with Scrum.)
- **Preparing the leadership of the organization** to receive information on impediments for removal. The impediments are obstacles to the teams' goal of delivering working software in a predictable and reliable manner. Getting the executive leaders ready to receive and remove these impediments is an essential first step. (Scrum provides a very clear protocol for identifying and removing impediments.)

And while changing the way decisions get made at the team level may look difficult, consider how difficult all of this is going to be, when the time comes to scale this change across the entire organization.

Your Company Is Not Ready for Transformation of Any Kind

Your company has built up all kinds of "structures" that support the current misaligned, out-of-sync, inefficient decision-making that is impeding the flow of value in your value streams. Some of these impeding and problematic structures include:

- Departments with budget and decision-making authority
- Department Heads who approve spending, hiring and firing
- Existing policies such as Performance Review policies
- Current reporting structures (formal hierarchies)

What's obvious is that most of the people holding authority in your organization have a vested interest in keeping everything the way it is. Every employee with any kind of authority whatsoever is, by definition, invested in the status quo. It includes the roles, rules, artifacts and events that are currently in place to support decision-making. Your departments, your budgeting and HR policies, your current reporting structures...all of this existing structure conspires against any change in the way decisions get made.

Changing decision-making to support and not impede value stream flow is a complex and difficult undertaking.

Inviting Leadership is the Solution

Ideally, all impediments to the flow of value are identified and removed, and your organization experiences 2X, 3X and 4X improvement in some key and measured business outcomes. For this to happen, people who are currently invested in the status-quo must be enlisted to help. Because if they are not, they will consciously and unconsciously resist the change, a change that is redefining many job descriptions.

So, you *do* actually need to enlist everyone, especially those with a big stake and a vested interest in the way things are.

Especially those who currently have substantial authority to make decisions in your organization!

And so, the key question becomes: how exactly will you enlist them?

Inviting participation in the design and the introduction of the change is the best way. By issuing invitations instead of impositions, you can and will achieve the following objectives:

You will:

- Be able to confidently and clearly determine how ready the organization is for change
- Identify those who are willing to help
- Identify those who are not really supporting the change right now
- Gain traction, by differentiating between willing and unwilling participants, and by working with (and through) the willing participants

The Inviting Leadership method, with its focus on opt-in and 100% voluntary participation and the ability to produce immediately actionable feedback, is one of the fastest ways possible to reduce resistance to the changes you are planning.

Leadership Semiotics

Everything hinges on your leadership skills, and leaders need to be ready for anything. That's why it's important to study domains that are related to leadership, domains that can help you effectively respond to all the various surprises you are sure to encounter when you are leading.

Two of these domains are semiotics and linguistics. Both of these domains are important for leaders to study.

Leadership Is Signaling

Semiotics is the sociological science of signals, symbols and signs. People make meaning and navigate the world using signals, symbols and signs.[12] Motorists, for example, rely on signals and signage to navigate to their destinations. Traffic *signals* regulate traffic *flow*. The traffic *signs* contain *symbols* (pictures and words) arranged in way that means something to the drivers who travel that road.

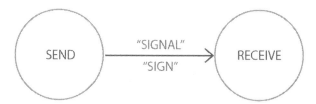

Figure 5.2: Signal Send and Receive

Leaders can help make meaning for followers by sending clear signals, creating signs, and making use of symbols. All of the signs, signals and symbols from leaders are assigned *meaning*. A primary task of a leader is to help followers make meaning and understand the "why" of executive actions. Leaders also need to help followers understand leadership direction, leadership intent and related leadership behavior. Clear signals leave little room for interpretation, while unclear signals can (and will) be "lost in translation." Since the decisions of leaders affect literally everyone in the organization, the behaviors of those in highly authorized leadership roles are always observed very carefully. Meaning can and will be assigned to all kinds of leadership behavior. That meaning may or may not be what the leader intended.

> *"When you are a Core Group member, your remarks are automatically amplified; people hear them as louder, stronger, and more command-like than they seemed when you uttered them."*[13]

---

[12] The science of semiotics is devoted to signals, symbols and signs. Good leadership has a lot to do with semiotics. For more information, see www.invitingleadership.com/book/links/#semiotics.

[13] *Who Really Matters*, by Art Kleiner, page 75.

Interactions are a medium for signaling. For example, the sending of an invitation starts an interaction with the receiver. The sending of invitations is a type of signaling behavior that can and will be assigned meaning by observers and followers.

Signals from leaders come from many sources:

Written communications include emails, memorandums, and the sending of invitations.

Verbal communications include conversations, speeches, announcements, and the offerings of invitations.

Communication *content* ("what is said") is routinely experienced as signal by followers. This includes stories about the past, present and future, statements about company direction and progress, and explanations about the "why" of company direction and progress.

Communication *form* ("how it is said") is often more important and includes verbal and nonverbal communication behaviors. *Verbal* communication behaviors include conversations, speeches, announcements, delegations, and invitations.[14] *Nonverbal* communication includes gestures, facial expressions, postures, and demonstrations of attention and inattention. For example, a leader may or may not pay attention at a meeting for the entire duration of that meeting. Or arrive late or leave early. The leader may interact with their cell phone when someone with less authority is speaking. This might be interpreted as disrespect of the speaker.

The sending of invitations by executives (the "formally authorized leaders") sends important signals about the levels of respect, openness and support for self-management.

Leadership Semiotics

Here we are introducing the term *leadership semiotics*. We define leadership semiotics as the study of how leaders use signals, signs and symbols. We believe that this sub-domain of semiotics is an

---

[14] Some verbal communications are "speech acts" and "illocutionary acts" and can be declarative, directive, or commissive. For more information, see www.invitingleadership.com/book/links/#speech-acts.

important one. Leaders help make decisions that affect the whole group. The most effective leaders use signals, signs and symbols to communicate and gain support for these decisions.[15]

Signal Broadcasting and Stigmergy

stigmergy *n.*

> An indirect coordination mechanism between independent agents in a biological or social system such as a mound of termites, a hive of bees, or a group of humans. Stigmergy relies on the unilateral broadcasting of signals by agents that do not require replies from the agents that receive the signal.

The basic idea of stigmergy is to broadcast a communication, message, or signal in such a way that everyone can receive it.

In stigmergy, independent agents in the population who receive the signal may respond to the signal, or not. They may communicate with the sender directly, or not. A stigmergy, a message is broadcast publicly and that message does not require a reply. It is sent with intent to influence the behavior of the group.

Social insects such as ants and bees engage in a wide variety of stigmergy. Ants that find food leave a chemical trail that others can follow. Bees that have located sources of nectar do a kind of dance inside the hive to signal they know where it is located.

Stigmergy[16] has quite a lot to do with self-management and higher performance. It is a very efficient technique for aligning the focus, attention and energies of a large organization. Inviting Leaders are in fact encouraging indirect coordination and collaboration ("stigmergy") when they broadcast invitations to the entire group.

---

[15] For more about semiotics, see
www.invitingleadership.com/book/links/#leadership-semiotics.

[16] For more information about stigmergy, see
www.invitingleadership.com/book/links/#stigmergy.

Sending Signals with Invitations

The Invitation chapter introduced the concept of *micro-authorization*, which occurs when a higher-authorized individual offers an invitation to a lower-authorization individual who is also a direct report. Invitation is not delegation or the assignment of responsibility. Delegation does not provide an option to decline while invitation does. Importantly, when an invitation is issued, the receiver is now the one with the authority to define the form, content and timing of the next interaction. This is micro-authorization.[17] It transfers a small yet significant amount of authority to the receiver.

A leader may for example make a standing status meeting optional to attend. Making that meeting optional amounts to an *invitation* to attend, rather than a *directive* or a command. It contains within it the micro-authorization to accept or decline.

When a "boss" issues an invitation to a direct report, it sends important signals about respect for people, emergence, control and inclusion.

Storytelling as Signal and Signage

If the people you are leading are able to convert your signals into meaning, their behavior will align faster with your leadership intent. As a leader you are always involved in signaling, whether you intend to or not. Everyone is listening on your "channel" and paying attention to the signals you are sending – deliberately or by accident. The best way to leverage this fact is to constantly be telling stories that support the direction you want the group to go. One definition of leadership is "the art of inspiring others to make a story come true." According to this definition, if you are leading people, you are telling them a story about the future, and inviting them to make that story a reality in the present.

---

[17] It's a good idea to review "Chapter 3 – Invitation" now if you are unfamiliar with the term *micro-authorization*.

Past, Present, and Future

When bringing any kind of change to any kind of organization, leadership storytelling is essential. The demand for a coherent narrative greatly increases during periods of change and transition. In the absence of intentional leadership storytelling, participants in the culture begin to construct *random* narratives to fill the gap. For this reason, "clear-signal" storytelling about the past, present and future is essential.

Stories about the past are *mythos*. When leaders tell stories about the ***past***, they can honor the people who took part in the past, convey essential core values, and begin to create a coherent present-tense narrative. They do this by naming *what* in the past is helping to create a positive outcome in the present. It is imperative that you avoid any invalidation of the past.

The past may be full of mistakes, but there is something positive from the past to refer to. Do this in all cases, because some in your audience are characters in that past-tense story. If you invalidate the past, you invalidate some individuals in the group who are characters in that story. This is a very serious error. Refer to some of the positive things from the past and build the present-tense story on that firm foundation.

Generative stories about the present are *celebrations*. Since all change happens in the ***present***, it is here that stories of experimentation and learning can be shared: who is trying new things, and what is the outcome? These stories speak to the value of learning and experiments.

Stories about the future are *visions*. These stories confirm the clear destination, and encourage the journey. Stories about the future are most effective when they state a clear goal and are confirmed by activity and effort in the here-and-now.

Story Generation through Intentional Behaviors

Formally authorized leaders can also trigger or generate stories through the acting out of deliberate and intentional behaviors. By engaging in deliberate, authentic actions and behaviors, leaders can generate stories about organizational change. To generate stories, leaders must intentionally behave in ways consistent with the wider narrative about change, and leave the storytelling to whoever will pick it up. Whatever formally authorized leaders pay attention to will signal importance to the rest of the organization. Making sense through change is what people look to their leaders for – and through deliberate leadership behaviors, change initiatives are more likely to actually take root and succeed.

Inviting Leaders leverage the power of storytelling. These leaders deliberately plan and generate specific stories, and construct and then express inspirational narratives about the past, present and future in very specific ways.

A large part of the culture of an organization is created through the stories told by its people. Stories about the past, the present and the future help create a coherent narrative of who and what the organization is. The life of the organization is made alive through the telling and retelling of these stories. A culture is a living system and is nourished through narrative.

Change Greatly Increases Demand for a Coherent Narrative

When an organization and its people are going through change, the group becomes "thirsty" for coherent and accessible narratives. *During times of change, the need for stories becomes greatly elevated and a large gap between demand and supply is created.* People naturally look to their leaders to fill this gap. If formally authorized leaders fail to provide a coherent narrative about change, the people will create stories themselves – *to make sense of the changes* they are experiencing. Since these stories are generated from reaction rather than intention, the new stories *will probably **not** be 100% aligned with the overall purpose of the change and may even work against the success of the change you are introducing.*

Leadership can easily sidestep this problem by engaging in purposeful storytelling and intentional story generation. Since those with the authority get the most attention, you can take advantage of this fact by crafting supporting narratives and repeatedly reciting them.

Lasting organizational change happens when the purpose of change is communicated well, through the coherent storytelling of formally authorized leaders.

Leadership storytelling and leadership inviting are forms of leadership signaling, and both are an essential aspect of effective leadership. Successful organizational change requires effective leadership storytelling and effective narrative management. Your risk of failure is high if you do not pay attention to this.

Liminality

The *liminal*[18] state is a transitional state of being. The root Latin word – *limens* – means "threshold" or "doorway." The *liminal* state is a "no-man's land" of transition, confusion, stress and vagueness. It is lacking in definition. No longer where you were, and not yet where you are presumably going, *liminality* has the potential to generate enough worry and anxiety to derail and stop progress. Completely.

Bringing change into your organization creates a liminal, "in-between," transitional state. Inviting Leaders address this reality by creating "guardrails" with well-defined boundaries that invite participation and give all the participants a clear sense of where they are, during the often-confusing process of organizational change.

This is an absolutely essential concept for the Inviting Leader to grasp. When change is introduced, the "previous story" is getting older and older as the "new story" is being introduced. "Transformation" and "transition" have the same root word, and any kind of authentic organizational change creates feelings of transition and liminality in those who are affected. As a leader you need to be aware of this. People make meaning through stories and narrative about what is happening. But during transitions, by definition, the narrative is being formed, in transition, "under

---

[18] Liminality is a very important aspect of organizational change For more information about liminality, see
www.invitingleadership.com/book/links/#liminality.

construction" if you will. This situation introduces a lot of stress because people are experiencing some discomfort and even some real confusion.

The Liminal State Demands a Coherent Story from Leaders

The liminal state of being can be defined as "the absence of a coherent story." When this situation occurs, the demand for a coherent story increases greatly. It is the duty and responsibility of leaders to create enough supply to meet this demand.

If you do not provide the narrative, others will do so. This means you must be proactive about storytelling. If you don't, there is a large risk that *other* stories from *others* sources may become the dominant narrative. These "alternative explanations" of what is going on can seriously undermine your leadership. Inviting Leaders understand *leadership semiotics* and understand the need for *leadership storytelling* to reduce the risk of resistance or even failure.

Specifically, consulting firms can tell a story that sounds good but is not really true. For example, your consulting firm may suggest that employee engagement is not really necessary for achieving authentic and lasting improvement. That's a narrative that is not really true; employee engagement is in fact *essential*.

Executive Leaders Also Find Comfort in a Coherent Story

Executive leaders are people. And people get worried when they do not have all the answers or "know the story." This can cause problems when choosing a consulting firm to assist with your organizational change. Business agility is in part about balancing planning with actual experience and then constantly adjusting to feedback. Planning is important, but cannot replace the essential aspect of learning through experience as the group makes progress. Organizational change is a complex endeavor and when in complexity, the best thing to do is to experiment and learn by experience. This is the essence of the agile approach applied to business.

Consultants Tell Stories

When a consulting firm offers you a step-by-step, "ABC" approach to organizational change, be careful. It does not actually work that way. Often the consultants will offer a coherent, "easy-to-follow" and "stepwise" process, explained with shiny info-graphics and slick presentations. All of which is OK. But if you do not see or cannot understand how the employees will be engaged in the change, caution is advised. If the consultants do not emphasize the essential nature of employee engagement, take a step back. *If the consultants do not explicitly address the issue of how they will engage employees, press the "pause" button and begin to get concerned.*

Forcing change and imposing new practices is not the path forward if your goal is authentic and lasting positive improvement in business outcomes. To achieve this goal, employees must agree to support the change.

Inviting Leadership is a means for achieving this end:

"Transformations can't be accomplished without others helping voluntarily, & people don't help unless you engage them first."
– Geoffrey Moore, author, ZONE TO WIN.

Say you are meeting with some consultants and they are explaining their approach. The presentation slides are up, and the shiny info-graphics are out and spread across on the table.

Here are two questions to ask when meeting with consultants that want to help you implement some positive changes. The first question is a set up for the second. The answer to the *second* question is the one you really want to listen for:

- Question 1: "Do our people actually have to be *engaged* in supporting this process, for this process to actually work? (NOTE: They almost always answer Yes to this question...)
- Question 2: *OK. What is your specific plan* for making sure that as many of our employees as possible are engaged, and that they continue to support the change?

Together, we have over 15 thousand hours of direct experience coaching executives and teams through the process of organizational change. And one thing we know for sure is that employee engagement is absolutely essential to any lasting success. Yes, it is possible to achieve temporary improvement without employee engagement. But lasting and authentic change is impossible without it.

The key skill for executive leadership is what we call "comfort in the discomfort." The expression refers to the empirical learn-by-experience approach. With this approach, the "story" is always under construction and the group as a whole is participating in constructing it.

It is often easy to accept a story that panders to our most cherished allusions about planning and control. But organizational change is a complex endeavor. And complexity science says that in complexity, the empirical, "learning-by-experience" approach is the one with the best odds of success.

Table 5.2: Organizational Change: Problems with Imposing vs Inviting

Enterprise-Change Approach	The Problems With That	Notes
Top executives mandate change	Low levels of employee engagement and much higher levels of active resistance	Employee engagement is essential and imposing mandates reduce it
Top executives do not experiment with using the change that the rest of the organization must accept	The behavior signals a "do as I say not as I do" approach from executive leaders	This signaling leads to questions about leaders, more resistance and even resentment. Leaders must go first

Enterprise-Change Approach	The Problems With That	Notes
External consultants set up camp and are authorized to begin "driving" the change and "define the how"	Much lower levels of employee engagement and self-management	Most of the positive results from Agile and digital transformation initiatives are a result of self-managed teams, not a result of engaging highly prescriptive and authoritative consultants.
The change is "rolled out" and there is no effort at getting explicit agreement from the execs, stakeholders and teams which are absolutely essential to any lasting change	Real resistance comes from those who are invested in the current status quo, especially those who occupy higher-authorization roles with decision-making authority and their direct reports	People in high-authority roles can and will block and impede any changes in decision-making

Enterprise-Change Approach	The Problems With That	Notes
The change is applied indiscriminately to all aspects of all operations	Typically there is resistance from those who are noticing that each part of the enterprise is unique and that "one size fits all" does not apply	Applying a change in the same way to every part of the operation will often cause more problems than it solves. Lasting change requires discernment on how much change to apply to each discrete area of business operations
The way decisions get made and who makes them does not actually change	The change is a change in name only, because authentic and lasting change involves change in the decision-making authority distribution schema	If decisions and who makes them does not change, then value streams will continue to suffer from a decision-making approach that impedes the flow of value

Enterprise-Change Approach	The Problems With That	Notes
The approach is not iterative, and has no planned periods of enterprise-wide inspections and whole-group reflection on the results-to-date	Increased resistance to a large and "until further notice" mandate of change, one that is perceived as having no end	Rapid change requires periods of integration and assimilation. By working in 45 to 90 day iterations, the entire workforce can commit to supporting the changes until the next inspection point. An iterative approach asks for less commitment and is easier to say YES to

Employee engagement is essential to achieving authentic and lasting change, and engagement of your employees has more to do with *invitation* than it does with *delegation*. Inviting Leadership creates the conditions where all the employees affected by the change are offered an opportunity to help design and shape how that change will actually work.

Invitation, Delegation, Signaling, and Change

The more change that is taking place in the business environment, the more you want to be adding invitation to your leadership practice. For example, if you are planning a digital or Agile transformation, you may decide to set up a meeting that focuses the whole group on starting that planning. You will then invite as many employees as possible into that event. *The invitation amounts to a signal that there is a "new story" unfolding, and that participation in "writing the story of the change" is highly desired.*

Every invitation is a small experiment. The outcome is unknown. Invitations generate decisions from receivers. That feedback is very valuable when there is a lot of complexity and you seek data about exactly what the situation is.

When the environment is not changing very much, delegation works great. When the environment is changing frequently, delegation is not as effective, and invitation works better because it generates more feedback and data for inspection.

Therefore it is important to monitor and understand the current pace of change, so you can use an appropriate mix of delegation and invitation. During periods of change, you'll want at least a 50-50 split of delegation and invitation. Figure 5.3 shows how this works:

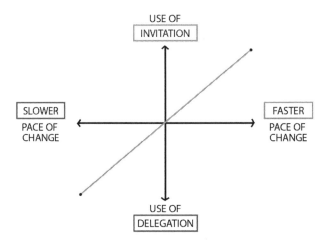

Figure 5.3: The Mix of Delegation and Invitation Depends on Context

Leaders who employ 100% delegation to get work done are at a very serious disadvantage. That's because invitation has the potential to increase your effectiveness during periods when the business environment is changing frequently.

Design

Design is the planning or intention that exists behind an action. When designing an organizational change, "big up-front planning" usually fails. While the narrative that is represented by the big up-front plan may be very comforting, there is always a flaw in the big up-front design. Big up-front plans typically have little if any allowance for responding to feedback as the plan is executed. This is a fatal flaw because it usually leads to an attempt at an authoritarian imposition of the big up-front plan and the change.

Where organizational change is concerned, the best leadership approach is as follows:

1. Have a solid idea of the set of outcomes you are looking for from any changes, and socialize alignment on those outcomes with the wider leadership group.
2. Begin making small moves in that direction by implementing a series of short-term (45 to 90 days in duration) 'safe to fail' experiments.

Inviting Leaders do not attempt to design enterprise change with big up-front planning, regardless of how tempting or alluring that option may be. Instead they work to generate and then inspect and act on the feedback of the last substantial action taken. Each small action is taken in the direction of the desired outcomes. The feedback generated is then used to inform decision-making about the next set of steps to take in that direction.

Invitations from leaders amount to a probe or stimulus that generates a reaction and a response. Those reactions and responses represent extremely valuable data, as they represent feedback from the very system you are working on changing for the better. The overall plan has a "true north" that represents the ideal set of desired outcomes. From there, a series of small but substantial actions is used to test the willingness and overall readiness and ability of the organization to make tangible progress in that direction. Those substantial actions in turn are designed, and composed of experiments which are delivered and presented as invitations. The invitations must be designed for easy understanding by those who receive them.

The design aspect of these invitations cannot be over-emphasized.

Leadership as Design

Using invitation in leadership means you are the one doing the initiating. When you initiate by sending an invitation, you need to be very clear about what you are inviting, otherwise your invitation (and your leadership) is hard to follow.

The best way to make sure your invitation is clear is to structure it as a game, with the goals, rules and progress-tracking aspects made very explicit. The chapter on Invitation introduced this material. Here we review it and go deeper on the idea of *leadership as design.*

When you invite, you are inviting the receivers to play your game. The content of the invitation (what you are inviting them into) must be structured *as a* game. Then, when that is done, the invitation itself is designed using the same FGS design template. Let's look at each part.

Designing the Game

Imagine if you will a large all-hands meeting where the goal is to explore a theme, something like "How Can We Be More Adaptive?" There are a few rules, like arriving at a certain time, the schedule for lunch, and so on. Meeting members track their progress by the passage of time, by progress on the agenda, and how much they are participating and learning. The whole deal is an opt-in affair with absolutely no sanctions or other consequences for opting out.

Here we have designed a game. It has goals, rules, feedback mechanisms, and opt-in participation. But so far, we have not invited anyone or even announced it.

The next step is to design the invitation using the same FGS template.

Designing the Invitation: The Game and the Story

Every invitation is an offer to go somewhere, or do something. We can also say with more than a little certainty that every invitation is an offer to be in a story, or play a game of some kind.

An example may serve: consider the basic dinner party. Just like a game, it has goals (good food and good company,) rules (arrive by 6PM, etc) and ways to track progress by time and task (how many courses are consumed, how many bottles of wine, and so on). And most dinner parties are not mandatory to attend; they are optional.

During the event, people interact and take up roles. One person may tell several stories; another may help with serving. Another may make people laugh by telling the funniest jokes. These are the *characters* in the emerging *story* of the dinner. Here we can see how an invitation to a dinner party is an offer to be a character in a story. Or even a kind of author of that story.

An invitation is:
- An offer to play a game
- An offer to be a character in a story
- An offer to be an co-author of a story
- A request to go somewhere, or do something

After the event, people talk. They recount and recall *the story* of the event. In all cases everyone who accepts the invitation is agreeing to the goals, rules and progress-tracking aspects of ... a game.

We might also say that the design of an invitation is game design. The invitation is an invitation to play a kind of game. For the game to be a good one, it must have the core game elements:
- A clear goal or set of goals
- Very clear rules
- A way to track progress (receive feedback)
- Opt-in participation

Leadership has a very large and predominant "game design" dimension. Leaders try to attract participants who are willing to play along.

Since every good game has opt-in participation, it is easy to see how games that are mandatory to play can be seen as less than inviting, potentially disengaging, or even repulsive. The game design concept and opt-in participation apply to the design of invitations. What we might call "leadership by invitation" is the art and discipline of bringing these ideas to life in your leadership work.

As described in detail in the chapter on Invitation, well-designed games and well-designed invitations deliver a sense of control, a sense of progress, and a sense of belonging. When the majority of your people experience these, the mood, the tempo, and the spirit of the organization will be "up," which is exactly where you want to be. You can get there as a leader by bringing the Inviting Leadership style into your leadership practice.

Employee Engagement and Invitational Engagement Models

engagement model *n.*
> Any pattern or set of patterns, reducible to practice, which result in more employee engagement, especially during the implementation of an organizational-change initiative.

Why You Need an Engagement Plan Based on an Engagement Model

During an organizational change, you need employee engagement or you will fail. Your engagement plan is the set of actionable steps you will take to engage as many employees as possible in the support and ongoing development of the change. An Engagement Model is a template that can be used as a starting point to develop your overall engagement plan.

An effective Engagement Model usually contains at least these elements:

- A set of *guidelines* ("do's and don'ts") for formally authorized leaders
- An *invitational* rather than purely directive approach
- An iterative approach, experienced as segments in a sequence, each of which has a beginning, middle and end
- Within each iteration, a timeline with steps, milestones, and empirical inspection points

- Clear articulation of all goals, rules, and progress-tracking (feedback) mechanisms
- A clear plan for identifying, observing, and enlisting emergent leaders
- A clear path forward for emergent leaders to participate in carrying the changes forward
- Guidelines/agreement on conditions under which formally authorized leaders may intervene to maintain the integrity of the defined boundaries and constraints
- Use of experiential meeting formats with whole group and subsets. Examples: Open Space, Fishbowl, World Café

An effective overall engagement plan based on a solid and proven engagement model will achieve the following outcomes:

- Reduced resistance to the change
- Reduction in risk of failure (an increase in the odds of success)
- Get more overall employee engagement
- Better ability to identify and reduce resistance as the change progresses
- Identification of enthusiastic supporters who will help promote and lead the change
- Better employee retention and ability to attract top talent

The Iterative Approach

One essential aspect of using an Engagement Model includes:

> *"An iterative approach, experienced as segments in a sequence, each of which have a beginning, middle and end."*

In "Chapter 3 – Invitation", you learned the technique of "reducing the ask by half." And in this chapter, you learned about the importance of frequently repeating a coherent story that clearly describes and explains the need for the change. One way of combining the ideas of "reduce the ask by half" and "tell a coherent story" is to use *iterations* for enterprise change.

The basic idea is to invite employees into working with a new set of rules for a clearly *limited period of* time, instead of "until further notice." The idea is that the "ask" is temporary and bounded by time, for example 45 to 90 days. An ask of short duration is easy to agree to, while an ask of a year or longer is a very difficult thing to commit to.

Whole-Group Inspection

Inspecting the progress of the enterprise change with the whole group (and not just the "higher-ups") is an essential aspect of the Inviting Leadership approach.

Iterations of change that end with a whole-group inspection have the following advantages:

- **A Coherent Story**
  - The iterations have a beginning, a middle and an end, just like any easy-to-follow story
  - By working in enterprise-wide iterations, "the story" of "where we are now" is easy for leaders to communicate, reiterate and explain
- **Easier Acceptance**
  - Asking for less means higher acceptance rates for your invitations to engage, and more participation in developing the needed changes
- **Quicker conversion of resistance to support**
  - By asking for less, you can guide the workforce toward direct experiences that reduce resistance and increase support, by quickly creating positive results
- **Predictable Inspection Points**
  - Everyone knows that they will be able to comment on the current iteration of experience and influence the next one

- **Opportunity for Leadership to Respond to feedback, and adjust to it**
  - ○ More frequent whole-group inspection means more frequent opportunities to collect feedback, and then adjust and adapt
- **Flexible plan**
  - ○ Instead of a static "forced march" kind of plan, the iterative approach allows for much more flexibility and a much more efficient allocation and deployment of scarce capital
- **Immediate Results**
  - ○ Short 45 to 90 day iterations allow for defining and achieving quick wins and KPI improvement based on evidence
- **Lasting Results**
  - ○ Because the workforce is engaged
- **A Greatly Reduced Consulting Spend**
  - ○ Because the workforce is engaged, those who answer your call to champion the change can and will lead it, reducing dependency on external consultants

By communicating an iterative approach to change that includes whole-group inspection points, Inviting Leaders can do much more with much less, by triggering employee engagement and getting better results at much lower cost in terms of time, effort and money.

Engagement Models are Essential to Inviting Leadership

The whole idea of Inviting Leadership is that invitations from leaders will tap into a great reserve of latent energy that is already present in the workforce. When you tap that energy, it can be made available for the work itself. The predictable result is more effectiveness as a result of your leadership practice.

Invitational Engagement Models[19] like OpenSpace Agility (see below) provide a proven template for leveraging the power of invitation. Most of the time, you are inviting large numbers of people to participate in opt-in meetings that are focused on either discussing the changes or implementing the changes that you are introducing.

Engagement Model vs Framework

The idea of an Engagement Model emerged inside the Agile industry during the 2013/2014 time period. Agile practices like Scrum and Kanban[20] were working really well at the team level, and larger organizations wanted A-B-C guidance on "scaling Agile up and across the enterprise." Frameworks such as Disciplined Agile Delivery, Large Scale Scrum and the Scaled Agile Framework suddenly sprouted and grew, in response to demand for guidance on "how to scale Agile" across the enterprise.

The basic problem with all of these frameworks is that any specific guidance on exactly how to engage employees was completely absent. The basic assumption was that if the framework was implemented, results would improve and everything would work out fine. This was rarely the case, in part because the critical success factor- employee engagement- was completely ignored.

In September 2013 Daniel was the keynote speaker at the Global Scrum Gathering in Paris France. During that presentation he introduced the concept of the Engagement Model and introduced the very first example, called OpenSpace Agility or "OSA."[21] OpenSpace Agility is the engagement model of choice for those favoring the invitational approach to enterprise change.

---

[19] For more information about Engagement Models, see www.invitingleadership.com/book/links/#engagement-models.

[20] For more information about Scrum and Kanban, see Appendix F and Appendix G in addition to www.invitingleadership.com/book/links/#agile.

[21] For more information about OpenSpace Agility, see Appendix H and www.invitingleadership.com/book/links/#openspace-agility..

Engagement Models: Key Takeaways

- You need a plan for engaging employees in the change. Employee engagement happens by intention and is not a random event.
- Invitation is your best tool for engaging people.
- By focusing on engaging as much of your total workforce as possible in the act of changing, your job as leader becomes far easier as your overall effectiveness greatly improves.
- By engaging the workforce in the overall change, you are encouraging innovation. This will create products and services that move in the direction of delighting your customers.
- The invitational approach creates advantages in hiring. It helps you retain your best people and reduce overall employee turnover. Over time you will attract and retain more of the best talent sourced within the locations where you operate.
- By focusing on engaging your workforce during a period of change, you will reduce the risk of failure, and improve the odds of rapid and lasting success with your current change program.
- An engagement *model* is a template for developing the structure and timeline of an overall engagement *plan*.
- Employee engagement is an essential aspect of any rapid and lasting change. Designing and implementing a clear engagement plan is essential. Engagement Models offer a template for this kind of planning.
- Leaders must define and communicate the "Why," advise and influence the definition of the "What," and refrain from defining the "How." Always leave the "How" for your workforce to define, within well-defined "guardrails." Inviting the people to "define the How" is a core aspect of the Inviting Leadership approach.

- It is a myth that executive leadership is "giving up authority" when others are invited into "defining the How." By inviting others in a structured way to "define the How," you are creating the conditions where the workforce can become energized about advancing the organizational-change process.

- Frameworks for business agility transformation are distinct from the Engagement Model that is used to implement them.

- Most frameworks are silent on the issue of employee engagement and do not offer any kind of plan for engaging the workforce. A robust Engagement Model such as OpenSpace Agility is designed to work with any framework you might choose to implement.

- If you cannot name your Engagement Model, you probably do not have one, and you are probably not focusing on employee engagement as a critical success factor in your overall plan for implementing change.

Leadership and Management

Clear agreements and clear boundaries are a big part of the Inviting Leadership approach. When leaders invite participation, higher levels of employee engagement and self-management are the result.

You might be wondering about the management function, and how it plays out when using the inviting style of leadership. We cover that next.

Management Is A Function, Not A Role

To manage is to direct and control. It might sound odd, but in the new world of work, management work is more important than ever. The key difference is this: *management is a function, and not a role.*

Part of the problem with management is that we normally associate it with a person in a role. Someone in a management role is responsible for "directing and controlling" the time, the cost, or the features. This is the domain of the "project manager." There is a "manager person." But what if everyone is engaging in self-management? What if executives encourage this kind of self-management behavior?

Inviting Leadership invites individuals and teams to manage many of the decisions at their level of scope. Leaders provide authorization, and the limits and boundaries of this decision-making authority. Self-management is team-level management of most but not all decisions that affect that whole team.

When leadership defines boundaries and issues invitations, the dynamics of self-management can and will play out.

One business consequence of this invitation-driven self-management is a dramatic reduction in costs, as strict hierarchies give way to a more fluid and networked approach to decision-making.

What, Why, and How

Executive Leadership Sets Direction and Defines "Why"

Inviting Leaders who are top executives are responsible for *why*. They define direction and explain the *why* of that direction. But they do not interfere with the definition of *what*. That work is left to those who lead Product and Services. This boundary is self-imposed. The Inviting Leader knows that decisions amplify employee engagement. That's why the Inviting Leader invites others to define the *what*.

Product Leadership Defines and Describes "What"

Product people and the people who deliver services define *what* will be in the product and *what* the services are. Inviting Leaders at this level seek feedback from paying customers, and roll that feedback into the process of defining the *what* of new products and services. Inviting Leaders at this level refrain from defining *how* products will actually be built, or *how* services will actually be delivered. Those decisions are left to the product engineering teams and the folks who deliver services. If the people responsible for *what* go too far and start defining the *how*, the Teams will not and cannot fully engage. This is because they are not making any more *how* decisions.

Teams Define and Execute on "How"

Teams are invited by Inviting Leaders to "define the *how*." This includes technical approaches and the overall internal design and organization of the product or service being delivered. If teams are invited and clearly authorized to "define the *how*," they have at least the potential to deeply engage in the process of making *how* decisions. This process of self-managing team-level decision-making is absolutely essential to the Inviting Leadership approach.

Releasing Authority: All or Nothing?

There is a set of false beliefs that are held by many formally authorized leaders. These beliefs go something like this:

"If I authorize any substantial decision-making, I am giving away all my authority to make decisions and to lead."

"If I authorize any substantial decision-making, I will introduce chaos."

"If I authorize any substantial decision-making, I will lose all control."

"If I authorize any substantial decision-making, I will be making myself and my role obsolete and therefore no longer needed."

The Inviting Leadership approach is optimized on generating employee engagement in service to generating much higher levels of self-management. But it does not reduce leadership control, introduce chaos, or require you to "give it all away." It does not make you or your role obsolete. On the contrary, it makes you and your role more important than ever. This is because you are defining the total environment for work by clearly defining the boundaries of any invitation that you issue. *You are the designer of a kind of game where the goal is measurable improvement.* You are the designer of a kind of game that has very clearly described rules and boundaries. You are the designer of a kind of game that provides everyone with frequent feedback and a way to track their progress continuously. You are the designer of the best kind of game, the kind where people opt-in to play.

Bounded Containment

Inviting Leaders issue very clear invitations to engage. These invitations are highly structured in the FGS format introduced in the Invitation chapter (goals, rules, progress feedback, and opt-in participation.) These invitations set very clear boundaries on what the receiver is being invited into. The rules aspect is where Inviting Leaders define the enabling constraints and make sure the authority being offered is clearly explained, and has very clear limits and boundaries.

These boundaries are designed to allow enough freedom for creativity and decision-making while also being constraining enough to define overall direction and focus the group.

When authority boundaries are too tight, no self-management can happen. When these same boundaries are too loose, there is too much freedom and there is potential for confusion or even chaos. This idea is depicted in Figure 5.4.

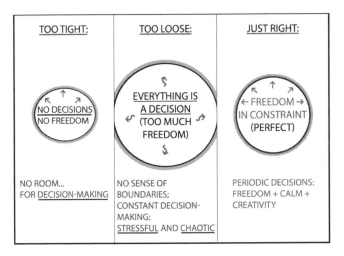

Figure 5.4: Boundaries in Three Sizes

Inviting Leaders know something that others do not. They know how to compose invitations that create the potential for generating 100 units of employee engagement in exchange for every one very well-defined unit of decision-making authority. They achieve this 100-to-1 return by building competency and know-how in the domains of authorization, boundary management, invitation, self-management, and leadership.

Recap

- Agreements
- Authorized Decision-Making
- Authority Structure Defines Culture
- Aligning Decisions With Value Streams
- Leadership Signaling & Storytelling
- Liminality`
- Engagement Models
- Management as a Function- Not a Role
- Trading away small units of decision-making authority in return for large increases in engagement, self-management, and results

PART III-
APPLICATION

Chapter 6 – Leadership Invitations

This chapter provides a template for applying the Inviting Leadership approach to organizational change. We also introduce and explore the essential subjects of leadership signaling and leadership storytelling.

Chapter 7 – Toolkit

Inviting Leadership is about the design of experiences that engage and enlist the entire workforce. In this chapter we offer tools for architecting and implementing your experience designs.

Chapter 8 – Guidance

Organizational change occurs in context. This context often includes common patterns. In this chapter we list some of these patterns and offer guidance on how to address them with the Inviting Leadership approach.

Chapter 6 – Leadership Invitations

This chapter provides a template for applying the Inviting Leadership approach to organizational change. We also introduce and explore the essential subjects of leadership signaling and leadership storytelling.

Overview

Summary Review of Key Concepts

This chapter provides ingredients, plans, and "recipes" that include all of the elements of Inviting Leadership presented in this book:

- Authority
- Boundary
- Invitation
- Self-Management
- Leadership

The applications you will find here are action plans that are compositions of these elements. In this chapter we build on the concepts previously introduced, and we identify and explain specific tools (mostly meeting formats and designs) that can be used in your practice of leadership. We explain the "why" behind these compositions, so that you yourself can design and construct your own compositions as needed, compositions that more precisely fit your context and application needs.

The following summarizes many of the most important points developed throughout this book:

- A leadership invitation triggers a decision on the part of the receiver. This decision-making creates engagement; the receiver must focus attention on the invitation to properly consider it and make the yes-no decision.

- In organizational change initiatives, it is people and not practices that power most all of the improvement. People also power most all of the obstacles and all of the impediments to success. It is therefore people that need to be the focus of the effort.

- Transformational organizational change means a change in the way decisions are getting made, and who makes them. If there is no change in the way decisions are getting made, there is no "transformation" of anything at all.

- Organizational change tends to create employee turnover. Since this is the reality, we want to influence what *kind* of turnover is generated. Any successful approach to change must address the issue of *how to engage and retain the best people.*

- The best people have career options and are constantly getting offers. The best people are also the very people who can help to create truly transformational results. Because they have options, they will begin "loitering by the exits" and will quickly vacate if they sense anything that "doesn't add up."

- Leadership invitations assume that the best people are in fact volunteers and that an inviting style is the best way to lead an "at-will," high-performance workforce.

- Forcing compliance can and will produce temporary positive effects. But lasting change is not really possible with force, since force tends to disengage the very people who are necessary to propel real change and improvement, namely: those high performers.

- Leadership invitations encourage very high levels of self-management and engagement. Authentic agile and digital transformation requires that employees engage in the process of change. Lasting change is possible only when employees engage, and leadership invitations are a primary mechanism for manifesting engagement, self-management, and self-organization.

Invitation, Persuasion, and Manipulation

Persuasion is an important topic and also an important skill in selling, in leadership, and in overall effectiveness in life. If we can't "get" people to do what we want, we can't experience progress in our plans and (at least in theory) cannot experience more and more success "in the real world."

The larger question is: what exactly is persuasion?

Wikipedia says that "persuasion is an umbrella term of influence. Persuasion can attempt to influence a person's beliefs, attitudes, intentions, motivations, or behaviors."

The dictionary provides this definition:

persuade *v.*
1. To cause someone to do something, through reasoning or argument.
2. To cause someone to believe something, especially after a sustained effort; convince.
3. To provide a sound reason for someone to do something.

Now what is interesting about persuasion is the opt-in, volitional aspect of it. No one "makes" you be persuaded. You agree to be. You consent to be. You decide to be. You *opt in* to being persuaded, to "suspending your disbelief." You choose it.

Here's some data from 42 psychology studies that generated data on 22,000 tested individuals:[1]

"...Across all the studies, *freedom to choose was found to double the chances that someone would say 'yes' to* the request."

Leadership invitations leverage this psychological reality. A leadership invitation can be persuasive. For this reason, a leadership invitation is often superior to leadership delegation, when the following conditions exist:

1. The work is mostly "knowledge work"
2. The people doing this work are mostly top performers with career options
3. The business environment is constantly in flux and moving
4. There is an organizational-change being implemented or already underway

When these conditions exist, you want to favor invitations.

The Abuse of Leadership Invitations

Is it possible for you, the leader, the sender, to abuse a leadership invitation?

We believe the answer is: yes.

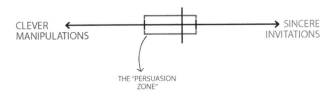

Figure 6.1: Outright Manipulation vs Sincere Invitation

We believe that quite a lot of *persuasion* is actually a subtle form of *manipulation*. Let's look at the definition of this word, *manipulate*:

---

[1] For more information about this study and others like it, see www.invitingleadership.com/book/links/#freedom-and-persuasion.

manipulate *v.*

To control or influence (a person or situation)
cleverly, unfairly, or unscrupulously.

Insincere or unscrupulous leadership invitations can and will backfire. *So be careful not to tilt into excessive levels of persuasion with your invitations.* Be sincere.

If you want rapid and lasting support for your plans and leadership, you'll need to form coalitions with other like-minded leaders and followers. After you've done that, you'll need to define a clear and actionable strategy for enlisting as much employee support as possible. Leadership invitations can be used as part of that overall approach.

Figure 6.2 illustrates how sincere leadership invitations are superior when you want genuine and lasting support for your plans:

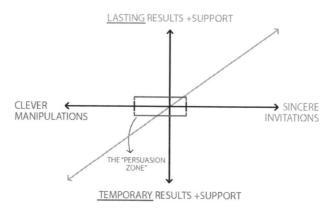

Figure 6.2: Lasting vs. Temporary Results and Support

Some of the range of sincere invitation does in fact fall into the "persuasion zone." You'll need to be mindful about this as you design your invitations, and make sure your designs avoid tipping into attempts to control or manipulate others. Simply engage in good invitational design, issue sincere invitations and go from there, and everything will be OK. Be careful.

Be sincere, because most people do have a way of sensing when you aren't.

Do not ever knowingly engage in any abuse of your leadership invitations.

Design and Management of Boundaries with Respect to Leadership Invitations

The "boundary design" aspect of overall invitation design is your primary tool for tailoring and tuning your leadership invitations. Engaging in good boundary design is essential.

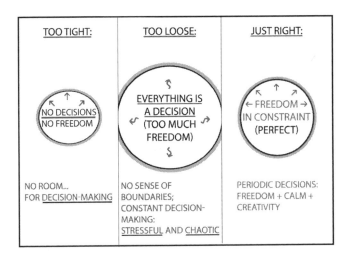

Figure 6.3: Boundaries in Three Sizes

You the leader have to get this right: if your leadership invitation is properly bounded with clear and explicit constraints, the receivers can quickly size it up and make a decision. But if the constraints are vague or implied, or the list of constraints is not complete, you can expect trouble. Much will be lost in translation.

The receivers of your invitations need to understand the following:

1. The goal of the activity (what is "in it" for *them*)
2. The constraints (also know as "the rules," from a game-design point-of-view)
3. How progress will be experienced (for example: progress across time, task, or territory)

4.   Opt-in participation

Enabling constraints[2] ("boundaries") enable self-organization and self-management by forming a kind of container. The container is formed by the set of constraints and boundaries that you define. If the constraints are too confining or "tight," the receivers will be slow to accept your invitation.

On the other hand, if the constraints are too loose, you'll be introducing some potential for confusion or even some chaos. When the constraints are properly sized, there is room for decision-making inside your clearly defined set of enabling constraints.

Designing and Defining Effective Leadership Invitations

Effective invitations from leaders require several elements:

1.   **A style of delivery** that makes it clear that there are absolutely no sanctions for opting out
2.   **A style of structuring** the invitation that makes it very plain what is and is not being invited
3.   **Boundaries and constraints** that are loose enough to invite real participation but also tight enough to clearly define what the invitation is (and is not) offering, and to focus the group

Here we focus on the details of designing, defining and issuing *leadership invitations.* We assume that you are a leader in an organization and you want to use the Inviting Leadership style to encourage more employee engagement in service to great results.

Goals, Rules, and Feedback on Progress

Every great leadership invitation needs to express clear goals, rules, and how progress is experienced. Without all three of these essential elements, your invitation will be lost in translation. Tight constraints tend to reduce the number of people who accept your invitation. Loose constraints make it difficult for the invitees to

---

[2] For more information about enabling constraints, see www.invitingleadership.com/book/links/#enabling-constraints.

respond with an unambiguous "yes." Designing and issuing a leadership invitation is not as easy as it sounds.

Sample Leadership Invitations

Here are some examples of well-formed leadership invitations. These invitations have all the elements, especially very carefully defined rules and constraints. The constraints invite participation while at the same time defining limits and the overall invitation.

Make a Meeting Optional

Making a meeting optional is a great way to get started with leadership invitations. Doing so signals that you trust the invitees to allocate their valuable time where it can do the most good. Optional attendance also gets the truly interested people in the room, generates data on who is most interested, and encourages self-management. You can define who must attend and explicitly state that everyone else is optional.

Here is how that invitation might be structured.

Invitation: Optional Sales Meeting

Meeting details and agenda:

Meeting Owner:	*Stacia Araya*
Facilitator:	*Harold Jorgensen*
Date & Time:	*October 18 10AM–12AM*
Subject:	*Sales*
Purpose:	*Sales Management (6-month projections)*

- *Formal Check In*
- *Quick Review of Sales Data*
- *Projections (next 6 months)*
- *Likely near-term deals (next 30 days)*
- *Marketing update from BobL*
- *Engineering update from JonT*

- *Discussions*
- *Planning (next 60 days)*
- *Formal Check Out*

The following people are needed and must attend:

- *Bob LeRoux- Sales Manager*
- *Jon Terrell- Head of Engineering*
- *Stacia Araya- VP Marketing and Sales (meeting owner)*

This meeting is optional for everyone else. If you elect to attend, please be sure to honor these ground rules:

- *Invitees only (you may elect to attend if you are on the distribution)*
- *Starts on Time (door closes at 10:01AM)*
- *Stick to the Agenda (listed above)*
- *10-minute break at the 50-minute mark*
- *Ends on Time*

Invite Leadership Learning

Change in organizations requires alignment of the entire leadership team. A good way to begin achieving that is by scheduling a learning event for leadership team members, and making it plain that the event is optional. Such an event can help you gauge overall support for the change among leadership.

Here's how that invitation might go. You've arranged a learning event. It's three hours long. It includes a substantial amount of experiential learning with group exercises. Assume the nature of the change is a pivot towards business agility across an entire business unit and that you are leading this business unit:

Invitation: Business Agility

As part of our wider resolve to improve results, I have arranged for Mark Davis of Davis Research to come and provide an experiential leadership learning workshop in business agility. You are invited. The details are as follows:

Date and Time: March 18
Subject: Business Agility: what it means for our organization
Agenda:

> *0830AM Check in, coffee, continental breakfast*
> *0900AM Quick overview and group exercise on business agility*
> *1000AM Break*
> *1015AM Whole group experiential learning (exercises) in business agility*
> *1215PM Formal check out*
> *1230PM Done*

The facilitator Mark Davis has written several books on business agility and is a noted authority in the field.

We are at a pivotal point in our development as an organization. We face a range of challenges and opportunities. The purpose of this learning event is to address these challenges, orient the leadership team, raise issues and questions, and prepare for our eventual move to a business agility stance.

I've invited a cross-section of about 40 executives, directors, and managers. If you know other executives, directors, and managers who can benefit from learning more about business agility, please feel free to invite them (the room can handle 60++ people.) We will have coffee, juice, and breakfast items available the whole time.

> *This event is optional: if you have something else going on that is important, go and do that instead. However, we are purposely scheduling this over 1 month in advance, to make it easier for you to adjust your schedule. I do need to know by March 16 (two days before the event) to plan the beverages, food, and seating. Please RSVP by then if you intend to participate.*

All the elements of a good invitation are present: clear goals and objectives, clear rules, an agenda that makes it easy to track progress, and opt-in participation. As you can see, leadership invitations need not be clinical or dry to be effective. The goals, rules, and progress tracking can be easily described in conversational language. It is much better to simply include clear goals, rules, and progress tracking rather than to label them. Simply make sure that all three elements are present in your invitation, and make sure the receiver understands there are no sanctions for opting out.

Invite Leadership to use the New Approach to Leadership Work

One way to generate support across the organization is to have the executive leadership team actually implement the contemplated change *first*, at the leadership team level. Doing so sends important signals to the wider organization about leadership-level resolve and intent.

Here's how that invitation might go. Assume that some leadership prep has already been done, the results are positive, and the time has come for probing leadership willingness further, with this invitation.

Invitation: Leaders Go First

Greetings All,

This message is about leadership agility and how it relates to our wider intent to achieve a business agility footing across the entire organization.

A primary way to achieve rapid and lasting change is to begin with the leadership team. We've done a lot of work in this area already and now we are in position to consider some options. Having some of the leadership teams work in an agile way is one of those options. As you know, it is a good practice to try the new changes with a set of "pilot" teams, to try everything out, get direct experience, and learn from that. I think a great way for us to do this is for some of the leadership teams in the functional areas to actually be those pilot teams.

It's very important for the pilot teams to be willing to participate in the experiment. Participation is 100% optional. Here is the offer:

We have scheduled some training in the new practices for the week of December 10th. The first three departmental teams from the nine on this distribution will receive the training. The training is in about six weeks. I need to hear from you not later than November 20, so we can plan. If you elect to bring your group into this training, you are committing to the following:

1. *Attending the training event and participating fully*
2. *Working as needed with the consultant we have engaged to get set up with the new way of working and the new practices*
3. *Being one of the pilot leadership teams who will work to get on a business-agility footing during January and February*

> 4. *Participating in a retrospective inspection of the experience with me and all other participating teams during the week of March 3*
>
> *If your group wants to be one of the pilot teams as described above, please let me know before November 20. We will use the results of these pilots to inform next steps, guide our plans, and customize and tailor our approach to change as we go forward.*
>
> *Regards,*
>
> *[Your name here]*

If you offer an invitation like this, consider how it will be received if your immediate team has *already* taken the first step and led by example.

Invite Leaders at All Levels to Explore an Issue in Open Space

After leaders are engaged in dialogue about change, some will naturally have objections. This is to be expected. It is very important to surface and process those objections. The Open Space meeting format is a great way to do that. The invitation might look like this:

> ## Invitation: Transforming Decision-Making?
>
> *Greetings,*
>
> *As part of our ongoing effort to improve, we've taken several important steps, including working hard to align the company leadership around business agility principles and practices. We have identified several obstacles that stand in the way.*

One of these is the perception from many on the leadership team that our current decision-making process is working well and does not need to change. This is a significant obstacle to moving forward. We know from our consultant Mark Davis that real change means a change in the way authorized decision-making happens. We need to align our decision-making to improve flows of value, innovation, company learning, and higher satisfaction scores from customers.

To process this issue as a whole leadership team and begin working towards resolution, I am inviting you to a whole-group event using the Open Space facilitated meeting format. The event is planned for May 18 from 1PM to 4PM. The theme is "Transforming Decision-Making?"

- *Can we make progress without making any changes to the way decisions get made?*
- *Are we happy with 10% or 15% improvement?*
- *Can we engage employees at every level of authority in this company if they are not actively involved in making at least some decisions that affect their work?*
- *How do we change for the better?*

These are some of the questions we hope to ask and answer at this meeting. You are not required to attend. On the other hand, if you have a strong interest in this topic, I certainly hope to see you there. We need to go to work on making progress and improving.

The work product from this meeting is a book of Proceedings that documents what was said and done during each session. We will use the feedback from these

> *Proceedings to determine what happens next with our improvement initiatives.*
>
> *This is an "Open Space" meeting with a theme. We will build an agenda together on the day of the event. Multiple sessions with open dialogue will be going all day. You can learn more about the Open Space meeting format here:*
>
> www.invitingleadership.com/book/links/#what-is-ost
>
> *Everyone who is a Manager or higher in this business unit is getting an invitation. If there are others in the organization who you think should be invited, please email or see me so we can discuss who needs to be invited.*

Invitations from highly authorized executives to other leaders in the organization are a very powerful way to sense and respond to the tone, opinions and overall tempo or "vibe" of the overall leadership group. The above invitation is a good example of what such an invitation looks like.

Invite Help and Engagement In Leading The Change

Geoffrey Moore, one of the greatest management thinkers, has this to say about introducing change:

> *"Transformations can't be accomplished without others helping voluntarily, & people don't help unless you engage them first."*
> *-Geoffrey Moore, author, Zone to Win*

One way to increase engagement is to invite people to help. One positive change you can make to create some improvement is to use facilitators for meetings. In the following invitation, this is explained and the invitee is invited to help. The context is that you have a specific initiative in mind and you are looking for volunteers to help get is started.

Invitation: "Will You Help?"

Greetings,

You are receiving this email as an invitation to help me and my leadership team achieve specific objectives in the 4th quarter. Will you help?

We are looking for 12 individuals who want to learn and execute on meeting facilitation. We believe that facilitated meetings are more efficient, and in fact superior to, non-facilitated meetings. Instead of bringing in facilitators from outside our company, we intend to develop in-house facilitators. Here is the basic idea:

1. *Facilitators from one department will offer facilitation services to meeting owners from other departments (facilitators cannot have any loyalty to anything or anyone except the meeting owner, whom they are serving).*

2. *Those who do this work will have their schedules opened up a bit to accommodate this new and important work. Facilitators can be from any level up to Director in the organization since Directors and above have substantial authority that might work against their effectiveness in the facilitator role.*

3. *A 1-day training program will kick off next month; the first 20 people to*

express interest in this program will receive the training.

4. *If you express interest, you are making a 6-month commitment. Your manager will be informed that you have elected to do this, and 10% of your schedule will be opened up for doing this work. You will continue to work 40 hours per week, 90% in your current job and 10% in this new role.*

5. *An online scheduling tool is under development which will allow meeting owners from all departments to find and engage facilitators from other departments.*

6. *At the end of the 6 months we will invite everyone to a half-day meeting to inspect the results and help inform the decision about whether to continue.*

This is an experimental program designed to help us improve the effectiveness of our in-house meetings.

You can learn more about facilitation via these links:

{List of links}

If you want to give it a try, please respond not later than September 15 to be considered for participation in this program.

Regards,

[Your name here]

With an invitation of this type, you are in fact delegating substantial yet temporary authority to those who opt-in and volunteer. With this type of invitation, it is absolutely necessary that you design the constraints around that authority very deliberately and carefully, and totally support the execution of those who accept the invitation.

(Note: Facilitated meetings are a very quick way to get great results. When your meetings are facilitated by a trustworthy person, you the meeting owner can devote more time to listening, observing, and picking up subtle signals from participants. You can learn more at www.invitingleadership.com/book/links/#facilitation.)

Invite the Whole Organization to Explore and Resolve an Issue in Open Space

Once the leadership team has been successfully prepared, the next step is to invite wider participation in the planning and development of the contemplated change. Once again, the very versatile Open Space meeting format can be used as the basic meeting structure for a large invitational meeting with a theme that focuses and engages the group. Here's how that invitation might actually look:

Invitation: "What Can We Improve in the Next 6 Months?"

As our company works to become more adaptive, we must consider and reconsider new ways of working. We must constantly respond to changes in our customers, our industry, and the wider changes brought about almost daily by technology. Our customers demand higher levels of service. Our competitors continue to improve and put pressure on us to be more adaptable every single day. As we grow we must not lose our ability to innovate. We face a range of opportunities and threats. The markets we operate in are growing, but smaller venture-funded competitors with nothing to lose are pressuring us to update our technologies and customer service. Large and established competitors are upping their game and are gaining market share. To prosper we need to attract and retain the best talent we can find.

No one person or leader has the complete answer to these challenges. However, we are confident that our people know how to best respond.

In this spirit I invite you to attend a large, all-hands-invited, "Open Space" meeting to engage in dialogue and problem-solving around these opportunities and threats.

The work product from this meeting is a book of Proceedings that documents what was said and done during each session during the day. We will use the data and feedback in these Proceedings to determine what happens next with our enterprise-wide improvement initiatives, and our journey towards authentic business agility.

This meeting has a theme, but no set agenda. The theme we will explore is "What Can We Improve in the Next 6 Months?"

We will build an agenda together on the day of the event. Multiple sessions with open dialogue will be going on all day. You can learn more about the Open Space meeting format here:

www.invitingleadership.com/book/links/#open-space-technology

I hope you can clear some time on your schedule for the meeting six weeks from now, on Wednesday, February 22. I am sponsoring the event. A consultant

> *named Mark Davis will lead us through the process of working in Open Space.*
>
> *I hope to see you there!*

Whole-group Open Space events generate dialogue, ideas, and actual Proceedings which then can become the basis for some decision-making and action steps.

The entire idea of this book emerged from our collective experience of over 15 years using this 100% invitational meeting format in organizations. Open Space is an extremely effective tool when combined with other forms of unambiguous and clear leadership signaling.

For more details about the design of the Theme and Invitation of an Open Space meeting, see "A Brief User's Guide to Open Space Technology" in Appendix E.

Organizational change requires a plan for engaging employees at every level of authority. Open Space is used as the foundation of the Prime/OS and OpenSpace Agility Engagement Models. Engagement Models like these provide a template or starting point for an overall engagement plan. For more detail on Prime/OS and OpenSpace Agility, see "OpenSpace Agility Introduction" in Appendix H.[3]

Summary

The definition of the rules, boundaries, and constraints is an essential aspect of designing and sending leadership invitations. Be careful to size the constraints and rules just right. If they are too confining you can expect to get a low response rate. On the other hand if those constraints are too loose, the invitees will lack

---

[3] Employee engagement is essential to achieving rapid and lasting business agility. To learn more about Engagement Models that use Open and invitational approaches to organizational change, see www.invitingleadership.com/book/links/#engagement-models. To learn more about the invitational Open Space meeting format, see www.invitingleadership.com/book/links/#open-space-technology.

enough guidance about your intended plans and direction. This will cause stress and make it difficult for the invitees to make a good decision about whether to accept the invitation. There is no set way to get this right. You will need to use your best judgment, within your context, with respect to defining the rules in your invitations structured in the 4-part game format: goals, rules, progress tracking, and opt-in participation.

Leadership, Experience Design, and Leadership Invitations: Inviting Leadership as Game Design

As leader of a change initiative, you are designing the "total experience" for all the people in the enterprise. You are the highly authorized leader and you are in fact in charge of the majority of the experience design. You are authorizing almost everything regarding the experience of change. Take your responsibility for the overall experience design very seriously.

The primary thing to focus on is the enabling constraints: the rules and guardrails that you design into the overall experience. This kind of experience design is in fact *game design*. Since you plan to be issuing leadership invitations, you need to define the related boundaries, rules and guardrails carefully. Be very specific about what is invited, and the boundaries on that invitation. Your receivers will be paying very careful attention to these constraints as well. Engineer these enabling constraints very, very carefully: not too tight, and not too loose. Approach boundary and experience design as a leadership art.

Recap

- Invitation, Persuasion & Manipulation
- Designing Invitations with Boundaries and Constraints
- Goals, Rules & Feedback
- Six Suggested Leadership Invitations to Try
- Leadership as Game Design; Game-Design Thinking

Chapter 7 – Toolkit

Inviting Leadership is about the design of experiences that engage and enlist the entire workforce. In this chapter we offer tools for architecting and implementing your experience designs.

Inviting Leadership Applied

Inviting Leaders are always issuing invitations to employees in pursuit of feedback. During organizational change, these leaders issue the invitations to help define how the change is implemented and to help in leading various aspects of the change. Most of the time, this means issuing invitations to whole-group meeting events or to events in which an appropriate subset of the group convenes to discuss, plan, and implement iterations of change. During these meetings, some of the participants do signal their strong willingness to help lead the change.

We've offered a few suggestions about how to invite group conversations that lead to safe and pragmatic next steps. The Appendices contain the detailed descriptions of various meeting formats and tools you can use to go further in implementing Invitation-Based Change™ (IBC).

Applying and executing on Inviting Leadership involves understanding and using each of these tools to design group-level activities that are appropriate for the current state and context of your change program.

Here we briefly introduce the tools. Each tool is described in more detail in the Appendices.[1]

---

[1] For more information about the full spectrum of tools for implementing Invitation-Based-Change, see
www.invitingleadership.com/book/links/#ibc-tools.

The tools are listed in the general order that you may need to consider them as you introduce change into your organization. You'll want to study these tools and meeting types carefully so you are familiar with them.

- "Ready for Agile" Checklist
- Authority Circle™
- Scrum
- Kanban
- Open Space Technology
- OpenSpace Agility™ and Prime/OS™

Some of these tools are meeting formats. It's important to keep in mind that most of the meeting formats in this toolkit assume a facilitator role. More on that later. Let's look at each in turn.

"Ready for Agile" Checklist

- A process we developed for socializing change by first obtaining explicit agreement from everyone on a) the new terminology used to describe the change and b) the new rules for decision-making[2]
- Used for dialogue and establishing of essential and enabling agreements
- The application can be generalized to help enable any kind of change

Authority Circle™

- An inviting meeting format that helps executive leaders gain experience in handing out small units of authority in a safe and pragmatic way via the use of invitations
- Helps the leadership group communicate clearly while at the same time inviting feedback from

---

[2] It's critically important to remember that "transformation" is actually about aligning decision-making with increasing the flow of value in a value stream. There is no "transformation" of anything at all unless and until the "who, what, and when" of decision-making actually changes.

lesser-authorized participants in a public and open manner
- Used when the dialogue phase is ending and the deciding phase is starting

Scrum
- An authority distribution schema developed by Jeff Sutherland and Ken Schwaber for aligning decisions with the goal of rapidly producing complex products and services
- Used for discussing and making decisions about the design and construction of complex products
- A minimal framework that includes specific events, roles, rules, and artifacts

Kanban
- A transparent rule-based method for managing work and workflow in a visual manner, such that both improve
- Designed to support dialogue, planning and execution of work flow

Open Space Technology
- A scalable and invitational meeting format discovered and developed by Harrison Owen that is appropriate for very large groups and encourages extremely high levels of self-management and self-organization
- A meeting design optimized for dialogue and ideation

Prime/OS™
- An invitational, general-purpose opt-in Engagement Model that uses Open Space to define iterations of enterprise-level change that run for 45 to 90 days
- An Engagement Model helpful for implementing lasting organizational change in

which each 45 to 90 day iteration begins and ends with a whole-group Open Space meeting

OpenSpace Agility™

- A specific derivative of Prime/OS that is focused on rapidly delivering transformational change based on the four values and twelve principles of the Agile Manifesto
- An Engagement Model in which each iteration of implementing enterprise-wide Agile change starts and ends with a whole-group Open Space meeting

The Challenges and Opportunities of Organizational Change

Now let's take a look at Table 7.1, which shows some of the challenges and opportunities that organizational change (and the use of these tools) can bring to your leadership practice.

Table 7.1: Inviting Leadership Addresses the Challenges and Opportunities of Organizational Change

Challenge	Opportunity	Notes
Employee engagement is essential to success and our scores are low	Create more employee engagement to reduce the risk of failure and increase the chances of success	Decisions are engaging and Inviting Leaders understand how to use invitation and clear boundary definitions to solve this problem

Challenge	Opportunity	Notes
The way we are making decisions no longer is optimal and it is actually impeding the flow of value to our customers and stakeholders	Invite a whole-group inspection of value stream flows and related decision-making	Inviting Leaders know how to design and implement meeting and event designs that build support (and employee engagement) in desirable change
Many of the senior leaders are invested in the way things are, and are not actually supporting change	Design invitational, facilitated, and private meeting events for the leadership team that encourage expression of objections, get good agreements, and align senior leaders in preparation to communicate and encourage enterprise-wide change	Inviting Leaders understand that the leaders are the first group that must confront the difficult issues of resistance … inside their own team. They also know how to address and reduce this resistance through invitation
Competitors are adapting to change faster and as a result they are attracting and hiring away our best people	Use invitation to enlist the help of top talent and improve employee retention	Inviting Leaders know how to design and deliver the kind of leadership invitations that are attractive to top talent

Challenge	Opportunity	Notes
Our business must follow regulatory and compliance rules; as a result our culture is not very open and not very adaptable. Change happens very slowly	Use invitation and whole-group events to create more openness and adaptability	The Inviting Leadership approach provides a method to gradually open up a culture in stages, based on action, inspection and feedback
We can make many simple changes but changing *policies* (like HR policies regarding performance reviews) requires more authority than we have	Aligning performance review policies with the goal of more self-management can reduce overall costs, increase the overall flow of value, improve morale, and make it easier to attract top talent	Inviting Leaders understand that continuous feedback to and from employees makes the entire organization more adaptive
Our culture values the role a person occupies over the person occupying that role; this is resulting in very low psychological safety as the change happens	Use leadership signaling and actions to communicate that the organization values the people in the roles over the roles themselves	The Inviting Leadership approach uses direct and whole-group meeting experiences to communicate values and culture, rather than using memos or one-to-many speeches

Whole Group Experiential Learning vs. Classroom Lectures

Learning events where an entire group is active in exercises and experiential learning have advantages over lecture-based classroom learning. This is especially true when the group participating is a group of leaders. Leadership in an organization is a group activity and does not occur in isolation. For this reason, a very strong technique is to get all of the formally and informally authorized leaders in one room and take them through some important group-level learning experiences. These events are best executed with the help of a facilitator. Such social learning events also provide you with an important opportunity for sending a leadership invitation to potential participants.

Some of the meeting types described in this chapter can be used for whole-group leadership learning experiences.

Here are some of the advantages of the whole-group leadership learning approach:

- You can observe the interactions between all of the individuals in the leadership group. This provides you with important data on those relationships and how they are currently trending.

- You can participate directly as a member, and be observed by your own leadership peers and direct reports. This allows you to send important leadership communication and clear leadership signals.

- The group can achieve progress in both dialogue and deciding, in stages, by progressing through a series of activities designed for that purpose.

- The leadership group can save substantial time, effort, and budget by meeting together for as little as three hours at a time. Doing so substantially reduces communication delays and accelerates leadership group decision-making and alignment.

- The entire leadership group can gauge its level of readiness to engage in authentic organizational change. This information can be used when considering options, and in the planning and execution of distinct segments or phases of ongoing change initiatives.

Transformation of the Leadership Group Comes First

Leading the organization through important transitions requires very clear leadership signaling throughout the process. This signaling is a group activity rather than the activity of one solitary leader. If the signals of the entire leadership group are consistent, then the wider organization will experience those signals as one clear and coherent leadership communication. If the signaling from the leadership group is mixed, the intent of the top leadership, as experienced by the wider organization, becomes *lost in translation*. Beginning an enterprise-wide transformation without first successfully transforming the leadership group is an expensive exercise in futility.

Since demand for a coherent story greatly increases during times of organizational change, it is essential that the leadership group is aligned on the essential and core narrative that supports the wider intent of the change effort. Without this, the change effort can and will fail. This cannot be overstated. Across the organization, during a phase transition, everyone listens for the consistencies and the inconsistencies in leadership communications. Alignment and ultimately transformation of the leadership team must therefore occur first.

The whole-group techniques employed to transition and align the leadership team can then be used in the same way to generate movement and transition across the enterprise as a whole. A very big advantage of this approach is that the formally authorized leaders and influencers all become familiar with the experiential, incremental, whole group approach. This means they are ready in advance for when the time comes to begin transitioning the entire organization via whole-group events.

Transitioning the Wider Organization

The basic pattern is to use the whole-group experiential learning approach with the leadership group first, and then later use many of the same meeting formats and techniques with the wider organization. For example, the leadership group may be at a point where it needs to engage in dialogue before an important decision about the next stage of change for the organization. To advance progress in the direction of these design decisions, you may decide to schedule a meeting of the entire leadership team that looks like this:

> 0900 AM Welcome and focusing of the group
> from the top executive
> 0915 AM World Café[3] or Open Space on the
> specific issue(s)
> 1115 AM Authority Circle
> 1200 PM Done

This type of designed whole-group experience generates important and immediate work product for the leadership team. That work product output includes the generation of common knowledge,[4] important group-level discussions, and some important boundary-design and boundary-management by the top leaders. This meeting creates important direct experience with the very same meeting formats that will be experienced by the entire organization in the next phase of the enterprise transformation.

Meetings, Culture and Experience Design

Standing meetings provide an opportunity to introduce change in a small way at first. In Daniel's first book on organizational change, *The Culture Game*, he describes how every meeting can be improved by using the FGS structure (goals, rules, feedback, and

---

[3] World Café is a specific and robust kind of meeting format with the potential for wide application. For more information, see www.invitingleadership.com/book/links/#world-cafe.

[4] Common knowledge is an important tool for large-group coordination. For more information about common knowledge, see www.invitingleadership.com/book/links/#common-knowledge.

opt-in). This structure is also described in the Invitation chapter of this book. The key takeaway here is that every meeting produces a small culture or a *microculture*. This is why standing meetings can be used as a starting point for introducing change.[5]

Meetings in general represent a significant point of leverage and a basic building block of the Inviting Leadership approach. Because meetings can contain segments and span hours or days, and can be intentionally designed and composed, re-designed meetings can accelerate change. The key is to incorporate the power of invitation throughout the "experience design" of these meetings.

For example, making a meeting optional means that participants are invited (and not compelled) to participate.

Costs of Meetings vs. the Cost of Resistance to Change

Invitational meetings and invitational meeting formats have the power to greatly reduce resistance to change. Such meetings can convert active resistance into active support in the shortest possible amount of time. You might be thinking: "Meetings are expensive, especially large whole-group events. There is the venue and food costs, there is the cost of labor, and there is the fact that ongoing work must be 'put on hold' for such meetings to take place."

Inviting group experiences are essential for reducing resistance to change. And what is the cost of that resistance? When there is failure in an attempt at organizational change, the total cost of not addressing objections and resistance *up front* is equal to the sum of the following:

1. **Training**: The total cost of training everyone
2. **Consulting**: The total cost of hiring expensive external consultants to help guide and manifest the change
3. **Executive Time**: The total payroll paid to all of the executive leaders who spent their valuable

---

[5] For more about the connections between meetings, games and culture, see www.invitingleadership.com/book/links/#the-culture-game-book.

time discussing, planning, and implementing the change

4. **Workers**: The total payroll of all the other non-executive employees who spent time on any aspect of the change

5. **Hidden Costs**: All the other hidden costs (usually adding up to about 20% of the known costs).

These costs rapidly escalate into the tens of millions of dollars for the largest enterprises. A basic rule of thumb is that it costs at least $8000 per affected employee per attempt at enterprise-wide change.[6] That means that for every 1000 employees affected, the true total cost is north of 8 million dollars.

Given this reality, do you think it might be a good idea to gauge the organization's readiness for change before spending that money?

Let's compare those costs of "transformation" (8 million per 1000 employees) and compare it to the cost of gauging organizational readiness through the use of enterprise-wide, whole-group meeting events. The venue, the food, the labor cost, and all of the other indirect costs are generally less than one half of one percent of the full cost of any "enterprise transformation plan" roll out.

And since it is the unwilling people who power all the impediments to change, the initial step is to make this investment in employee engagement *first*, up front, to achieve the following:

1. Identify and enlist all the people who strongly support and will in fact carry the change successfully forward

2. Create the conditions where objections to the change can be freely expressed

3. Develop a gradual process of changing that is sensitive to feedback from the organization

---

[6] For more direct data on actual costs, see
www.invitingleadership.com/book/links/#expected-dollar-cost.

4. Create the conditions where resistant people can change their minds, and become more tolerant of the change

5. Create the conditions where those who are merely tolerant can become active supporters

Dialogue And Decisions

Any meeting is usually focused on one of two goals: either generating *dialogue* (exploring and discussing a course of action) or generating *decisions* (moving beyond dialogue to action).

A meeting about dialogue will benefit from the use of certain meeting formats, while a meeting focused on deciding will benefit from a different set of meeting formats. For example, the Open Space Technology format works very well for generating dialogue but it not ideal for deciding. You'll need a different meeting design to generate decisions and get support for those decisions. Inviting Leaders know these meeting formats and which meeting format is best to use. This chapter introduces you to how to use various other meeting formats and how to compose them to create whole-group events to achieve your objectives.

Composing Whole-Group Events with Meeting Types

Whole-group events afford an opportunity to design and create an experience that helps the whole group generate *dialogue* and then move on to *action*. This is done through intentional *event design* and intentional *meeting composition*.

For example, here is a plan for a 1-day meeting event for an organization that usually makes decisions without including any feedback from those who are affected. It is designed to open up the conversation a little bit, without making huge changes in who decides. The three segments are Opening Keynote, Open Space and Authority Circle™:

Goal:

- Gather feedback from workforce before finalizing a decision that affects the whole group

Context:

- Deciding which Agile framework to use for bringing Agile thinking and processes into the organization

Schedule and Flow:
    0900-1000AM:
    º Opening keynote by top executive
    1000-1015AM:
    º BREAK
    1015-1045AM:
    º Opening of the Open Space meeting. Theme: Do we need a framework?
    1045-0245PM:
    º Open Space Sessions and Closing Circle
    0245-315PM:
    º BREAK (Time for Execs to review Proceedings and reflect on the Open Space)
    315P-415PM:
    º Authority Circle™ with Top Executives

Using Composition to Design Half-Day and Full-Day Events

The main takeaway here is that various meeting designs can be connected in a sequence to create a progressive experience that achieves your goals for the whole group, while also staying very sensitive to feedback from your current culture and overall context. Over time, as the culture and the context change, you will also adjust your designs to match.

Depending on your current situation and local context, these meeting formats can be mixed and matched to compose the kind of events that advance your goals, gather rich feedback, reduce resistance to change, and accelerate progress in the direction you intend.

Predictability + Reliability = Trust

Organizational change is not simple. Periodic whole-group inspection of the results is essential. When whole-group meetings are scheduled in a periodic, predictable and reliable way, a sense of trust in the process can develop. Trust is essential for a high-functioning organization. When trust is low, organizational learning and overall results suffer. By scheduling recurring events that invite everyone to inspect the progress, and by using that feedback to make adjustments, the results can be rapid, impressive, and lasting. The alternative (forcibly "rolling out" the change program, not soliciting feedback from those affected, and imposing the change) does little to encourage participation. But when whole-group events are scheduled on a cadence, trust and participation in them (and in the process) does increase.

Another important aspect of a recurring event is that it may begin to be experienced as an important and recurring cultural *ritual*. This opens up opportunities to build "common knowledge."

Ritual, Prestige, and Leadership

Whole-group events create common knowledge. "Common knowledge" is knowledge that can be used to coordinate the actions of very large groups of people.

Common knowledge can be used for coordination of actions across your entire enterprise. Rituals play a part in generating common knowledge.

Michael Chwe, in his fascinating book *Rational Ritual*, has this to say about it:

> "...in order to coordinate its actions, a group of people must form 'common knowledge.' Each person wants to participate only if others also participate. Members must have knowledge of each other, knowledge of that knowledge, knowledge of the knowledge of that knowledge, and so on."

Ritual events can play a big part in developing common knowledge. In fact, ritual is a primary tool for leaders who wish to create and leverage common knowledge to help coordinate their groups. As the back of the book explains:

> "...Michael Chwe applies this insight, with striking erudition, to analyze a range of rituals across history and

cultures. He shows that public ceremonies are powerful not simply because they transmit meaning from a central source to each audience member but because they let audience members know what other members know…"

Whole-group events create common knowledge and common knowledge is essential for large-group coordination. This is why the Inviting Leadership approach places such a strong emphasis on the careful design and execution of whole-group events.

Ritual alone is not enough, however. These events need to be structured as optional to attend, because the yes-no option generates the need for a decision … and the making of decisions can elevate the level of human engagement. The yes-no option also generates substantial feedback and "big data" that can be inspected later, to gauge the current state of enthusiasm for the change. The big data generated from invited whole-group events can also be used to inform decision-making and increase the quality of those executive decisions.

Carefully designed, whole-group ritual events and the use of invitation are both important aspects of the Inviting Leadership approach.

Ritual Events Enhance Leader Prestige

Ritual events tend to enhance the prestige of leaders.[7] This is especially true when participation in the ritual event is based on invitation rather than compulsion or mandate. Rituals can deliver feelings of shared identity, shared commitment, shared emotional energy, and a stronger culture.

Rituals can be scaled up and down to effectively build common knowledge. For example, a simple "check in" ritual[8] at the start of

---

[7] For more information about ritual and leadership prestige, see www.invitingleadership.com/book/links/#ritual-and-prestige.

[8] A "Check-in" ritual is a way for each person to acknowledge their current state and state their intent to follow the team's protocols for behavior during the meeting. For more information about team protocols, see www.invitingleadership.com/book/links/#the-mccarthys.

10-person staff meeting can help develop sense of shared identity and membership in that meeting. At the other extreme, large-scale ritual events such as a carefully designed, monthly "all-hands" meeting can also deliver on a sense of membership, commitment, and productive, goal-aligned behavior.

Recurring and periodic whole-group meeting events can help with more than generating common knowledge. These events can also substantially reduce the anxiety and worry that is associated with wide-scope organizational change. Reducing those worries can go a long way towards creating the conditions where resisters become tolerant of the change, and eventually support the changes being made. Ritual helps people make sense of what is happening.

Engagement Models Revisited

Employee engagement is essential for any lasting change. We introduced this concept in Chapter 5 and extend that discussion here.

> **engagement model** *n.*
> Any pattern or set of patterns, reducible to practice,
> which result in more employee engagement,
> especially during the implementation of an
> organizational-change initiative.

An Engagement Model is a kind of template that can be used for building and tailoring an employee engagement *plan*. One instance of an Engagement Model is called OpenSpace Agility.

A cycle of OpenSpace Agility is 45 to 90 days long, and starts and ends with a large "all hands" meeting. Open Space meetings are whole-group invitational meetings, where participants explore and discuss current organizational changes, and offer suggestions on how to best introduce and implement new changes.

A highly authorized leader functions as the Host by first *inviting* everyone to the event. Then, on the big day, that same leader welcomes everyone, focuses the group, and kicks off the meeting by introducing the facilitator. A facilitator guides the group initially and then launches them into an immersive experience of dialogue and planning.

These whole-group Open Space meetings are usually at least a full day. They build common knowledge, reduce employee anxieties during the change, and enhance the prestige of the highly authorized leader who brings it all together.

Because the Open Space meeting format is an invitational meeting format that can scale to thousands of participants, it figures prominently in the Inviting Leadership approach. For this reason, you will want to turn to the Appendices and refer to the basics of Open Space (and the OpenSpace Agility Engagement Model) as you examine this chapter.

Prime/OS[9] and its more specialized derivative OpenSpace Agility[10] are Tools for Implementing Inviting Leadership. They embody many of the concepts introduced and explained in this book, including:

- Iteration, Inspection and Adaptation: Learning by Experience
- Invitation
- Ritual
- Common Knowledge
- Self-Organization and Self-Management
- Bounded Containment and Enabling Constraints
- Psychological Safety

For all of these reasons, if you are considering an Agile or digital transformation effort, or are in the midst of one, it is a good idea to investigate OpenSpace Agility and Prime/OS. These are robust tools that enable Invitation-Based Change (IBC.) Both scale up to handle groups as large as 3,000 or more. You can learn more about OSA in Appendix H.

---

[9] For more information about Prime/OS, see www.invitingleadership.com/book/links/#prime-os.

[10] For more information about OpenSpace Agility, see www.invitingleadership.com/book/links/#openspace-agility.

Working in Enterprise Iterations

OpenSpace Agility uses iterations of 45 to 90 days to execute larger plans in steps, followed by inspection, adaptation, and re-planning. When embarking on an enterprise change effort, working in iterations is extremely important. The reasons include:

- **Working in iterations is an absolutely core aspect of an overall agile approach.**
  - ○ By using iterations, you are implementing your changes in an agile way, using an agile approach to change. Iteration allows an inspection point.
- **To make steady progress with enterprise level change and hold those gains, the people need time to integrate the new learning before going further.**
  - ○ Iterations provide those integration points as part of the process.
- **Change in organizations is unpredictable. Iterations allow for here-and-now collection of essential feedback.**
  - ○ The leadership group can use that valuable feedback to inform next-step decision-making.
- **Working the enterprise transformation in iterations demonstrates leader intent.**
  - ○ It clearly signals the intent of leaders to apply empirical approaches across the entire enterprise, in service to generating rapid and lasting improvement.
- **Iterations provide an opportunity to schedule whole-group events that can be focused on inspection of the results and the process.**
  - ○ Whole-group events create common knowledge. Common knowledge is important for coordinating very large groups of people. Recurring whole-group events are perceived as ritual. Ritual is an important

cultural device for reducing anxieties &
fears during period of transition.

For all of these reasons, it is desirable to have a desired "end-state," but not a fixed plan for getting there. Instead, to save time, effort and money, you want to define stepping-stone goals inside a reasonable timeframe for achieving them, followed by inspection and more planning. This is the essence of the business agility approach.

There is plenty of precedent in other areas of endeavor that support this approach.

Let's look at some of them:

The OODA Loop from the US Air Force (John Boyd)

The OODA loop is a strategy for successfully engaging in fighter jet combat. Defined by the legendary fighter pilot trainer John Boyd, it consists of four steps:

1. Observe: Take in all the data and observations that are available now
2. Orient: Enumerate a set of possible options
3. Decide: Eliminate all the alternatives until only one is left
4. Act: Execute your plan

PDCA – The Deming Cycle (W. Edwards Deming called it the Shewhart Cycle)

- Plan: Enumerate a set of options and eliminate each until only one is left
- Do: Execute on your plan
- Check: Inspect the results
- Act: Also referred to as "enact," in this step adjustments are made based on the "Do" and "Check" steps

Agile Software Development

The Agile Manifesto defines four values and twelve principles for effective software development.[11] Here are the values and principles from the Agile Manifesto that also support the idea of working in iterations at the enterprise level, with willing people: (paraphrased for brevity)

- Values:
  - Individuals and interactions over processes and tools
  - Responding to change over following a plan
- Principles:
  - Welcome feedback and changes, even late in the process of executing
  - Deliver frequently
  - At regular intervals, reflect, tune and adjust as needed
  - Great results emerge from self-organizing teams
  - Identify and build upon motivated individuals

Here we see how the Agile Manifesto embraces the same ideas as those from John Boyd, W. Edwards Deming, and others. In light of this background, it is easy to see how the complex nature of organizational change is best handled using an empirical, iterative, "inspect and adapt" approach. Have a direction, keep an idealized end-state in mind, but be flexible enough to respond to new data, new information, and change as you go. Engage in multiple iterations of mid-course correction and adjustment in light of the latest feedback and information.

---

[11] For decades, software development was viewed and approached as a manufacturing process. As software became more critical to business, it became obvious that software development is much more like cultivation. The environment for growth must be established first: rich soil, sufficient sunlight, and plenty of water. For more information, see www.invitingleadership.com/book/links/#agile.

Recap

Change is hard. Many people resist it, especially when they do not have a voice in how the change is implemented. Inviting Leaders use the tools in this chapter to design experiences that engage and enlist the entire workforce in successful change. These tools focus on whole group experiential learning that can surface resistance and inform the best ways for moving your change initiative forward.

Chapter 8 – Guidance

Organizational change occurs in context. This context often includes common patterns. In this chapter we list some of these patterns and offer guidance on how to address them with the Inviting Leadership approach.

The Guidance
The guidance that follows here is brief and to the point. It assumes you have a solid understanding of the concepts and facilities already introduced in this book, in particular the essential nature of employee engagement in affecting lasting and effective change. It also assumes that you are familiar with the various tools and meeting formats and types described in the Appendices.

Common Scenarios in Moving Towards Business Agility
Now let's now look at various scenarios you will encounter as a leader who is part of a leadership team attempting to implement an organizational change. When we say "the top executive" we mean the formally authorized leader that is in authority with respect to the entire group of people affected by the change. This can be a subset of the whole enterprise, such as a business unit, division, or department. In the case of the entire enterprise, the top executive will be the person occupying the role of CEO, President, etc.

1. Imposed Change Initiative In Flight
2. Top Executive's First Transformation
3. Transform with Current Decision-Making
4. Transformation Assuming Direct Reports Will Follow
5. Transformation With Less Than100% Leader Support
6. Top Leader New to Iteration and Inspection
7. Gain Support from the Workforce

People and their interactions power real progress. The scenarios that follow describe how to prepare a leadership team for real progress. Read the scenarios below to get a sense of the kind of leadership work that needs to be done to achieve rapid and lasting change. Then use Open Space (or something better, if you can find it) to restart your enterprise-change initiative.

Scenario #1: Imposed Change Initiative in Flight

Context:

> You have a change initiative such as Agile already in flight. Now you understand that it was imposed and not invited. You have lost some good people and now have low levels of engagement. You need a reboot. The leadership team acknowledges this reality, has been reoriented, and is now focused on employee engagement. Now an execution plan is needed for the restart across the whole enterprise.

Objectives:

- Restart the enterprise transition.
- Focus on invitation instead of delegation or imposition.
- Retain the best people.
- Create more enthusiasm and better results and outcomes.

Options:

- Hold an open meeting for the leaders only. Make it an open and invited meeting. Do not demand attendance from all leaders; invite them instead. Use a facilitator to design an event lasting three hours, one which takes the leadership team through an important and realistic learning experience by inspecting the results-to-date.
- Go back and do all the steps that need to be done with the wider leadership team, steps that prepare the leaders for leading a large increase in employee engagement (see the additional scenarios in this list).
- Arrange and execute an invited enterprise-wide all-hands Open Space meeting with a theme of "Now What?" or similar. Invite everyone in the organization to weigh in on the experience-to-date with respect to the

process of changing. Make the subject of the meeting the very process of changing, to bring as many people as possible into the conversation with intent to engage them.

Reasons and Rationale:

- o It's a common mistake to assume that practices power improvement when in fact people do. These steps acknowledge reality.
- o Leaders with substantial authority are often the biggest impediments to change. By starting with the leadership team, once again we are acknowledging reality.
  - People in the organization are very sensitive to signaling from formally authorized leaders, so alignment and harmonization of the content of overall leadership signaling is essential. This alignment is only possible if the entire leadership group has first gone through a period of transformational learning with the outcome of substantial group alignment, well in advance of beginning the process of introducing change to the wider organization.
- o Authentic and lasting organizational change depends on engaged, committed, and active supporters. By inviting rather than imposing change, the conditions for employee engagement in the process of changing can actually appear.

Summary:

Starting with imposition and delegation instead of invitation is a very common scenario. Large consulting firms often agree with and recommend this approach. But transformation means transformation of many aspects of organizational life, especially decision-making.

Scenario #2: Top Executive's First Transformation

Context:

Top executive wants transformational change but has never done this before, and:

- ° May not fully understand the implications.
- ° Does not want to change the way decisions are made (and who makes them).

Objectives:

- ° Help the top executive fully understand the implications of transformational change.
- ° Help the top executive fully understand (in particular) that transformational change means changes in the way various decisions are currently being made.

Options: If you are this top executive you may want to:

- **Invite Optional Meetings:** Start experimenting with making some meetings optional to attend. Use all feedback to inform your next steps. Who did attend? Who did not? What was the optional meeting like? What kind of results were generated?

- **Invite Whole-Group Learning Events:** Engage a reputable consultant to come and teach for ½ day on this change you are looking to make. For example if you are considering the use of a specific framework for the contemplated change, engage a teacher of that framework to come in, or find an employee who can teach it and engage them.

  - Make this training optional for your direct reports.
  - Optionally, allow those that you invite, to invite one additional person from the organization to attend this training.
  - Tell the trainer you will meet their minimum student count, and the final invoice is dependent on how many

attend, up to the maximum. In this manner you can retain the services of the consultant without knowing the exact student count in advance.

Reasons and Rationale:
- Get direct experience with using invitation for meetings and training.
- Identify willing people who can help your contemplated change succeed.
- Socialize your current best ideas by signaling with the training in the direction of your intent.
- Gather "big data" on the support (or lack of it) for your ideas.

Summary:
- Consider suggesting these options if you are a direct report or a peer of this top executive.
- Invite the leader to get started with invitational approaches and get learning via direct experience as well as very focused and formal training.
- The biggest implication of transformational change is that there will be changes in the way decisions are made. It will take time to socialize this to the leadership team.

Scenario #3: Transform with Current Decision-Making

Context:

As the top leader of the group, you want transformational change, but do not want to change the way decisions are currently made and/or who makes them.

Objectives:

○ Begin actual org-level transformation by assigning decision-making to support value stream flows.

Options: If you are this top executive you may want to:

○ Study the rules of Kanban and notice how these rules represent a change in the way decisions get made with respect to work assignment, and work flow.

• After studying and understanding these new rules about decision-making, invite your direct reports and others to do the same.

• Schedule training in the Kanban method and make it clear that participation is 100% optional for everyone you invite.

○ Study the rules of Scrum and notice how these rules represent a change in the way decisions get made with respect to work priority, assignment, and work flow.

• After studying and gaining an understanding the rules about decision-making in Scrum, invite your direct reports and others to do the same.

• Schedule training in Scrum and make it clear that participation is 100% optional for everyone you invite.

- Initiate a series of short and 100% invitational Lean Coffee[1] meetings with your direct reports to discuss topics related to the transformation of decision-making across the enterprise.

- After successfully using the Lean Coffee format with your direct reports, consider use of the Authority Circle meeting format for closed-door meetings that generate detailed discussions and feedback between the various influencers, your direct reports, and yourself.

  - Schedule a series of these meetings and make sure they are well facilitated.

  - Make participation 100% optional for all your invitees.

Reasons and Rationale:

- Learn about how decisions-making changes under the rules of Kanban and Scrum.

- Prepare for these changes. This includes:

  - Preparing as the leader.
  - Preparing as a wider leadership team.

- Start to understand Kanban and Scrum from a business agility perspective, instead of strictly an IT/engineering perspective.

- Identify sources of objections and other tensions in the leadership team.

Summary:

The fact that transformational change means changes in the authority distribution schema is a fact that must be consistently and repeatedly socialized. As stated previously in this book, decision-making that is out of

---

[1] For more information about Lean Coffee, see www.invitingleadership.com/book/links/#tools.

alignment with the flow of value represents
a serious impediment to improvement. The
current policies for decision-making often
represent the biggest impediment to genuine
transformational change.

For authentic transformational change to occur and to last,
two things must be true:

- The whole leadership team must be aligned in support of the changes to decision-making.
- An invitational rather than an imposed or delegated approach must be used at the leadership level and the wider enterprise level.

These steps are the starting steps for moving in the direction of improvement.

Scenario #4: Transformation Assuming Direct Reports Will Follow

Context:

> As the top leader of the group, you want transformational change and understand most of the implications. You assume that all other members of the leadership team and the wider organization will align 100% with whatever you say and will follow your lead.

Objectives:

- o Learn that objections and resistance from people in high-authority roles represent what is (by far) the largest set of impediments to leadership-level and enterprise-level transformational change.
- o Learn that the use of the inviting approach at the highest levels of authority can help generate useful feedback to help determine who is fully supportive and who is not.
- o Develop skills for leading direct reports and other leaders and colleagues through difficult learning experiences.

Options:

- o Study: Examine the available literature on imposing change, and the very low success rates associated with that type of approach.
- o Get Coached: Invite a coach who has experience leading digital and agile transformations to provide guidance and counsel. Make up your mind to allow them to lead you through acquiring some new beliefs about delegation and imposition vs. invitation.
- o Use Open Space: Create a small Open Space event that explores the idea of bringing agile and digital transformation.

Invite as many influential, direct reports and
essential stakeholders as you possibly can.

- Make sure the event is 100% opt-in
  with no sanctions whatsoever for opting
  out.
- Observe the meeting carefully.

Reasons and Rationale:

o Study and coaching is essential for
  effective leadership. If you purport to lead
  a transformational change, you must engage
  in these behaviors if you are to be up to the
  challenge. Enterprise transformation is not
  simple.

o Assuming your positional authority can force
  support for substantial change is dangerous.
  Those in positions of authority (such as
  your direct reports) are the people who can
  most effectively block and impede change.
  These are the people with direct reports and
  budgets. These are also the people who can
  and will use existing leverage points, such as
  the performance reviews of subordinates, to
  sanction those who do not also quietly and
  passively oppose the change.

o Open Space events with the entire
  leadership group allow you to size up where
  everyone stands. Genuine engagement is
  hard to fake. The Open Space events allow
  you to observe all the leaders interacting
  on key aspects of enterprise change. These
  observations are essential.

o People do change their minds, and periodic
  Open Space events can help you to gauge
  what kind of movement, if any, is taking
  place on the leadership team.

Summary:

It is essential to create the conditions where opposing views and objections can be expressed inside the leadership group. It is up to you to create that kind of environment. Leadership is large part invitational game design. Mandatory-to-play games are not fun, and as a leader you are the overall "leadership game designer." You must assume everyone has objections if you are to effectively lead an enterprise-wide transformation effort. Therefore: design compelling invitations and make sure they are authentic with no sanctions for opting-out. Use the data and feedback generated by your well-formed invitations to plan your next phase of change.

Scenario #5: Transformation With Less Than 100% Leader Support

Context:

> As the top leader of the group, you want transformational change and know for sure that some of the leadership team is *not* 100% on board. You know that their support is essential.

Objectives:

- o Identify the objections held by members of the leadership team.
- o Address the objections held by members of the leadership team.
- o Socialize transformational change with the leadership team.
- o Gain support from members of the leadership team.
- o Prepare the leadership team for the wider effort of encouraging and implementing change.
- o Use agile techniques to prepare the leadership team for these same techniques at every level of authority across the enterprise.

Options:

- o Meet to Invite Objections: Schedule closed-door sessions with the leadership team to invite objections to change, and actually listen to them. By inviting objections, important issues can be identified and raised in these open forums that you create. It is best if the meetings are facilitated, short, and 100% optional to attend. Gather feedback from these meetings with the leadership team, to inform the pace and timing and content next steps.

- o Address Objections: After objections have been identified, it is essential to address them. Addressing objections from leadership team members is an iterative process. You'll be asking:
  - "What would it take to get you in?"
  - "What needs to be true in the future that is not true now, to get you in?"
- o Use Lean Coffee: The Lean Coffee meeting format is a fantastic format for convening small-group meetings that are invitational and focused on a specific set of topics. This means Lean Coffee is fantastic for inviting and addressing objections from members of the leadership team. See Appendix I for details on this meeting format.
- o Use Authority Circle: This meeting format can help you to clearly explain your position while opening space for alternative points of view. Use it to socialize the changes and your reasons for making them, across the whole leadership team. See Appendix B for details on this meeting format.
- o Use "The Debate" meeting format[2] with the leadership team: "The Debate" is a great meeting format for discussing and exploring potentially divisive issues. It can be used in a space of time as short as 30 minutes or as long as 3 hours.
- o Consider using the Core Commitments:[3] The Core Commitments are a set of norms that encourage rational and results-

---

[2] For more information about "The Debate", see www.invitingleadership.com/book/links/#tools.

[3] For more information about The Core Commitments, see www.invitingleadership.com/book/links/#tools.

oriented behavior. Consider inviting these norms. For example, under the Core Commitments, a participant in a decision-making process cannot object to the current proposal credibly if they do not offer a clear alternative. These norms can help speed up the identification and addressing of objections to change.

Reasons and Rationale:

- When the change is initiated, as an Inviting Leader, you will be inviting the rank and file later to express their objections. Unexpressed objections to change are the #1 impediment to it.

- It is essential to invite objections to change from members of the leadership team. People in high authority are in a position to block change from happening.

- People on the leadership team (department heads, direct reports, and 1-off direct reports) have a lot at stake when a change is introduced. If you repress their objections, you will miss an opportunity to gather essential feedback.

- The whole leadership team needs to understand the Inviting Leadership approach to organizational change. By using it first and foremost with the leadership team, you gain the advantages of using an inviting style as you work with them. You also are teaching them valuable lessons in how the inviting style actually works.

Summary:

No matter what, don't move forward without inviting objections from members of the leadership group and gaining the explicit support of as many of those leaders as possible.

Scenario #6: Top Leader New to Iteration and Inspection

Context:

The whole leadership team has been heard, objections within that leadership team have surfaced, and now they need processing.

As the top leader of the group, you want transformational change, but you are new to the idea of working in enterprise-wide iterations followed by enterprise-wide inspections.

Objectives:

- Reduce objections by asking for commitments that are short, and followed by inspections.
- Work in well-defined increments, each with a clear narrative that has a clear beginning, a middle, and end.
- Start experimenting with the change at the leadership-team level, by working in the same iterations that the whole enterprise will soon be using.
- Give the leadership team direct experience working in iterations of change; get them comfortable with the process.

Options:

- Leaders Go First: Lead by example and have your direct reports working in a way that embodies the changes. Do it on an experimental basis and follow with inspection. If the change is a move into business agility, start working in an agile way: use a Kanban board, build a backlog, conduct a short daily meeting, deliver a demo at the end of the month to the rest of the organization.
- Invite Departments to Try Using a Business Agility Approach: Invite but do not force

Department heads and other leadership teams in the organization to try the new way of working and to apply it to their work. Invite them to select and try some new practices for a month or two on an experimental basis. Locate sources and make available skilled facilitators, who can and will help the leadership teams enjoy the new experience of change.

o   Invited Half-Day Open Space Events for the Whole Leadership Group: Periodically pull the whole leadership team together, for face-to-face or online Open Space events to discuss the shift to business agility from a leadership point of view. Make these about the biggest issues inside the leadership team, invite and do not impose, and use an outside facilitator to keep everything very open.

Reason and Rationale:

o   Iterations that are short and followed by inspections make it simple for people to accept. This includes the leadership teams. Small commitments are easier to say yes to. Small and invited commitments are superior to large and delegated obligations where leadership engagement in change is concerned.

o   Since the leadership teams are essential to success, start by setting up iterations of change with them first. Do this to increase support, reduce resistance, and set the stage for rapid and lasting success with your overall agile or digital transformation program.

o   Doing leadership work by what is contemplated for the whole organization is an extremely effective way for leaders to signal, and to generate the emergence of supporting narratives across the organization. People can, will, and do *talk*. These discussions and emerging narratives socialize the change, in advance of inviting the whole enterprise into the process.

○ Learning by doing is a very fast way to identify points of leverage and impediments. By immediately starting with the leadership teams, you will more rapidly identify where the points of leverage are, and where the pain points are.

Summary:

Leaders and leadership teams in many organizations have a belief that "agile or digital change is for the I.T. delivery teams, but not for business functions or the executive management team." Nothing could be further from the truth. If you put even one delivery team on an agile footing, almost immediately that begins to affect the decision-making of stakeholders and the wider organization. Add to this the increase in the velocity of change in the business environment and it's obvious that "change is for the delivery teams only" is a very dangerous false assumption.

By aligning the leadership teams first and helping them gain direct experience, you set the stage for authentic success with authentic business agility across the entire organization.

Scenario #7: Gain Support from the Workforce

Context:

As the top leader of the group, you understand enterprise-iteration, all objections from leaders have been heard and addressed, and the entire group of formally authorized leadership agrees to support the change using iterations followed by whole-group inspections. The time has now come to gain support from the rest of workforce: all formally authorized leaders, team members, and other employees who will be affected.

Objectives:

- o Sense and respond to the organization's current level of *willingness* to change.
- o Sense and respond to the organization's current level of *readiness* to change.
- o As a leader, work with the topmost leadership team to design and define an organizational-change game that everyone in the organization wants to play.
- o Initiate the first enterprise-wide iteration of change, and base it on the concepts of Inviting Leadership and leadership invitations.
- o Identify the passionate and the responsible, the people who can make the whole thing happen.
- o Generate and socialize narratives and storytelling that positively support the change.

Options:

- o Invite willing teams into formal training programs.
- o Use an enterprise Engagement Model such as OpenSpace Agility to initiate the first wave of change.

○   Informally socialize Open Space meetings across the organization.

○   Identify champions of change across the enterprise who will in fact carry the change forward, socialize it, and create enthusiasm and results.

Reason and Rationale:

○   The leaders have now been through a process that is very similar to what is about to be experienced by the enterprise as a whole. This means the leadership team is ready to lead (and in fact invite) a very substantial change.

○   People power all the impediments to change. People also power all the progress and improvement. By telling a coherent and iterative story of change, and by asking for medium-sized (not large) commitments that are bounded by time, the leadership team is reducing risk of failure and increasing the chances of success.

○   Inviting enterprise-wide iterations of change followed by enterprise-wide inspections creates the conditions for enterprise-wide adaptations. This is the formula for creating steady gains and holding on to them. This is the recipe for rapid and lasting success.

○   Working with willing teams is essential to success. Whether working enterprise-wide or with pilot teams, this aspect is essential. Remember: People power all the impediments and also all the progress and improvement.

Summary:

Being willing and being able ("ready") are two different things. We need the organization to be both willing and able. This means a certain level of preparation. The leadership team has prepared. Now it is time to prepare the organization to literally "change itself." The leaders have created the fertile conditions. This fact and the subsequent use of leadership invitations means the organization has a legitimate shot at rapid and lasting success with digital and agile transformation.

Recap

Business Agility Transformation Scenarios:

- Imposed Change Initiative In Flight
- Top Executive's First Transformation
- Transform with Current Decision-Making
- Transformation Assuming Direct Reports Will Follow
- Transformation With Less Than100% Leader Support
- Top Leader New to Iteration and Inspection
- Gain Support from the Workforce

APPENDICES

Here you can find resources and tools that can be applied to the Inviting Leadership style. The content here includes meeting formats, frameworks for organizing, and some important essays that have strongly influenced the development and definition of the Inviting Leadership style.

Appendix A – "Ready for Agile" Checklist

Appendix B – Authority Circle™

Appendix C – The Tyranny of Structurelessness

Appendix D – The BART System

Appendix E – A Brief User's Guide to Open Space Technology

Appendix F – The Game of Scrum

Appendix G – Kanban Introduction

Appendix H – OpenSpace Agility Introduction

Appendix I – Additional Tools

Appendix A – "Ready for Agile" Checklist

NOTE: The Ready For Agile Checklist is the result of a full collaboration with our colleague Joseph DeAngelis, a prominent Agile coach and Agile community organizer from the greater Boston, Massachusetts area. We are thankful to Joseph for noting the complete lack of an actionable definition for the "Ready" state ahead of any enterprise Agile transformation effort. Organizations are seldom prepared for what transformation implies, and a definition of "Ready" is essential. The Ready for Agile Checklist is a direct result of Joe's keen thinking and creativity during our collaboration on this. You can learn more about Joe DeAngelis and his work at www.invitingleadership.com/book/links/#coach-joe-deangelis.

Opening Notes

- In Agile work, **people** power all of the improvement and all of the impediments. We must therefore set the stage for success, by getting clear agreements about essential topics such as word definitions and rules. Without these essential agreements, we are inviting trouble almost immediately.
- Your Agile pilots worked in large part because **willing teams** were selected. Do not forget this. Keep this firmly in mind as you try to "scale Agile." You cannot scale the success of a pilot unless you are working with Teams that demonstrate the same level of enthusiasm as your original pilot teams. The challenge is how to create enthusiasm for change so that the

maximum number of Teams, Stakeholders, and Executives are willing to play along in an active way.

- People are flexible and do change their minds. If a person is resistant to change they may reconsider after a while, so do not give up on them.
- In all cases, endeavor to work with *willing people* at every level in the organization. The willing people power almost all of the **improvement**, while the unwilling people power almost all of the **impediments**.
- Summary of steps:
  - ○ Socialize and set agreements on the terminology (Scrum, Agile, Kanban)
  - ○ Discuss the rules of the methods to be used (Scrum, Agile, Kanban)
  - ○ Prepare executive leaders for what is about to happen, and what is fully expected of them

Step #1: Socialize & Get Agreement on Key Definitions (Agile, Scrum, Kanban)

Notes:

- **Agreements about word definitions are key agreements in Agile work.** By testing the organization's willingness to agree to word definitions, you can learn a lot about context, org-level readiness to proceed, etc.
- **It is common for the more resistant people to have objections to agreeing on simple word definitions.** Thus asking for agreement on word definitions for Agile, Scrum and Kanban generates "big data" that is useful for the coach, the in-house Agile champion, etc.

- **This step might look easy, however be prepared for real resistance, which is much more common than you might think.** For example, if executives are unwilling to allow the time needed for everyone to do this together, you can (clearly) expect trouble with your Agile effort in that company. (See also "Step #3: Prepare Executive Leaders for What is about to Happen, and What is Now Fully Expected of Them")

Part A: Agree on a Shared Definition of Agile

☐ For all affected **Teams**: socialize the Agile Manifesto as the definition of the word "Agile." Get clear and explicit agreement.

☐ For all affected (in-scope) **Stakeholders**: socialize the Agile Manifesto as the definition of the word "Agile." Get clear and explicit agreement.

☐ For affected (in-scope) **Executives**: socialize the Agile Manifesto as the definition of the word "Agile." Get clear and explicit agreement.

Part B: Agree on a Shared Definition of Scrum

☐ For all affected **Teams**: socialize *The Scrum Guide* as the definition of the word "Scrum." Get clear and explicit agreement.

☐ For all affected (in-scope) **Stakeholders**: socialize *The Scrum Guide* as the definition of the word "Scrum." Get clear and explicit agreement.

☐ For affected (in-scope) **Executives**: socialize *The Scrum Guide* as the definition of the word "Scrum." Get clear and explicit agreement. (See also "Step #3: Prepare Executive Leaders for What is about to Happen, and What is Now Fully Expected of Them")

Part C: Agree on a Shared Definition of Kanban

☐ For all affected **Teams**: socialize the *Kanban from the Inside* book from Mike Burrows as the definition of the word "Kanban." Get clear and explicit agreement.

☐ For all affected (in-scope) **Stakeholders**: socialize the *Kanban from the Inside* book from Mike Burrows as the definition of the word "Kanban." Get clear and explicit agreement.

☐ For affected (in-scope) **Executives**: socialize the *Kanban from the Inside* book from Mike Burrows as the definition of the word "Kanban." Get clear and explicit agreement. (See also "Step #3: Prepare Executive Leaders for What is about to Happen, and What is Now Fully Expected of Them")

Step #2: Discuss & Agree on How These Rules of Agile, Scrum & Kanban Will Impact Behaviors, Operations & Decision-Making

Notes:

- For each group (Teams, Stakeholders, and Execs) this step can be done immediately after agreeing to each definition that was socialized to the group. That is, during the same meeting, ask everyone to *actually agree not only to play by those rules, the rules found in the Agile Manifesto, The Scrum Guide, and the Kanban definition, but also understand how these rules impact behaviors and mindset and the distribution of authority to make decisions.*

- Not everyone is happy about the changes that Agile brings. Real Agile brings changes to how *decisions* get made and by whom. This is going to trigger **fear** for just about everyone. Go in with that assumption.

- It is a good idea (and more efficient) to get everyone (Teams, Stakeholders, and Execs) in one big room for 3 hours to hammer all of this out. But this is not always practical so use common sense. But get it done!

- It is important to design an experience with group exercises to engage the people, to reduce worries, and (most importantly) to surface legitimate objections. Experiential meeting formats (Open Space, Lean Coffee, etc.) work well for this!

- There will be objections. Objections exist at every level across the company. People invested in the status quo always want to keep it that way. When the objections surface, it is important to allow those objections to be expressed freely and openly in a facilitated-meeting context. Encourage and honor the open expression of objections. As the facilitator, you must create the space for objections. The key question to pose to anyone objecting is: "what has to change to get you in?" Or, "what needs to be true in the future that is not true now, to get you in?"

- It is a good idea to create a simple one-page document that people can actually sign. When they sign it, they are agreeing (for "N" weeks or months, a limited time) to a) use these definitions, and b) be bound by what they say, and c) commit to do everything expected to support the Agile, the Scrum, the Kanban implemented by Teams in this organization.

- Naming a date when all of this is to be reconsidered and inspected is **always** an excellent idea. It reduces worries, and gets more people IN.

Part A: Agree to honor the four values and twelve principles of the Agile Manifesto and how they impact behaviors and authority

- ☐ For all **Teams**: agree to be bound by the rules contained in the definitions of Agile.
- ☐ For all impacted **Stakeholders**: agree to be bound by the rules contained in the definitions of Agile.
- ☐ For all impacted **Executives**: agree to be bound by the rules contained in the definitions of Agile.

Part B: Agree to follow The Scrum Guide rules and how these rules will impact the decision-making process and how teams and individuals work together

Notes:

- • This is where it gets sticky. Example: *The Scrum Guide* says "for the Product Owner to be successful, *everyone* in the organization must respect his or her decisions" and "The Product owner is one person, not a committee."
- • Expect pushback. *Encourage* pushback. If you do not get any pushback, do an exercise that helps to elicit some pushback. Scrum is very strict about a few things. Make sure everyone *understands this.*
- ☐ For all **Teams**: agree to be bound by the rules contained in *The Scrum Guide.*
- ☐ For all impacted **Stakeholders**: agree to be bound by the rules contained in *The Scrum Guide.*
- ☐ For all impacted **Executives**: agree to be bound by the rules contained in *The Scrum Guide.*

Part C: Agree to honor "All" the rules of Kanban

Notes:

- There are many false beliefs about the Kanban Method. The Kanban Method is not just a rows-and-columns depiction of the work. It also contains process rules, such as work-in-process limits, pulling work from state to state, and defined Work Order Types.

- In the Kanban Method, an item does not get worked on until and unless it belongs to a specific Work Order Type with a specific Cycle Time. Make *sure* that everyone understands this.

- ☐ For all **Teams**: seek and obtain agreement to be bound by the rules contained in the definition of the Kanban Method.

- ☐ For all impacted **Stakeholders**: seek and obtain agreement to be bound by the rules contained in the definition of the Kanban Method.

- ☐ For all impacted **Executives**: seek and obtain agreement to be bound by the rules contained in the definition of the Kanban Method.

Step #3: Prepare Executive Leaders for What is about to Happen, and What is Now Fully Expected of Them

Notes:

- Everything hinges on leadership. You need agreement from the rank-and-file about the words Agile, Scrum, and Kanban, and also agreement on the rules for those items. Executive leaders must understand the definitions, agree to them, *and follow through*, especially when it gets difficult. This work must begin **no later than** your work with the Teams, or **preferably, well in advance** of your work with the Teams.

- You will observe the largest amount of fear from Leaders. This makes sense when you think about it; they must agree to give up some authority but are still accountable for key results!

- Leaders need to understand that the entire organization will sense and respond to any directives and executive behaviors that are inconsistent or directly contrary to this new Agile approach.

- Leaders need to understand that departments and policies can and will change as a result of confronting reality with Agile. For example, value stream mapping identifies departments, roles, and policies that are reducing the flow of value to customers. Scrum encourages the identification and removal of impediments. Kanban authorizes Teams to require that a Work Item Type is assigned to each item that is queued for work. Leadership prep is ongoing and a **very big deal.**

- Often executives believe the common notion that "Agile is only great for I.T." Be prepared to push back on this misconception. The reality is that Agile immediately affects and makes demands upon the entire organization!

- Just because the top executive wants Agile does not mean it is going to happen. People up and down the organization resist, including direct reports to the top leader. Make sure the top leader understands this. You don't want an **"Air Sandwich"** between the top leader and the teams executing Agility.

- Also make sure the top leader understands that it is not good enough for direct reports to merely comply; they must *agree* in fact to support with some enthusiasm.

☐ Explain to executive leaders the benefits of doing their leadership work in an Agile way, and how being public about that is a very good idea.

☐ Ask executive leaders to: work from a backlog, use a Kanban board, run a daily meeting, and/or present an end-of month demo to the organization. Offer to facilitate. Try to get them to agree to do this.

☐ If they say NO, reduce the ask by half and try again.

☐ Explain to executive leaders the essential nature of very clear and very consistent messaging and communication about the change.

☐ Explain to executive leaders the essential nature of very *frequent* ("early and often") messaging and communication about the change.

☐ Ask executive leaders to send out a weekly email that reports on and celebrates the wins that the Teams (and the organization) are achieving.

☐ If they say "No," reduce the ask by half and try again.

☐ Test the willingness of individual executives to be led through learning by asking them to read a small portion of a book you recommend, for example the book *Software in 30 Days* by Jeff and Ken. They will always say yes to the request but may not do the work. Provide a list of pages to read (about 40 or so), have them suggest a date when they can be done with the reading, and see if they actually do it.

☐ Explain to executive leaders that the benefits of Agile are not lasting unless the people are genuinely engaged.

☐ Explain to executive leaders that substantially all of the improvement comes from "individuals and interactions" and "motivated individuals" who are actively participating on self-managed (self organizing) teams.

☐ Explain that *employee engagement is essential!* Encourage pushback and objections and then cite the Gallup data on the horrific costs associated with low employee engagement.

☐ Explain that self-management is where the improvement comes from, and that self-managed teams are impossible to achieve unless the Team members are engaged!

Step #4: Work in Enterprise Iterations of Agile Transformation, Creating Natural Boundaries of Inspection & Adaptation

Notes:

- **Phased-gate "waterfall style"** implementations of Agile create the following disadvantages & problems:
  - ○ Transformation impacts people more than anything else in the organization. Everyone reacts differently to change; some embrace it but most people fear it. Depending on the culture in place, it is hard to predict when "real" transformation will take hold and produce better outcomes. Thus, trying to plan up front and predict when these longer-term outcomes will occur is fruitless!
  - ○ Typically rigidly planned up front, the phased-gate approach gives the impression that change cannot happen once the decision is made to follow a specific transformation strategy. And worse, those who are impacted by these changes were not even given a seat at the planning table to begin with, leading to disengagement and ... poor results and even failure.

- **Enterprise iterations** achieve the following advantages & solutions:
  - ○ Each iteration creates natural boundaries for Experimentation, Inspection, and Adaptation. When people believe that they can try something, learn from it, and adapt it as needed, they are much more willing to be *in*!
  - ○ The organization can react more rapidly to a Big Opportunity if one arises instead of being stuck in the midst of a transformation that cannot react to change.
  - ○ Each iteration has a clear goal and we know what "Done" looks like because it is measurable, not with vanity metrics by actionable metrics!
- Therefore, make sure these items are checked off before you begin:
- ☐ Agree to work in 45-60 day enterprise iterations. At the end of each iteration, invite everyone to review what happened during the past iteration and agree on what if any changes should be made. Again, a meeting format like Open Space or World Café work great for such meetings.
- ☐ Be sure each enterprise iteration has a minimum of one SMART (Specific, Measurable, Attainable, Relevant, and Timely) goal. It is best for this goal to be set with those affected (almost everyone) participating. Various meeting formats and facilitation methods can be used to do this.
- ☐ Define Actionable Measurements to help you realize true progress towards achieving your SMART goal. Beware of "vanity metrics" that can mislead you on how far along your Agile transformation is! Example of a vanity metric: how many teams we trained, "stood up," etc.

Closing Notes

You might be doing a "reboot" or a "remake." If you are, simply follow these instructions. But first set the stage with a message about *why* we are taking these steps. If you can also time this "reboot" to happen at a time when other changes are taking place, so much the better. For example if the leadership team is changing in some way, *that* is a perfect time to introduce the "Agile reboot."

Appendix B – Authority Circle™

When and Why to Use the Authority Circle

Authority Circle is a meeting format. It is a severe variation (a mutation) of the plain-vanilla Fishbowl format. Use it when you are aiming at the following goals and objectives:

- You want to create "common knowledge" across the entire group about key items the group is working on
- You want to allow the wider group to listen in on authority conversing with itself, about issues of importance
- You want to create a very real sense of convergence around a set of issues, in advance of launching the group into either
  - a deeper-convergence activity around taking action, or
  - a divergence activity such as Open Space
- A common belief held by many executives is that releasing any amount of decision-making authority opens the door to disorder and a loss of control. But the reality is that good boundary design, good boundary implementation, and good boundary management can create an environment where the transfer of very small amounts of decision-making authority can create very large increases in the desired results: more self-management, more employee engagement, more innovation, and higher performance.

- You want to focus the leadership authority figures on how to leverage the power of authority and authority distribution dynamics, to discover "persons of interest" and emergent leaders in the wider group; people who are led to "speak *to* authority" or even "speak *as* authority" on the most important issues

How to Use the Authority Circle

Roles

Original set of inner circle authority figures
Current inner circle member
Current outer circle member
Facilitator

Events

Authority Circle start
Inner circle member vacate
New inner circle member arrival (occupies an empty seat)
Inner circle discussion
Topic change

Required Elements

- Time: 30 to 90 minutes without a break; up to 180 minutes with 1 or 2 breaks
- Topics: A set of issues that are very hot for the group, a minimum of 3, maximum of 10
- Microphones for larger groups

Steps

1. How Space is Arranged and Materials Needed
   o Arrange an inner circle and an outer circle of chairs. The inner circle contains a small ring of chairs; the outer circle is larger

and encircles and contains the inner circle completely.

o   The outer circle has one or more rows of chairs, with enough seats for all of the other less-authorized participants.

o   Inner circle contains at least 2 microphones for larger groups.

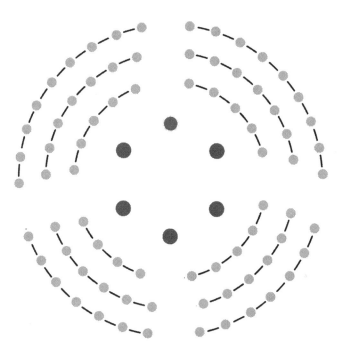

Figure B-1: Authority Circle Setup

2. Structuring the Invitation

    o   Populate the inner circle with the people occupying the highest-authority roles in the group. Ask them to discuss a set of hot topics, listed on the wall, one by one with each in a strict time box of at least 10 minutes each. Invite them to converse with each other as if the audience was not there. Ask them to avoid presenting to the audience.

- ○ Invite the people outside the Authority Circle to listen and observe, and optionally participate directly by occupying the blank "hot seat" if and when if becomes available (see below).

3. How Participation is Distributed
   - ○ Everyone in the inner circle may speak.
   - ○ Everyone in the outer circle may listen, and if the "hot seat" is open, they may step in and take it.

4. How Groups are Configured
   - ○ One inner circle group of 3 to 7 participants, with one blank chair in that circle.
   - ○ One outer circle with everyone else seated.
   - ○ Rules apply for the original N members of the inner circle:
     - All original inner circle members stay inside the inner circle at all times.
     - When someone from the outer circle takes the hot seat:
       - Conversation stops.
       - That person gets the microphone, has the floor, and may speak a comment, question, or concern.
     - This is a facilitated event. For each topic queued up to be addressed by the inner circle, it goes like this:
       - Phase 1:
         - Identify the next issue to discuss.
         - Clear the "hot seat" (open it up so there is one seat open in the inner circle).
         - Brief discussion of the topic by the authority figures inside the

inner circle; everyone in the outer circle listens.
- Phase 2: Outer circle members are authorized to take the hot seat. What that happens:
  - Discussion stops.
  - New inner-circle member gets a microphone.
  - New inner circle member speaks a question, comment, or concern.

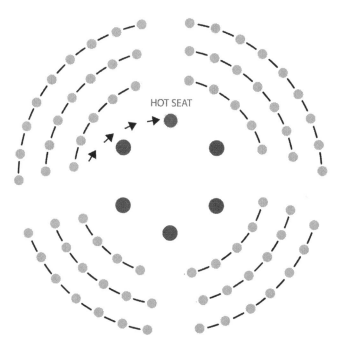

Figure B.2: Outer Circle Member Takes a Seat

Sequence of Steps and Time Allocation

- Time: 30 to 90 minutes without a break; up to 180 minutes with 1 or 2 breaks

- For each topic addressed by the inner circle, it goes like this:
  - Phase 1: Brief discussion inside the circle; everyone in all rows of the outer circle listens.
  - Phase 2: Outer circle members may come forward and occupy the hot seat. When this occurs, then:
    - Discussion stops.
    - New inner-circle member gets a microphone.
    - New inner circle member speaks a question, comment, or concern.

Tips and Traps

- When a new person takes the hot seat by moving from the outer circle to the inner circle, they may change the subject. For this reason, it is important to work in the Phase 1 / Phase 2 format. This allows the leaders to say what *they* want to say in Phase 1 and then allows for the randomness and subject changes that may ensue in Phase 2.
- For Authority Circle to work, the event must be competently and firmly facilitated.
  - The timebox for each discussion item must be kept.
  - The rules for 'the originals' must be maintained in a strict way. In this default setup, original inner-circle members must remain seated inside the inner circle.

Riffs and Variations

- Variation 1: An Original Inner Circle Member Vacates
  - You can open up more than one seat in the inner circle by allowing some of the original

inner circle members to vacate. For example, one of the original members may get up and join the outer circle. The rule is that at least "N" of the original authority figures must remain in the inner circle at all times, so the center contains a high concentration of authority and authorization. Example: The original group is seven and six must be present inside the inner circle at all times (N=6). There are now six originals remaining. None of them may vacate the inner circle until the authority figure who left the inner circle returns to the inner circle. This rule allows the opening up of a maximum of two seats in the inner circle: the original vacant "hot seat" and the seat opened up by one of the original authority figures.

- o It is a good idea to tag each of the original inner circle members with a special nametag that identifies them as one of the originals. This makes it easier to facilitate the inner circle as original members move in and out.

- o Be careful when opening up multiple seats. Only do it when you want more openness. There is a high potential for disorder when you do this. Multiple open seats can be hard to manage as a facilitator, and may introduce substantial randomness to the conversation. When using Authority Circle with multiple open seats, the current topic and conversation can tend to stop and start as new participants enter the inner circle. This can be "bumpy" at times. Subjects change more frequently. To reduce randomness and make facilitation easier, a single hot seat (single empty seat initially) is recommended for the first time you try Authority Circle.

- Variation 2: Phase 1 Contains all Subjects:
  - ○ No open chairs for most of the event; instead have the top leadership in the inner circle converse and articulate their positions on the issues one by one. Then, later, have a Phase 2 where a single chair can open up.
- Variation 3: Concentric Ring Seating:
  - ○ For large groups over 50 or so, use multiple concentric rings for the outer circle. Create at least four aisles so participants can quickly move to or from the center.
- Variation 4: Authority Layers:
  - ○ For a very large group, populate the first row of the outer circle with direct reports of the original inner-circle members. And for each topic, run it in three phases:
    - Inner circle discussion.
    - Inner circle discussion, with an option for those in the first row of the outer circle to take any empty inner-circle seat.
    - Inner circle discussion, with an option for anyone to take any empty inner-circle seat.

Examples

- You are assisting with establishing a change in a rather hierarchical organization. Use Authority Circle with the top 40 or 50 company leaders, to teach them how to measure out small units of authority to gain several large units of employee engagement
- You are designing a large company retreat or corporate planning event. Use Authority Circle after the CEO keynotes and before launching

the group into a problem-solving activity, for example before the use of Open Space

- You are designing a large company retreat or company planning event. Use Authority Circle after an Open Space to build common knowledge of how the group of key authority figures responds to the content of the event and the Proceedings.

- The group is facing a set of problems that only the whole group knows how to solve. Create a three-hour event with a beginning, middle, and end. Use Authority Circle in the middle segment of the event to build common knowledge about the issue. Discover (as a group) what the authority figures think about it, in service to making a mid-course correction or adjustment as a whole group, based on what "authority has to say" about the hottest issues.

Appendix C – The Tyranny of Structurelessness

Authors' Notes

This essay by Jo Freeman (aka Joreen) is one of the foundational essays in the emerging discipline of Authority Studies.[1] It clearly deconstructs and then explains the dynamics and mechanics of informal authority distribution, especially in groups where there is an aversion to any kind of formalized hierarchy. This essay is a significant work that makes an important contribution to the Authority Studies literature.

While the subject and context of the essay is the state of the women's movement in the 1970's, the lessons found here apply to any group.

This essay is particularly useful for making sense of the informal, unwritten, and unseen rules about how authority is actually distributed in a so-called "unstructured group." As the author points out, "contrary to what we would like to believe, there is no such thing as a structureless group."

Near the end of this fascinating essay, the author offers a set of properties that small, high-functioning, task-oriented, "structureless" groups tend to exhibit.

The following is a verbatim copy of the essay from the author, Jo Freeman. We include it here with permission of the author. We have bolded some of the more important statements and sentences for emphasis.

---

[1] For more information about Authority Studies, see
www.invitingleadership.com/book/links/#authority-studies.

This highly detailed essay is long and takes time to digest; the estimated reading time is about 20 minutes. While it describes aspects of the "structureless" women's movement of the 1970's, this essay does a good job of explaining what happens when boundaries on authority by role are not clearly specified. Enjoy.

Notes on the Essay from the Original Author, Jo Freeman

The earliest version of this article was given as a talk at a conference called by the Southern Female Rights Union, held in Beulah, Mississippi in May 1970. It was written up for Notes from the Third Year (1971), but the editors did not use it. It was then submitted to several movement publications, but only one asked permission to publish it; others did so without permission. The first official place of publication was in Vol. 2, No. 1 of The Second Wave (1972). This early version in movement publications was authored by Joreen. Different versions were published in the Berkeley Journal of Sociology, Vol. 17, 1972-73, pp. 151-165, and Ms. magazine, July 1973, pp. 76-78, 86-89, authored by Jo Freeman. This piece spread all over the world. Numerous people have edited, reprinted, cut, and translated "Tyranny" for magazines, books and web sites, usually without the permission or knowledge of the author. The version below is a blend of the three cited here.

The Original Paper

The Tyranny of Structurelessness

During the years in which the women's liberation movement has been taking shape, a great emphasis has been placed on what are called leaderless, structureless groups as the main -- if not sole -- organizational form of the movement. The source of this idea was a natural reaction against the over-structured society in which most of us found ourselves, and the inevitable control this gave others over our lives, and the continual elitism of the Left and similar groups among those who were supposedly fighting this overstructuredness.

The idea of "structurelessness," however, has moved from a healthy counter to those tendencies to becoming a goddess in its own right. The idea is as little examined as the term is much used, but it has become an intrinsic and unquestioned part of women's liberation ideology. For the early development of the movement this did not much matter. It early defined its main goal, and its main method, as consciousness-raising, and the "structureless" rap group was an excellent means to this end. The looseness and informality of it encouraged participation in discussion, and its often supportive atmosphere elicited personal insight. If nothing more concrete than personal insight ever resulted from these groups, that did not much matter, because their purpose did not really extend beyond this.

The basic problems didn't appear until individual rap groups exhausted the virtues of consciousness-raising and decided they wanted to do something more specific. At this point they usually foundered because most groups were unwilling to change their structure when they changed their tasks. Women had thoroughly accepted the idea of "structurelessness" without realizing the limitations of its uses. People would try to use the "structureless" group and the informal conference for purposes for which they were unsuitable out of a blind belief that no other means could possibly be anything but oppressive.

If the movement is to grow beyond these elementary stages of development, it will have to disabuse itself of some of its prejudices about organization and structure. There is nothing inherently bad about either of these. They can be and often are misused, but to reject them out of hand because they are misused is to deny ourselves the necessary tools to further development. We need to understand why "structurelessness" does not work.

FORMAL AND INFORMAL STRUCTURES

Contrary to what we would like to believe, there is no such thing as a structureless group. Any group of people of whatever nature that comes together for any length of time for any purpose will inevitably structure itself in some fashion. The structure may be flexible; it may vary over time; it may evenly or unevenly distribute tasks, power and resources over the members of the group. But it will be formed regardless of the abilities, personalities, or intentions of the people involved. The very fact that we are individuals, with different talents, predispositions, and backgrounds makes this inevitable. Only if we refused to relate or interact on any basis whatsoever could we approximate structurelessness -- and that is not the nature of a human group.

This means that to strive for a structureless group is as useful, and as deceptive, as to aim at an "objective" news story, "value-free" social science, or a "free" economy. A "laissez faire" group is about as realistic as a "laissez faire" society; the idea becomes a smokescreen for the strong or the lucky to establish unquestioned hegemony over others. This hegemony can be so easily established because the idea of "structurelessness" does not prevent the formation of informal structures, only formal ones. Similarly "laissez faire" philosophy did not prevent the economically powerful from establishing control over wages, prices, and distribution of goods; it only prevented the government from doing so. Thus structurelessness becomes a way of masking power, and within the women's movement is usually most strongly advocated by those who are the most powerful (whether they are conscious of their power or not). As long as the structure of the group is informal, the rules of how decisions are made are known only to a few and awareness of power is limited to those who know the rules. Those who do not know the rules and are not chosen for initiation must remain in confusion, or suffer from paranoid delusions that something is happening of which they are not quite aware.

For everyone to have the opportunity to be involved in a given group and to participate in its activities the structure must be explicit, not implicit. The rules of decision-making must be open and available to everyone, and this can happen only if they are formalized. This is not to say that formalization of a structure of a group will destroy the informal structure. It usually doesn't. But it does hinder the informal structure from having predominant control and make available some means of attacking it if the people involved are not at least responsible to the needs of the group at large. "Structurelessness" is organizationally impossible. We cannot decide whether to have a structured or structureless group, only whether or not to have a formally structured one. Therefore the word will not be used any longer except to refer to the idea it represents. Unstructured will refer to those groups which have not been deliberately structured in a particular manner. Structured will refer to those which have. A Structured group always has formal structure, and may also have an informal, or covert, structure. It is this informal structure, particularly in Unstructured groups, which forms the basis for elites.

THE NATURE OF ELITISM

"Elitist" is probably the most abused word in the women's liberation movement. It is used as frequently, and for the same reasons, as "pinko" was used in the fifties. It is rarely used correctly. Within the movement it commonly refers to individuals, though the personal characteristics and activities of those to whom it is directed may differ widely: An individual, as an individual can never be an elitist, because the only proper application of the term "elite" is to groups. Any individual, regardless of how well-known that person may be, can never be an elite.

Correctly, an elite refers to a small group of people who have power over a larger group of which they are part, usually without direct responsibility to that larger group, and often without their knowledge or consent. A person becomes an elitist by being part of, or advocating the rule by, such a small group, whether or not that individual is well known or not known at all. Notoriety is not a definition of an elitist. The most insidious elites are usually run by people not known to the larger public at all. Intelligent elitists are usually smart enough not to allow themselves to become well known; when they become known, they are watched, and the mask over their power is no longer firmly lodged.

Elites are not conspiracies. Very seldom does a small group of people get together and deliberately try to take over a larger group for its own ends. Elites are nothing more, and nothing less, than groups of friends who also happen to participate in the same political activities. They would probably maintain their friendship whether or not they were involved in political activities; they would probably be involved in political activities whether or not they maintained their friendships. It is the coincidence of these two phenomena which creates elites in any group and makes them so difficult to break.

These friendship groups function as networks of communication outside any regular channels for such communication that may have been set up by a group. If no channels are set up, they function as the only networks of communication. Because people are friends, because they usually share the same values and orientations, because they talk to each other socially and consult with each other when common decisions have to be made, the people involved in these networks have more power in the group than those who don't. And it is a rare group that does not establish some informal networks of communication through the friends that are made in it.

Some groups, depending on their size, may have more than one such informal communications network. Networks may even overlap. When only one such network exists, it is the elite of an otherwise Unstructured group, whether the participants in it want to be elitists or not. If it is the only such network in a Structured group it may or may not be an elite depending on its composition and the nature of the formal Structure. If there are two or more such networks of friends, they may compete for power within the group, thus forming factions, or one may deliberately opt out of the competition, leaving the other as the elite. In a Structured group, two or more such friendship networks usually compete with each other for formal power. This is often the healthiest situation, as the other members are in a position to arbitrate between the two competitors for power and thus to make demands on those to whom they give their temporary allegiance.

The inevitably elitist and exclusive nature of informal communication networks of friends is neither a new phenomenon characteristic of the women's movement nor a phenomenon new to women. Such informal relationships have excluded women for centuries from participating in integrated groups of which they were a part. In any profession or organization these networks have created the "locker room" mentality and the "old school" ties which have effectively prevented women as a group (as well as some men individually) from having equal access to the sources of power or social reward. Much of the energy of past women's movements has been directed to having the structures of decision-making and the selection processes formalized so that the exclusion of women could be confronted directly. As we well know, these efforts have not prevented the informal male-only networks from discriminating against women, but they have made it more difficult.

Because elites are informal does not mean they are invisible. At any small group meeting anyone with a sharp eye and an acute ear can tell who is influencing whom. The members of a friendship group will relate more to each other than to other people. They listen more attentively, and interrupt less; they repeat each other's points and give in amiably; they tend to ignore or grapple with the "outs" whose approval is not necessary for making a decision. But it is necessary for the "outs" to stay on good terms with the "ins." Of course the lines are not as sharp as I have drawn them. They are nuances of interaction, not prewritten scripts. But they are discernible, and they do have their effect. Once one knows with whom it is important to check before a decision is made, and whose approval is the stamp of acceptance, one knows who is running things.

Since movement groups have made no concrete decisions about who shall exercise power within them, many different criteria are used around the country. Most criteria are along the lines of traditional female characteristics. For instance, in the early days of the movement, marriage was usually a prerequisite for participation in the informal elite. As women have been traditionally taught, married women relate primarily to each other, and look upon single women as too threatening to have as close friends. In many cities, this criterion was further refined to include only those women married to New Left men. This standard had more than tradition behind it, however, because New Left men often had access to resources needed by the movement -- such as mailing lists, printing presses, contacts, and information -- and women were used to getting what they needed through men rather than independently. As the movement has charged through time, marriage has become a less universal criterion for effective participation, but all informal elites establish standards by which only women who possess certain material or personal characteristics may join. They frequently include: middle-class background (despite all the rhetoric about relating to the working class); being married; not being married but living with someone; being or pretending to be a lesbian; being between the ages of twenty and thirty; being college educated or at least having some college background; being "hip"; not being too "hip"; holding a certain political line or identification as a "radical"; having children or at least liking them; not having children; having certain "feminine" personality characteristics such as being "nice"; dressing right (whether in the traditional style or the antitraditional style); etc. There are also some characteristics which will almost always tag one as a "deviant" who should not be related to. They include: being too old; working full time, particularly if one is actively committed to a "career"; not being "nice"; and being avowedly single (i.e., neither actively heterosexual nor homosexual).

Other criteria could be included, but they all have common themes. The characteristics prerequisite for participating in the informal elites of the movement, and thus for exercising power, concern one's background, personality, or allocation of time. They do not include one's competence, dedication to feminism, talents, or potential contribution to the movement. The former are the criteria one usually uses in determining one's friends. The latter are what any movement or organization has to use if it is going to be politically effective.

The criteria of participation may differ from group to group, but the means of becoming a member of the informal elite if one meets those criteria are pretty much the same. The only main difference depends on whether one is in a group from the beginning, or joins it after it has begun. If involved from the beginning it is important to have as many of one's personal friends as possible also join. If no one knows anyone else very well, then one must deliberately form friendships with a select number and establish the informal interaction patterns crucial to the creation of an informal structure. Once the informal patterns are formed they act to maintain themselves, and one of the most successful tactics of maintenance is to continuously recruit new people who "fit in." One joins such an elite much the same way one pledges a sorority. If perceived as a potential addition, one is "rushed" by the members of the informal structure and eventually either dropped or initiated. If the sorority is not politically aware enough to actively engage in this process itself it can be started by the outsider pretty much the same way one joins any private club. Find a sponsor, i.e., pick some member of the elite who appears to be well respected within it, and actively cultivate that person's friendship. Eventually, she will most likely bring you into the inner circle.

All of these procedures take time. So if one works full time or has a similar major commitment, it is usually impossible to join simply because there are not enough hours left to go to all the meetings and cultivate the personal relationship necessary to have a voice in the decision-making. **That is why formal structures of decision-making are a boon to the overworked person. Having an established process for decision-making ensures that everyone can participate in it to some extent.**

Although this dissection of the process of elite formation within small groups has been critical in perspective, it is not made in the belief that these informal structures are inevitably bad -- merely inevitable. **All groups create informal structures as a result of interaction patterns among the members of the group.** Such informal structures can do very useful things but only Unstructured groups are totally governed by them. **When informal elites are combined with a myth of "structurelessness," there can be no attempt to put limits on the use of power.** It becomes capricious.

This has two potentially negative consequences of which we should be aware. The first is that the informal structure of decision-making will be much like a sorority -- one in which people listen to others because they like them and not because they say significant things. As long as the movement does not do significant things this does not much matter. But if its development is not to be arrested at this preliminary stage, it will have to alter this trend. The second is that **informal structures have no obligation to be**

responsible to the group at large. Their power was not given to them; it cannot be taken away. Their influence is not based on what they do for the group; therefore they cannot be directly influenced by the group. This does not necessarily make informal structures irresponsible. Those who are concerned with maintaining their influence will usually try to be responsible. The group simply cannot compel such responsibility; it is dependent on the interests of the elite.

THE "STAR" SYSTEM

The idea of "structurelessness" has created the "star" system. We live in a society which expects political groups to make decisions and to select people to articulate those decisions to the public at large. The press and the public do not know how to listen seriously to individual women as women; they want to know how the group feels. Only three techniques have ever been developed for establishing mass group opinion: the vote or referendum, the public opinion survey questionnaire, and the selection of group spokespeople at an appropriate meeting. The women's liberation movement has used none of these to communicate with the public. Neither the movement as a whole nor most of the multitudinous groups within it have established a means of explaining their position on various issues. But the public is conditioned to look for spokespeople.

While it has consciously not chosen spokespeople, the movement has thrown up many women who have caught the public eye for varying reasons. These women represent no particular group or established opinion; they know this and usually say so. But because there are no official spokespeople nor any decision-making body that the press can query when it wants to know the movement's position on a subject, these women are perceived as the spokespeople. Thus, whether they want to or not, whether the movement likes it or not, women of public note are put in the role of spokespeople by default.

This is one main source of the ire that is often felt toward the women who are labeled "stars." Because they were not selected by the women in the movement to represent the movement's views, they are resented when the press presumes that they speak for the movement. But as long as the movement does not select its own spokeswomen, such women will be placed in that role by the press and the public, regardless of their own desires.

This has several negative consequences for both the movement and the women labeled "stars." First, because the movement didn't put them in the role of spokesperson, the movement cannot remove them. The press put them there and only the press can choose not to listen. The press will continue to look to "stars" as spokeswomen as long as it has no official alternatives to go to for authoritative statements from the movement. The movement has no control in the selection of its representatives to the public as long as it believes that it should have no representatives at all. Second, women put in this position often find themselves viciously attacked by their sisters. This achieves nothing for the movement and is painfully destructive to the individuals involved. Such attacks only result in either the woman leaving the movement entirely-often bitterly alienated -- or in her ceasing to feel responsible to her "sisters." She may maintain some loyalty to the movement, vaguely defined, but she is no longer susceptible to pressures from other women in it. One cannot feel responsible to people who have been the source of such pain without being a masochist, and these women are usually too strong to bow to that kind of personal pressure. Thus the backlash to the "star" system in effect encourages the very kind of individualistic nonresponsibility that the movement condemns. By purging a sister as a "star," the movement loses whatever control it may have had over the person who then becomes free to commit all of the individualistic sins of which she has been accused.

POLITICAL IMPOTENCE

Unstructured groups may be very effective in getting women to talk about their lives; they aren't very good for getting things done. It is when people get tired of "just talking" and want to do something more that the groups flounder, unless they change the nature of their operation. Occasionally, the developed informal structure of the group coincides with an available need that the group can fill in such a way as to give the appearance that an

Unstructured group "works." That is, the group has fortuitously developed precisely the kind of structure best suited for engaging in a particular project.

While working in this kind of group is a very heady experience, it is also rare and very hard to replicate. There are almost inevitably four conditions found in such a group;

1. It is task oriented. Its function is very narrow and very specific, like putting on a conference or putting out a newspaper. It is the task that basically structures the group. The task determines what needs to be done and when it needs to be done. It provides a guide by which people can judge their actions and make plans for future activity.

2. It is relatively small and homogeneous. Homogeneity is necessary to insure that participants have a "common language" for interaction. People from widely different backgrounds may provide richness to a consciousness-raising group where each can learn from the others' experience, but too great a diversity among members of a task-oriented group means only that they continually misunderstand each other. Such diverse people interpret words and actions differently. They have different expectations about each other's behavior and judge the results according to different criteria. If everyone knows everyone else well enough to understand the nuances, these can be accommodated. Usually, they only lead to confusion and endless hours spent straightening out conflicts no one ever thought would arise.

3. There is a high degree of communication. Information must be passed on to everyone, opinions checked, work divided up, and participation assured in the relevant decisions.

This is only possible if the group is small and people practically live together for the most crucial phases of the task. Needless to say, the number of interactions necessary to involve everybody increases geometrically with the number of participants. This inevitably limits group participants to about five, or excludes some from some of the decisions. Successful groups can be as large as 10 or 15, but only when they are in fact composed of several smaller subgroups which perform specific parts of the task, and whose members overlap with each other so that knowledge of what the different subgroups are doing can be passed around easily.

4. There is a low degree of skill specialization. Not everyone has to be able to do everything, but everything must be able to be done by more than one person. Thus no one is indispensable. To a certain extent, people become interchangeable parts.

While these conditions can occur serendipitously in small groups, this is not possible in large ones. Consequently, because the larger movement in most cities is as unstructured as individual rap groups, it is not too much more effective than the separate groups at specific tasks. The informal structure is rarely together enough or in touch enough with the people to be able to operate effectively. So the movement generates much motion and few results. Unfortunately, the consequences of all this motion are not as innocuous as the results' and their victim is the movement itself.

Some groups have formed themselves into local action projects if they do not involve many people and work on a small scale. But this form restricts movement activity to the local level; it cannot be done on the regional or national. Also, to function well the groups must usually pare themselves down to that informal group of friends who were running things in the first place. This excludes many women from participating. As long as the only way women can participate in the movement is through membership in a small group, the nongregarious are at a distinct disadvantage. As long as friendship groups are the main means of organizational activity, elitism becomes institutionalized.

For those groups which cannot find a local project to which to devote themselves, the mere act of staying together becomes the reason for their staying together. **When a group has no specific task (and consciousness raising is a task), the people in it turn their energies to controlling others in the group.** This is not done so much out of a malicious desire to manipulate others (though sometimes it is) as out of a lack of anything better to do with their talents. Able people with time on their hands and a need to justify their coming together put their efforts into personal control, and spend their time criticizing the personalities of the other members in the group. Infighting and personal power games rule the day. When a group is involved in a task, people learn to get along with others as they are, and to subsume personal dislikes for the sake of the larger goal. There are limits placed on the compulsion to remold every person in our image of what they should be.

The end of consciousness-raising leaves people with no place to go, and the lack of structure leaves them with no way of getting there. The women in the movement either turn in on themselves and their sisters or seek other alternatives of action. There are few that are available. Some women just "do their own thing." This can lead to a great deal of individual creativity, much of which is useful for the movement, but it is not a viable alternative for most women and certainly does not foster a spirit of cooperative group effort. Other women drift out of the movement entirely because they don't want to develop an individual project and they have found no way of discovering, joining, or starting group projects that interest them.

Many turn to other political organizations to give them the kind of structured, effective activity that they have not been able to find in the women's movement. Those political organizations which see women's liberation as only one of many issues to which women should devote their time thus find the movement a vast recruiting ground for new members. There is no need for such organizations to "infiltrate" (though this is not precluded). The desire for meaningful political activity generated in women by their becoming part of the women's liberation movement is sufficient to make them eager to join other organizations when the movement itself provides no outlets for their new ideas and energies. Those women who join other political organizations while remaining within the women's liberation movement, or who join women's liberation while remaining in other political organizations, in turn become the framework for new informal structures. These friendship networks are based upon their common nonfeminist politics rather than the characteristics discussed earlier, but operate in much the same way. Because these women share common values, ideas, and political orientations, they too become informal, unplanned, unselected, unresponsible elites -- whether they intend to be so or not.

These new informal elites are often perceived as threats by the old informal elites previously developed within different movement groups. This is a correct perception. Such politically oriented networks are rarely willing to be merely "sororities" as many of the old ones were, and want to proselytize their political as well as their feminist ideas. This is only natural, but its implications for women's liberation have never been adequately discussed. The old elites are rarely willing to bring such differences of opinion out into the open because it would involve exposing the nature of the informal structure of the group.

Many of these informal elites have been hiding under the banner of "anti-elitism" and "structurelessness." To effectively counter the competition from another informal structure, they would have to become "public," and this possibility is fraught with many dangerous implications. Thus, to maintain its own power, it is easier to rationalize the exclusion of the members of the other informal structure by such means as "red-baiting," "reformist-baiting," "lesbian-baiting," or "straight-baiting." The only other alternative is to formally structure the group in such a way that the original power structure is institutionalized. This is not always possible. If the informal elites have been well structured and have exercised a fair amount of power in the past, such a task is feasible. These groups have a history of being somewhat politically effective in the past, as the tightness of the informal structure has proven an adequate substitute for a formal structure. Becoming Structured does not alter their operation much, though the institutionalization of the power structure does open it to formal challenge. It is those groups which are in greatest need of structure that are often least capable of creating it. Their informal structures have not been too well formed and adherence to the ideology of "structurelessness" makes them reluctant to change tactics. The more Unstructured a group is, the more lacking it is in informal structures, and the more it adheres to an ideology of "structurelessness," the more vulnerable it is to being taken over by a group of political comrades.

Since the movement at large is just as Unstructured as most of its constituent groups, it is similarly susceptible to indirect influence. But the phenomenon manifests itself differently. On a local level most groups can operate autonomously; but the only groups that can organize a national activity are nationally organized groups. Thus, it is often the Structured feminist organizations that provide national direction for feminist activities, and this direction is determined by the priorities of those organizations. Such groups as NOW, WEAL, and some leftist women's caucuses are simply the only organizations capable of mounting a national campaign. The multitude of Unstructured women's liberation groups can choose to support or not support the national campaigns, but are incapable of mounting their own. Thus their members become the troops under the leadership of the Structured organizations. The avowedly Unstructured groups have no way of drawing upon the movement's vast resources to support its priorities. It doesn't even have a way of deciding what they are.

The more unstructured a movement is, the less control it has over the directions in which it develops and the political actions in which it engages. This does not mean that its ideas do not spread. Given a certain amount of interest by the media and the appropriateness of social conditions, the ideas will still be diffused widely. But diffusion of ideas does not mean they are implemented; it only means they are talked about. Insofar as they can be applied individually they may be acted on; insofar as they require coordinated political power to be implemented, they will not be.

As long as the women's liberation movement stays dedicated to a form of organization which stresses small, inactive discussion groups among friends, the worst problems of Unstructuredness will not be felt. But this style of organization has its limits; it is politically inefficacious, exclusive, and discriminatory against those women who are not or cannot be tied into the friendship networks. Those who do not fit into what already exists because of class, race, occupation, education, parental or marital status, personality, etc., will inevitably be discouraged from trying to participate. Those who do fit in will develop vested interests in maintaining things as they are.

The informal groups' vested interests will be sustained by the informal structures which exist, and the movement will have no way of determining who shall exercise power within it. If the movement continues deliberately to not select who shall exercise power, it does not thereby abolish power. All it does is abdicate the right to demand that those who do exercise power and influence be responsible for it. If the movement continues to keep power as diffuse as possible because it knows it cannot demand responsibility from those who have it, it does prevent any group or person from totally dominating. But it simultaneously insures that the movement is as ineffective as possible. Some middle ground between domination and ineffectiveness can and must be found.

These problems are coming to a head at this time because the nature of the movement is necessarily changing. Consciousness-raising as the main function of the women's liberation movement is becoming obsolete. Due to the intense press publicity of the last two years and the numerous overground books and articles now being circulated, women's liberation has become a household word. Its issues are discussed and informal rap groups are formed by people who have no explicit connection with any movement group. The movement must go on to other tasks. It now needs to establish its priorities, articulate its goals, and pursue its objectives in a coordinated fashion. To do this it must get organized -- locally, regionally, and nationally.

PRINCIPLES OF DEMOCRATIC STRUCTURING

Once the movement no longer clings tenaciously to the ideology of "structurelessness," it is free to develop those forms of organization best suited to its healthy functioning. This does not mean that we should go to the other extreme and blindly imitate the traditional forms of organization. But neither should we blindly reject them all. Some of the traditional techniques will prove useful, albeit not perfect; some will give us insights into what we should and should not do to obtain certain ends with minimal costs to the individuals in the movement. Mostly, we will have to experiment with different kinds of structuring and develop a variety of techniques to use for different situations. The Lot System is one such idea which has emerged from the movement. It is not applicable to all situations, but is useful in some. Other ideas for structuring are needed. But before we can proceed to experiment intelligently, we must accept the idea that there is nothing inherently bad about structure itself -- only its excess use.

While engaging in this trial-and-error process, there are some principles we can keep in mind that are essential to democratic structuring and are also politically effective:

1. Delegation of specific authority to specific individuals for specific tasks by democratic procedures. Letting people assume jobs or tasks only by default means they are not dependably done. If people are selected to do a task, preferably after expressing an interest or willingness to do it, they have made a commitment which cannot so easily be ignored.

2. Requiring all those to whom authority has been delegated to be responsible to those who selected them. This is how the group has control over people in positions of authority. Individuals may exercise power, but it is the group that has ultimate say over how the power is exercised.

3. Distribution of authority among as many people as is reasonably possible. This prevents monopoly of power and requires those in

positions of authority to consult with many others in the process of exercising it. It also gives many people the opportunity to have responsibility for specific tasks and thereby to learn different skills.

4. Rotation of tasks among individuals. Responsibilities which are held too long by one person, formally or informally, come to be seen as that person's "property" and are not easily relinquished or controlled by the group. Conversely, if tasks are rotated too frequently the individual does not have time to learn her job well and acquire the sense of satisfaction of doing a good job.

5. Allocation of tasks along rational criteria. Selecting someone for a position because they are liked by the group or giving them hard work because they are disliked serves neither the group nor the person in the long run. Ability, interest, and responsibility have got to be the major concerns in such selection. People should be given an opportunity to learn skills they do not have, but this is best done through some sort of "apprenticeship" program rather than the "sink or swim" method. Having a responsibility one can't handle well is demoralizing. Conversely, being blacklisted from doing what one can do well does not encourage one to develop one's skills. Women have been punished for being competent throughout most of human history; the movement does not need to repeat this process.

6. Diffusion of information to everyone as frequently as possible. Information is power. Access to information enhances one's power. When an informal network spreads new ideas and information among themselves outside the

group, they are already engaged in the process of forming an opinion -- without the group participating. The more one knows about how things work and what is happening, the more politically effective one can be.

7. Equal access to resources needed by the group. This is not always perfectly possible, but should be striven for. A member who maintains a monopoly over a needed resource (like a printing press owned by a husband, or a darkroom) can unduly influence the use of that resource. Skills and information are also resources. Members' skills can be equitably available only when members are willing to teach what they know to others.

When these principles are applied, they insure that whatever structures are developed by different movement groups will be controlled by and responsible to the group. The group of people in positions of authority will be diffuse, flexible, open, and temporary. They will not be in such an easy position to institutionalize their power because ultimate decisions will be made by the group at large. The group will have the power to determine who shall exercise authority within it.

Appendix D – The BART System

Overview

The following paper, which published in 2005, does an excellent job of exploring and explaining the relationships between four essential aspects of participation in organizational life: boundary, authority, role, and task.

The Group Relations Community

The BART paper that follows originates in the "Group Relations" community of practice. The Group Relations community worldwide conducts experiential conferences in which leadership and authority in groups can be explored in the here-and-now. These conferences create a "temporary institution" in which participants will find all of the dynamics and sociocultural elements found in their own organizations. As such, Group Relations conferences provide a "practice ground" and a rich source of knowledge about the exercise of leadership and authority in groups. The Group Relations community is based on the work of Alfred Bion, a distinguished psychiatrist who practiced and conducted substantial research during World War 1.

We have attended several of these conferences and can attest to their educational and practical value. Attending has shifted our thinking in very substantial ways. Our experience of these conferences leads us to conclude that attending a Group Relations conference is 100% aligned with the Inviting Leadership approach. You will profit from attendance in our view. We recommend that you consider attendance at a Group Relations conference.

The truth is that our experience studying Group Relations and attending the conference events continues to be a major influence in our own thinking and work. Group Relations work has the potential to transform your leadership practice and your own practice of the Inviting Leadership methods.

If you would like to explore the domain of Group Relations further, see www.invitingleadership.com/book/links/#group-relations.

The BART paper is included here with permission from the authors.

The Original Paper

This article is an unrestricted fair use draft document presented to the public to stimulate dialogue and discussion in as wide an audience as possible. The article may be reproduced in part or in whole for training and educational purposes so long as there is clear attribution to the authors in any such re-issue. Inquires about other uses of this intellectual property may be directed to René Molenkamp at rmolenkamp@ academy.umd.edu. The article itself may be found at www. invitingleadership.com/book/links/#BART

The BART System of Group and Organizational Analysis

Boundary, Authority, Role and Task

Zachary Gabriel Green and René J. Molenkamp (2005)
(in full collaboration)

Introduction

In the United States of America, group relations conferences, often termed "Tavistock" conferences, have been held since the mid 1960's. The method of learning is through experience and reflection upon one's experience. Theory of this method of learning has been described in many a publication (Bion, Banet & Hayden, Colman & Bexton, Colman & Geller, Cytrynbaum & Noumair).

This article provides an introduction to a key system within this tradition of learning, known as the BART system. BART is an acronym for four elements of group analysis:

- Boundary
- Authority
- Role
- Task

The authors wish to be among the first to stipulate that BART, while an exceptionally user-friendly tool, provides only a partial application of the type of learning that comes through the group relations work. The learning from such conferences can be powerfully personal yet has been found to have rich application to human systems analysis, ranging from a family dinner to board meeting to a multinational negotiation. Participants in group relations conferences may learn about aspects of group dynamics, such as the group's reaction to authority, resistance to the task, and response to leadership. Participants may also learn about internal personal dynamics, particularly their own proclivity to take up a leadership role and other roles that support and/or thwart the task of groups. This article offers BART as an example of readily useful constructs that tend to be consistently present in study and learning from the group relations perspective. The application of these insights is of particular interest to managers and executives, but is likely to have value to anyone who works in an organization, participates in work groups, or is on a professional team.

First one major caveat about the use of the BART system is needed. Group relations conferences have psychodynamic theoretical underpinnings that place emphasis on unconscious elements of systems. Through this method, trained consultants provide commentary or interpretation about their perception of the emergence of unseen and unarticulated events as they are happening in a group. Using the Gestalt therapy term, conferences give focus to "here-and-now" experiences, which by definition are ever fluid and changing. Such attention on the moment, with the unit of analysis being the group, creates regression in individual participants, providing them no familiar bearings for their experience. The anxiety that tends to emerge from this regression provides the conditions for profound learning in most participants and deep defensive resistance in others. These processes are the more subtle, ineffable, but foundational elements of group relations work. Some would argue that BART is unduly reductionistic, tending to make too facile dynamics that run quite deep and cannot be subject to a mechanistic acronym. The authors of this article accept these arguments. One is not able to extrapolate an understanding of group relations experiences simply with an intellectual grasp of BART. The effort here is to make accessible to more general audiences some of the key learning from group relations work that otherwise tends to be steeped in its own jargon.

The main focus will be on Boundary, Authority, Role and Task. We will describe the concepts and apply them to the organizational context.

Boundary

Boundary is the container for group work. We encounter boundaries constantly but may not experience them as such. Time, task, and territory provide the basis for the study of boundaries in group relations work. The conference metaphor for time is the strict adherence to the beginning and end of group sessions by staff consultants. It is not uncommon for a participant to be mid-sentence when a consultant appears to leave abruptly at the appointed hour. Participants get confronted with the rigidity of the time boundary and soon not only learn "when it is over, it is over," but upon examining their own reactions and the reactions of the group, the learning may become much richer. While conversation may continue after the departure of the consultant, the boundaries shift with the absence or presence of someone in a designated authority role.

In every day life we have deadlines, due dates, departure times, and the like to which we must adhere. Failure to attend to these time boundaries carries consequences, depending on the rigidity of the boundary. Anyone who has ever been late to a train station or an airport knows this fact. If you are not at the gate at the departure time, the doors will be closed and your travel plans will be altered. A missed deadline may have no or limited consequence in certain contexts while in others it may mean a lost opportunity or in more severe situations, the end of a professional role.

In a similar light, territory boundaries are easy to spot. They are the space in which work happens in a group. In most offices or organizations, we often speak of "turf battles," meaning the metaphoric territory where one person or group's responsibilities ends and another's begins. In every police drama, regardless of quality, there is inevitably a scene where there is a jurisdictional dispute about who is to take the lead on cracking the big case. In such instances, territory boundaries are tied to task, which will be detailed later.

The more common issue of territory as boundaries often comes in the form of more literal ones. If we look to nation states, on every continent there are currently and historically contentious issues about boundaries. Wars and unrest in global "hot spots" can be tied, among other issues, to disputes over the demarcation of territory between one group and the other. These spaces become markers of identity, carrying with them more than a geographic line in the sand. We need only to turn to different expression of conflict such as those in the Middle East between Israelis and Palestinians, or in Kashmir between India and Pakistan, or in Rwanda between the Hutus and the Tutsis, or in the United States between the "red states" and the "blue states" to see the power of territory boundaries—those that are physical and those that are in the mind—at work.

While territory and time boundaries are perhaps easiest to see, in group relations work, the task boundary is key. The way the work is understood and the manner in which it is to be conducted strongly influence nearly every aspect of group life. Turf wars provide a way of noting differences between groups about the nature of the task. The challenge is when there are different understandings of the task within groups. In day-to-day parlance, the task is akin to the mission of an organization, the terms of reference in a business contract, the syllabus for a course, or a work order in a repair shop. Within loose or tight parameters, the group is to do its work. Yet most of us can think of examples from our own experience where the clearest delineation of the task has resulted in varied and at times undesired outcomes. From the renovation of our home that is not yet really complete, to the work team that produced a less than desirable deliverable, to the board that emphasized funding over organization values and focus, to the engineers that designed a bridge that collapses, the task somewhere got lost, or the boundary as it relates to the task was undermined, subverted, or simply violated.

Boundary considerations extend beyond time, task and territory. Included in this analysis are boundaries of resources, roles and responsibilities. The most important of these, resources, often determines the capacity of individuals and organizations to complete even the most rudimentary tasks. We can think of resource boundaries expressed and represented by basic survival elements such as air, food and water. Absent attention to resource boundaries, there is no life. Other resources, such as money in family budgets, the number of team members available to work on a project, or the kind of relief available to disaster ravaged areas, all are influenced by the kind of boundary involved. (In-)adequacy of resources and the management of them co-determine the success or failure of a project.

Some groups or organizations work better with relatively rigid time, task and territory boundaries, others prefer to work with more fluid ones. Key is that there is clarity about boundaries of an organization. In addition it helps to understand the boundary culture within an organization. For example, a newspaper-publishing agency needs to have the newspaper print ready at a certain time, yet it needs to be flexible until the last minute in order to report the latest news.

Boundaries can be seen as a container that 'holds' the task. If the container is inadequate or has holes in it, it will not support the task. Although the concept of boundaries is rather simple and therefore conceivably easily dismissed, the consequences of diminishing the importance of boundaries can be far reaching. Attention to solid boundaries is in service of the task. It is crucial that boundaries are:

- *Clearly specified*

Clear specification of time, task and territory boundary should answer the questions: "When?" "What?" and "Where?" During a specific time, in a specific location we will work on this particular task. Examples of inadequate boundary management are: two meetings may be scheduled at the same time in the same space, or two consultants are working independently on a similar policy because the task boundary between the two was not clarified.

- *Agreed upon*

Although a boundary may be clearly outlined, invested parties need to come to some agreement about what the stated time, task or territory boundary is or how they interpret it. If disagreement persists, there may be at least agreement on who the authority is that calls the boundary. This is where boundary and authority converge and where people in robes and uniforms – judges, umpires, police officers – can be very helpful. More will be discussed under the heading authority.

- *Adhered to*

If boundaries are taken as guidelines, rather than clear instructions in support of accomplishing the task, an organizational culture can become rather chaotic – for example meetings hardly ever start on time, tasks are forgotten or done twice, people are unclear on where the next meeting will take place. Especially in situations like this it may be helpful for an organization to ask what their use of boundaries represents.

We like to introduce the concept of boundary as a region (and acknowledge Charla Hayden who used the term in the A.K. Rice Institute National Conference in 1998), where the space, time or task boundary is seen as a transition or bridge space. In terms of time boundary, the one event has not quite ended, yet the next event is already in people's mind. Or an event has just started but people are still somewhat preoccupied with whatever happened before. One way of acknowledging the transitional nature of the beginning of a meeting is to do a check-in on state of mind – the length of the check-in depending upon the length of the meeting – so that attendees are in a position to acknowledge what they bring to the meeting, which generally speaking makes them more available for the present task. The entrance space to a person's office or a meeting room is an example of a territory boundary transition region. In terms of task boundary, two departments with different tasks may have subtasks that are closely related and will need to manage that transition space or region. Seeing the boundary as a region allows for a transition function prior to and subsequent to the boundary and it may prevent the boundary from either becoming rigid or chaotic. Understanding boundaries as a region, may highlight the delicate nature of boundaries and the attention that requires. At times it is helpful to reflect upon the representation of how individuals and groups in an organization deal with boundaries.

Authority

We define authority quite simply as the right to do work. In his book Leadership without Easy Answers, Ronald Heifetz defines authority as "conferred power to perform a service" (p. 57). When a person takes up her authority we assume that she takes responsibility and that she is accountable for her actions. We make a distinction between formal authority and personal authority.

Formal or Delegated Authority

Formal authority may be derived from a group or body – the Board of Directors of a non- profit agency or corporation -- or from an individual such as one's immediate supervisor or manager. Authorization involves one person or group giving over or delegating some of their own formal authority so that another might do certain work on their behalf. For example, formal authority may be given to someone through a job description outlining his role in an organization, the role of manager comes with a particular job description of for example evaluating, hiring and firing people.

It is crucial that formal authority is:

- *Clearly defined*

Authority needs to be clearly defined by the body that is granting it and understood by the person or body that is receiving it. Lack of clarity about the scope of authority a person has been given may result in unattended tasks. Incomplete job descriptions or incomplete instructions by a person's supervisor may result in incomplete tasks or may cause an employee to do tasks that he is not officially assigned to do.

- *Taken up accordingly*

People are clear about the formal authority they have received but for some reason do not take up some of the authority that they have or take up too much authority. For example the Program committee not only has provided a program but also organized a fundraising event. Or the president of a non-profit organization has been given authority by the bylaws to name committee members but only with the consent of committee chairs. If she names committee members without the chairs' consent, she has exceeded her formal authority.

- *Accompanied by tools to exercise it*

It is not uncommon that people are authorized to do a certain task, but they lack the tools to complete the task successfully. In a non-profit context an example may be that a person is authorized to organize a lecture by the Executive Committee, but the committee does not make available any funds to support that lecture.

Personal Authority

The way an individual takes up formal authority we call personal authority. Personal authority is how we execute our formal authority. Personal authority is influenced by many different factors, i.e. our psychological make up, our social identity, our cultural - background, etc. For example, the well-known Myers-

Briggs Type Indicator in terms of extraversion and introversion, intuition and sensing, feeling and thinking, judging and perceiving influences how we take up our personal authority. An extraverted executive may consult many employees in groups and meetings while in a decision-making process, whereas an introverted executive may delegate some of the consultation with employees to her subordinates and receive feedback through the subordinates prior to making the actual decision.

After formal authority has been established and clarified, a person has to take up her personal authority to execute her formal authority. Important considerations are what helps and what hinders a person in taking up their personal authority? Group relations work teaches that many factors play a role in how we take up our authority, and they span a continuum of things that are known to things that are unknown to us. For example a person may take up more or less authority depending upon how he thinks the persons affected by his authority will value his behavior. In such a case a manager may postpone an unpopular decision endlessly. People make decisions in part because of desires and fears that have little to do with task, but more with managing anxiety, particularly related to ambition, competition, political correctness, etc. The more individuals know about the elements that influence their authority, the more likely they may exercise personal authority in relation to the task.

Role

People occupy roles. The span of these roles is rather transitory yet robust, ranging from mere moments to a lifetime. Roles can be achieved, acquired, assigned, and/or ascribed to us. According to the goodness of fit, roles can be reflections of or equated with our identity. The link is made clearer through the distinction of formal and informal role.

Formal Role

A formal role is much like a job description. It defines the duties to be performed, the parameters for completing tasks, the people and processes with which interaction must take place, and often the outcomes or deliverables that mark the tangible successful performance of the role. Typically some external authority assigns these roles to us. Our bosses, managers, teachers, supervisors, and the like also serve as the arbiters of how well we take up these roles—and at times, determine whether we will continue in them. If the role comes through merit or privilege, we may have more range in how we take up our role compared to someone who is newly assigned a role. In other words, a history of exceptional performance and/or personal attributes (such as race, gender, age, etc.) that are valued by the organization or particular authority figure influence how the role is perceived and filled.

A perhaps easier way to think of formal authority is in terms of those individuals we call "authorities" more colloquially. Police officers are a clear example of where role, authority and task converge. We expect the police to fight crime, maintain general order, and give us tickets for traffic infractions. These authorities are readily recognized in their role by their uniforms and a general social agreement about the nature of their task.

Other roles where such social agreements are clear can be seen when certain people put on their robes (Sorenson, 1999). The vestments of clergy and the robes of judges come with some understanding of the nature of their formal role. When wearing these robes, there is authority ascribed to such individuals and clarity on the tasks they perform. These examples help us in understanding formal roles, yet many of the roles we take up don't have robes to go with them. It requires that individuals understand their roles and can clearly communicate what that role is. Clarity about one's role is not only important for the person who takes up the role, but also for the people who work with the person in a particular role. Misperceptions about roles occur frequently.

In addition, it is essential for a person in role to know how other people perceive her in that role and how that influences their behavior. Given that role is intricately connected with authority and boundaries, a misperception of the role may result in a misperception of authority and boundaries. For example, the role description of a team leader may include evaluation of team members and recommending them for promotion. It is likely that if team members are not aware that this is part of the team leader's role, they may give him less authority and their performance may be affected.

Finally, we want to say a few words on role shifts and on occupying multiple roles. With role shifts we mean moving from one role to another more permanently, for example the promoted colleague becoming manager, or the former professor being a friend. The former role influences how the current role is viewed and vice versa. Awareness of these role shifts may assist both parties in making the transition. Shifting between multiple roles requires that a person maintain clarity both for oneself and for the people the person is interacting with about what role one is in at any particular moment.

Informal Role

The informal roles people take on are not found in a job description or in any contract between employer and employee. Nonetheless individuals take on roles that serve to fill the gaps of authority and tasks abandoned, yielded, or implicitly ceded to them by the organization or group. These roles range several continuums: from simple to complicated, from more implicit to more explicit, and from conscious to unconscious. Let us give some examples. The care taking roles: who makes the coffee in the morning, or who changes the light bulbs in the office. A coordinating role – there are five project managers in an organization but no one has been designated to coordinate the projects, what persons steps forward to do so. The antagonist role is one example— the person who always questions every decision, procedure and change.

Both informal as well as formal roles are in part dictated by what our valence is. Valence refers to a person's tendency to take up particular roles in groups. For example a person may have the valence to be "the quiet observer" or "the practical voice" or a person may be "the emotional one." Given that a person's valence is an unconscious dynamic that gets activated to regulate anxiety, an individual's valence does not change much from one group or another, although it may be more or less activated in one or the other group. Generally speaking a person's valence influences both their formal and informal role.

For example, a person with a leadership valence is likely to have a formal leadership role, or when that is not the case to take an informal leadership role.

One of the authors, René Molenkamp, has developed The Metaphor Method for Role Analysis, a method of becoming clearer about one's informal role by making use of the unconscious through images and metaphors. Although the method was developed within group relations conferences, it has been applied to working groups. A brief description of what the method involves: a group member is interested in what informal role she plays in the group. All members of that group are silent for a moment and think of an image or metaphor for the person's role and write it down, including the person herself. Then, one by one, people share their images and metaphors and give a brief explanation of why they think that image or metaphor came to mind.

Two things are particularly important. One is to try to make links between the different images and metaphors and to see what they have in common (for example, movement, height, distance, elements, detailed descriptions). The second is to pay attention to how the person's own image or metaphor fits with the images and metaphors she received from other people. There may be discrepancy between how the person perceives herself and how other people perceive her, which can be painful initially but a significant learning experience.

To summarize, essentials related to role are:

- *Complete description*

An accurate and complete description and understanding of the formal role avoids role confusion and potential conflict with colleagues.

- *Understanding of both one's formal and informal roles*

Understanding how one's informal role gets activated and how it influences our formal role is the foundation of the ability to make different choices about group participation in the future.

Task

From a group relations perspective, the next task has never been done before. Yes, we may have a technical "fix" for a variety of circumstances, but the task remains dynamic. While a similar task may have been done previously, the change in the time boundary alone makes it different. Each person involved with the task also brings his or her perceptions to the moment. Conflicts arise when perceptions of the task differ from person to person or from group to group. In other words, we tend to import our histories and experiences to a task. Group relations work calls on us to be conscious of what we bring into a situation. In reality, most of us are engaged in curious enactments of past triumphs and tragedies related to similar tasks. What we have not resolved or what we have learned will work in other settings we will replay. In the former case we await some new outcome. In the latter, we seek to have our reality yet again confirmed. In short, if there is an absence of consciousness about what is being imported, we can be assured that what will be exported will be inconsistent with the true nature of the task.

We distinguish different kinds of tasks. There is the primary task (also referred to as functional task or work task), which corresponds with the mission of an organization. Most organizations face multiple tasks all vying to be expressed in the service of the primary task. This is the point where authority becomes central, i.e. the person who decides what task has priority. It is the authority boundary in conjunction with the task boundary that helps the task become clear and for the work of the group to be taken on successfully. Absent clarity at the authority boundary, destructive chaos is likely to result and the survival of the group is in peril. While in some instances such a collapse is desirable for the new to arise and for the task to be met. Yet from the perspective of the group that dies, the loss continues to live well after the time boundary passes.

When a group works on a task, members of the group always – albeit mostly unconsciously – have the survival of the group in mind. We call this the survival task of the group. "Although this fundamental task is frequently disguised or masked, survival as a group becomes the primary preoccupation and latent motivating force for all group members..." (Hayden and Molenkamp, 2002, p. 7). The primary task and the survival task co-exist, at times the survival task is in service of the primary task and complimentary but mostly it is in conflict with the primary task.

This survival instinct of group members is the foundation for off task behavior. Off task behavior can be distinguished in four categories: dependency, pairing, fight/flight or oneness (in group relations terms these categories are called basic assumptions). Dependency is when the group waits for one person to take leadership, as if other members don't have those skills. Pairing is when the group uses a pair to produce the solution in the form of a prophetic idea or person, oftentimes this happens in the form of a fight which may eventually result in some solution (thesis, antithesis, synthesis) or in the form of some emotional connection that 'enlightens.' Fight is when the group starts a conflict about relatively inconsequential things and flight is when the group either literally or metaphorically distances itself from the task, for example by members starting to take personal phone calls during a meeting, or by entering into fantasy land and thinking about the next dream vacation. Oneness is when the group acts totally undifferentiated, as if there is no difference of opinion let alone conflict within the group.

Finally, we want to discuss the process task. The purpose of the process task is to give attention to the survival task without necessarily acting it out. It provides an opportunity for members of a group to look at their own dynamics, including dependency, pairing, fight/flight and oneness behavior, issues of competition and authority, interpersonal relationships, trying to understand the meaning of behavior of an individual for the group, or group behavior as such. When a certain time is set to work on the process task it is likely to reduce the amount of off task behavior and it may enhance the work of the primary task. Attention to the process task can take place at the end of a regular meeting, or it can be a regularly returning meeting as part of a group's ongoing work together, depending upon the size of the group and the intensity of its work together.

It is crucial that

- All parties have great clarity about the task
- Someone in the group can distinguish the different kinds of tasks
- To realize that the task is always fluid because of factors that influence the way a person perceives the task

A BART analysis of a workgroup or an organization may assist in preventing loss of valuable resources, off task behavior, productivity decrease, not to mention stress, frustration and potential interpersonal and intergroup conflicts. The consequences of any of these problem areas are likely to impede or slow down the primary task and may ultimately be destructive for the good of the organization.

References

Bion, W. R. (1961). Experiences in groups. New York: Basic Books.

Banet, A. G. & Hayden, C. (1977). A Tavistock primer. In J. E. Jones & J. W. Pfeiffer (Eds.), The 1977 annual handbook for group facilitators (pp. 155-167). La Jolla, CA: University Associates.

Colman, A. D. & Bexton, W. H. (Eds.). (1975). Group relations reader 1. Washington, DC: A. K. Rice Institute.

Colman, A. D. & Geller, M. H. (Eds.). (1985). Group relations reader 2. Washington, DC: A. K. Rice Institute.

Cytrynbaum, S. & Noumair, D. (Eds.). (2004). Group Dynamics, organizational irrationality, and social complexity: Group relations reader 3. Washington, DC: A. K. Rice Institute.

Hayden, C. & Molenkamp, R. J. (2002). "Tavistock primer II." Jupiter, FL: The A. K. Rice Institute for the Study of Social Systems.

Heifetz, R (1994), Leadership without easy answers. Cambridge, MA: Belknap Press. Sorenson, G. (1999). Taking the robes off: when leaders step down. In B. Kellerman and L. Matusak(Eds.), Cutting Edge: Leadership 2000. College Park, MD: Academy of Leadership Press, 1999.

Note:

This article is a work in progress. This is the first version. Updated publications will be marked as such.

Version: December 2005

Appendix E – A Brief User's Guide to Open Space Technology

Harrison Owen

Figure E.1: The Opening Circle and Marketplace Wall

(NOTE: This is a brief introduction to Open Space. For more information about the depth, details, and nuance of Open Space Technology, see www.invitingleadership.com/book/links/#open-space-technology.)

THE REQUIREMENTS OF OPEN SPACE

Open Space Technology requires very few advance elements. There must be a clear and compelling theme, an interested and committed group, time and a place, and a leader. Detailed advance agendas, plans, and materials are not only un-needed, they are usually counterproductive. This brief User's Guide has proven effective in getting most new leaders and groups off and running.

THE THEME

Creation of a powerful theme statement is critical, for it will be the central mechanism for focusing discussion and inspiring participation. The theme statement, however, cannot be a lengthy, dry, recitation of goals and objectives. It must have the capacity to inspire participation by being specific enough to indicate the direction, while possessing sufficient openness to allow for the imagination of the group to take over.

There is no pat formulation for doing this, for what inspires one group will totally turn off another. One way of thinking about the theme statement is as the opening paragraph of a truly exciting story. The reader should have enough detail to know where the tale is headed and what some of the possible adventures are likely to be. But "telling all" in the beginning will make it quite unlikely that the reader will proceed. After all, who would read a story they already know?

THE GROUP

The group must be interested and committed. Failing that, Open Space Technology will not work. The key ingredients for deep creative learning are real freedom and real responsibility. Freedom allows for exploration and experimentation, while responsibility insures that both will be pursued with rigor. Interest and commitment are the prerequisites for the responsible use of freedom. There is no way that we know of to force people to be interested and committed. That must be a precondition.

One way of insuring both commitment and interest is to make participation in the Open Space event completely voluntary. The people who come should be there because they want to be there. It is also imperative that all participants know what they are getting into before they arrive. Obviously they can't know the details of discussions that have yet to take place. But they can and should be made aware of the general outlines. Open Space is not for everybody, and involuntary, non-informed participation is not only a contradiction in terms, it can become very destructive.

This raises the obvious question of what to do with those people whom you want to involve, but who, for whatever reason, do not share your desire. There are two possibilities. The first is to schedule two sessions, and trust that the first one will be so rewarding that positive word of mouth testimony will draw in the recalcitrant. The alternative is to respect the wishes of those involved. In the final analysis it remains true that genuine learning only takes place on the basis of interest and commitment, and there is absolutely no way to force any of that.

The size of the group is not absolutely critical. However, there does seem to be a lower limit of about 20. Less than 20 participants, and you tend to lose the necessary diversity which brings genuine interchange. At the upward end of the scale, groups of 400 work very well, and there is no reason to believe that number could not be increased.

SPACE

The space required is critical, but need not be elaborate or elegant. Comfort is more important. You will need a room large enough to hold the entire group, with space to spare in which the participants may easily move about. Tables or desks are not only unnecessary, but will probably get in the way. Movable chairs, on the other hand, are essential.

The initial setup is a circle with a large, blank wall somewhere in the room. The wall must be free from windows, doors, drapes, and with a surface that permits taping paper with masking tape. The wall should also be long enough so that the total group may stand before it, and never be more than three to four deep. The center of the circle is empty, for after all we are talking about Open Space.

If the room is very large, additional break-out areas may not be required, but they are always helpful. Best of all is the sort of environment in which there is an abundance of common space. If you are going to use a conference center or hotel, find one with plenty of conversation nooks, lobbies, and open grounds, where people may meet and work undisturbed, and without disturbing others.

TIME

The time required depends on the specificity of result you require. Even a large group can achieve high levels of interaction combined with a real sense of having explored the issues in a matter of eight hours. However, if you want to go deeper than that, reaching firm conclusions and recommendations (as would be the case for strategic planning or product design), the time required may stretch to two or three days.

More important than the length of time is the *integrity* of the time. Open Space Technology will not work if it is interrupted. This means that "drop-ins" should be discouraged. Those who come must be there at the beginning, and stay for the duration if at all possible. By the same token, once the process begins, it cannot be interrupted by other events or presentations. These might come before or afterwards, but never in the middle.

THE BASIC STRUCTURE

Although it is true that an Open Space event has no predetermined agenda, it must have an overall structure or framework. This framework is not intended to tell people what to do and when. Rather, it creates a supportive environment in which the participants can solve those issues for themselves. Minimal elements of this framework include: Opening, Agenda Setting, Open Space, and Conclusion. These elements will suffice for events lasting up to a day. Longer events will require the addition of Morning Announcements, Evening News, and probably a Celebration.

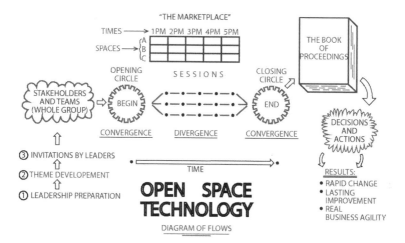

Figure E.2: The Basic Flow of Open Space, from Preparation to Proceedings

A standard Open Space Design, using all these elements appears below. If the event you anticipate lasts longer than the time indicated, simply replicate the middle day. If shorter, you will find that an Opening, Open Space, and Conclusion will suffice. Generally speaking, the minimum time required is five hours, but that is cutting it rather close.

OPENING

We have found that a very informal opening works well, especially if the group involved is an intact work group. An evening meal and a time for catch-up conversation will effectively set the stage. Should the group not have any prior association, the simple device of having all the participants introduce themselves by giving their names and telling a short story from their lives to illustrate who they are will usually do the job. Detailed and involved "icebreaking" exercises do not seem to work very well, and more to the point, set the wrong tone. After all, we want Open Space.

AGENDA SETTING

This is the time for the group to figure out what it wants to do. The details for this procedure are given below.

OPEN SPACE

Is exactly what the words imply, open space and time for the group to do its business. There is literally nothing here at the start.

ANNOUNCEMENTS

A short period every morning for the group to catch up on what it is doing, where, when, and how. Nothing elaborate, no speeches, just the facts, nothing but the facts.

EVENING NEWS

This is usually a time for reflection and occasionally fun. Not to be confused with a formal report-out session, the approach is "What's the story?" -- with participants voluntarily providing the tale.

CELEBRATION

If your Open Space event is like all the ones we have seen, particularly multi-day affairs, by the last night it will time to celebrate, otherwise known as having a party. Even in "serious" undertakings like preparation of the corporate strategic plan, when it is over, it is over, and people will enjoy celebrating that fact. We suggest doing the celebration in the spirit and manner of the rest of the event. All of which means don't plan it in advance. It may be worthwhile to have some taped music if your people are inclined to dance, but other than that you will undoubtedly find that the talent you need is already available in the folks you have. Use it. Skits, songs, humorous reviews of what has happened, will amply fill the evening, and add to the learning experience.

CLOSING

We try to keep the closing simple and serious. Simple in that there are no formal presentations and speeches. But serious, for this is the time for announcing commitments, next steps, and observations about what the event has meant. The closing event is best conducted in a circle with no "head table." Start anywhere, and go around the circle allowing each participant, *who wants to,* the opportunity to say what was of significance and what they propose to do. But do make it clear that nobody has to say anything. In very large groups, hearing from everybody is obviously impossible, but two or three folks may be asked to volunteer.

FORMAL REPORTS

The formal report-out session has apparently become a fixture of conference life. However, we find it to be boring and generally non-productive. There is never enough time for each group to say all they wanted to, and if sufficient time is allocated, the majority of conference participants are uninterested at any given time. As an alternative, we recommend using a simple word processing system, a computer conferencing system, or both.

In a recent conference 200 participants created 65 task force reports (a total of 200 pages) which were available as the participants left the conference. Mechanically, all that is required is a bank of computers (low-powered laptops will do) and a request to each group organizer to enter the results of their deliberations into the system. They can either type it in themselves, or for the "non-typables," a small group of secretaries will do the job. We print out each report as it is entered and hang it on the wall, providing an ongoing, real-time record of the discussions. The obvious advantage here is that participants find out what is happening, as it is happening, rather than waiting until the end when it is too late. Of course, having the proceedings at the end of conference, rather than six months later, is a pleasant and positive surprise.

Figure E.3: The Newsroom, Where the Open Space Proceedings Are Generated

MEALS

You will notice that meals are not listed on the agenda, nor are there any coffee breaks. The reason is quite simple: once the conference starts to operate in small groups, there is usually never a time when something of substance is not going on. And in accord with the Third Principle, it will take place in its own time. All of this creates a small, but not insoluble, problem for such things as meals and coffee-breaks. Our solution has been to have coffee and other refreshments available in the main meeting room, so people partake when they are ready. No need for the whole group to get into lockstep, and stop an important discussion just because it is coffee-break time. Likewise with meals. We suggest buffets, open and available over a several hour period, so people can eat when they want to. There are two exceptions to the flexible meal/coffee-break schedule: an opening dinner if there is one, and dinner on the last night.

The whole point is that the pacing and timing of the conference must be determined by the needs of the group and its learning process, and not by the requirements of the kitchen.

LEADERSHIP

The leadership of an Open Space event is at once absurdly simple and very tricky. The simplicity derives from the fact that the group itself will, and must, generate its own leadership. The tricky part comes in *letting* that happen. The demands placed upon the initial group leader are therefore limited and critical. Dealing with the limited aspects of group leadership is easiest and may therefore be done first. The functions here are to set time, place, and theme. Time and place are simply a question of where and when, both of which have been discussed above. Setting the theme involves creating the written theme statement describing where the group is starting, and where it hopes to go in general terms.

Now we come to the tricky part. Leadership in Open Space requires a style that some may find uncomfortable and counterintuitive. This is especially true for those who equate leadership with control. There is no question that when we know exactly what we are doing, and where we want to go (as is presumably the case, for example, in a manufacturing process), tight controls are essential. In fact, control is the very heart of good management. We get into trouble, however, when we understand leadership simply as advanced management, and therefore, if the manager controls, the leader must control absolutely. Sensitive leaders today, in a world marked by progressively expanding Open Space, know all too well that most of what they have to deal with is beyond their control, and maybe out of control.

Leadership defined as control can only fail. But that is not the only definition. Gandhi described the leader as one who intuits which way the parade is moving, and then races to reach the head of it. The function of leadership is to provide a focal point for direction, and not to mandate and control a minute-by-minute plan of action. The details must be left to the troops, which means amongst other things, the troops must be trusted. In no case can any leader possibly solve all problems or direct all actions. Leadership in Open Space requires that one set the direction, define and honor the space, and let go.

There are Four Principles and One Law which serve as guides to the leader and all participants. The principles are: Whoever comes is the right people. Whatever happens is the only thing that could have. Whenever it starts is the right time. When it is over, it is over.

The first principle reminds everyone of the obvious fact that those present are the only ones there. Whatever gets done will get done with them, or not at all. There is little point, therefore in worrying about all those who should have come, might have come, but didn't come. It is essential to concentrate on those who are there. The experience is that, in some strange way, the group present is always the right group.

In more practical terms, it has been discovered that if the group is deeply involved in the issue at hand and excited by the possibilities, that involvement and excitement are contagious, and others will soon join in. Even if the technical expertise present is not of the highest order, a committed group will find the needed expertise. However, if all the time is spent in telling each other that the group is neither right nor competent, it is always the case that the group will live down to it expectations.

None of this is to suggest that effort should not be made before the gathering to be sure that invitations are extended to critical people. Or indeed that those critical people should not be specially urged to attend. However, when the gathering starts, it is unarguably true: those who came are the ones who came. Whatever gets done will be done by them, or not at all. They will be the right people.

The second principle is yet another statement of the obvious. Given the theme (job) at hand and the people in attendance, whatever happens is the only thing that could have. Change the people, time, place, or theme, and something different will result. It is, of course possible that the result of the gathering could be a miserable failure, but experience shows that such a negative result is usually the product of negative expectations. Expect the worst, and you will very often get it.

Expectations are in fact critical. Be prepared to be surprised -- positively. Those who come to an Open Space event with a precise and detailed list of intended outcomes will be frustrated. More than that, they will inevitably miss the positive and useful things that occur. Never before, and never again will the assembled group gather in that time and place. No one could possibly predict the synergism of effect that will take place when those particular people assemble. Some of what happens will be non-useful. But it is the special function of the leader to raise the expectations of the group, and heighten their sensitivity to the opportunities at hand, whatever they may be.

Here is the most difficult and important point about leadership in Open Space. *The leader must truly trust the group to find its own way.* Attempts on the part of the leader to impose specific outcomes or agenda will totally abort the process. Any person who is not fully prepared to let go of their own detailed agenda should not lead.

The third principle will seem essentially wrong to those whose lives have been dictated by the clock, which is basically all of us. The conventional wisdom says that if you want to get something done, you must start on time. The conventional wisdom is right so long as you know what you are going to do, and how. On the other hand, when creativity, and real learning are involved, the clock can be more of a detriment than an assist. Things will start when they are ready, and whenever they start is the right time. In fact, when the creative learning moment arrives, it seems to create its own time, or put another way, clocks don't seem to matter much anymore. The Open Space environment provides the nutrient setting for creative activity, and those who would lead in that environment must keep their eye on the creative process and forget about the clock. When "it" happens, it will happen in its own time, and scheduling a breakthrough for 10 am is not only an exercise in futility, it is consummately destructive of Open Space.

Open Space Events do, of course, occur in time, which means that there must be a time of beginning and a time for closure. But everything in the middle must be allowed to run its own course.

The final principle, "When it is over, it is over," again states the obvious, but it is a point we may forget. Deep learning and creativity both have their own internal life cycle. They may take more or less time, but when they come to completion, they are over. Occasionally this means that we have to spend more time than we had planned, but more often than not, the reverse is true. The creative moment has a nasty habit of occurring very quickly, and just because the session or meeting was scheduled to take two hours is no reason to sit around and waste time after the moment has passed. When it is over, it is over.

Finally we come to the One Law of Open Space. It is a law only in the sense that all participants must observe it or the process will not work. We call it the Law of Two Feet. Briefly stated, this law says that every individual has two feet, and must be prepared to use them. Responsibility for a successful outcome in any Open Space Event resides with exactly one person -- each participant. Individuals can make a difference and must make a difference. If that is not true in a given situation, they, and they alone, must take responsibility to use their two feet, and move to a new place where they can make a difference. This departure need not be made in anger or hostility, but only after honoring the people involved and the space they occupy. By word or gesture, indicate that you have nothing further to contribute, wish them well, and go and do something useful.

WHEN NOT TO USE OPEN SPACE TECHNOLOGY

As there are individuals who should not lead in Open Space, there are also situations in which Open Space Technology is not appropriate, and in fact may be counter-productive. Open Space Technology is effective when real learning, innovation, and departure from the norm are required. When you aren't quite sure where you are, and less than clear about where you are headed, and require the best thinking and support from all those who wish to be involved, Open Space Technology will provide the means.

On the other hand, if the present state, and future position are crystal clear, along with all the intervening steps, Open Space Technology is not only a waste of time, it will be very frustrating. Using a very mundane example, if the task at hand is the implementation of a known technology, such as a word processing program, or an established office procedure, inviting people to be creative and inventive is quite beside the point. They simply have to learn the skills and methods required. There is no mystery. Just do it.

(NOTE: This is a brief introduction to Open Space. For more information about the depth, details, and nuance of Open Space Technology, see www.invitingleadership.com/book/links/#open-space-technology.)

Appendix F – The Game of Scrum

Overview

Scrum is a teamwork framework that defines three roles, five events, three artifacts, and a few rules that bind these elements together. Recent updates have changed a few of these definitions yet the essentials of Scrum have not changed very much in ten years. Scrum emerged as a solution to the problem of how to develop and ship working software on time. It is also used in many other areas including hardware development, marketing, schools, and more.

This overview is a quick summary of Scrum. It is not intended to be comprehensive.[1] It is designed to orient readers who are new to the framework.

Scrum omits many details. The idea is to not be too prescriptive with people and teams. Instead, Scrum defines essential elements of a social (team) structure that encourages focus, commitment, courage, respect, and openness. These values are associated with greatness in teams and organizations.

Introduction

When developing products, we wish that the customers know what they want, the developers know how to build it, and that nothing changes along the way. In reality, customers discover what they want, the developers learn how to build it, and many things change along the way.

---

[1] For the definitive guide to Scrum, see
www.invitingleadership.com/book/links/#scrumguides.

Scrum is based on empiricism. It is a learning framework. Scrum Teams learn as they do the work and use that learning to improve results. Using feedback to make changes to your assumptions is an example of double-loop learning.

Scrum employs iterations. Iterations are spaces bounded by time during which teams perform work. It is important to recognize this time-bounded container. In Scrum, each iteration is called a *Sprint*. A Sprint is usually two weeks, but it can range from one to four weeks long. At the end of each sprint, the team inspects their results. They will continue to do things that went well. The team discards things that did not go so well, in favor of trying something new that might work better. This process continues, sprint by sprint. Frequent iterations lead to frequent and explicit inspections, which help teams improve. Questioning everything is part of what happens inside teams that do Genuine & Authentic Scrum. This inspect-and-adapt approach encourages dialogue, respect for people, and continuous improvement.

Three great strengths of Scrum are that it has very clear goals, clear structure for rules, and clear way to track progress as a team. Scrum has the potential to make working with others become a very satisfying and enjoyable experience. It is important to notice that Scrum is a game played as a group. The object of the game is to produce great results – as a team.

Three Roles

Scrum has three roles:

- Product Owner (PO)
- Development Team
- Scrum Master (SM)

The Product Owner serves the business. The Product Owner creates a list of features to deliver. This to-do list is called the Product Backlog. The PO prioritizes items in this list by moving items of highest value to the top. The team uses the prioritized Product backlog as a starting point to plan an iteration of work. You may think of the Product Backlog as an announcement of intention for the Product's characteristics. The Product Backlog is a kind of vision statement expressed as a list of features to be developed and built into the Product (or Service, if you are a service organization).

The Development Team serves the Product Owner and each other in pursuit of great results. The Development Team considers the work described in the Product Backlog. The Development Team then selects as many items from the top of the Product Backlog as the Development Team believes it can complete in one Sprint. This forecast is the Sprint Backlog. Then they commit to only work on items that are in the Sprint backlog. Only the Development Team may add items to the Sprint Backlog.

The Scrum Master serves the Team by helping them. The Scrum Master facilitates Team meetings, and reminds everyone about their agreement to follow Scrum rules. (People often need to be reminded about their commitments.) The Scrum Master protects the Development Team from distractions. If they need anything, the Scrum Master goes and gets it. The Scrum Master identifies and removes obstacles that are in between the Development Team and greatness. Finally, *The Scrum Guide* states that the Scrum Master serves the organization by "*Leading and coaching the organization in its Scrum adoption*" and "*helping employees and stakeholders understand and enact Scrum and empirical product development.*"

It is important not to tamper with these three roles. Everyone in the situation needs to find a place as a PO, an SM, or a Development Team member.

Five Events

Scrum contains five events:
- The Sprint
- Sprint Planning
- Daily Scrum
- Sprint Review
- Sprint Retrospective

The Sprint serves as a container for the other four events. The PO is the authority in the Sprint Planning meeting. Sprint Planning is where the PO presents the Product Backlog to the Team. The Team looks at it, and selects as much of the work from the top as it thinks it can complete in one Sprint. If your Sprint length is two weeks, the Team loads the two-week Sprint with work during this selection. Ideally, during this meeting the Product Owner is not hatching anything on the Team, but rather has socialized the contents of the Product Backlog well in advance of the Sprint Planning meeting.

After the Team selects the work, the Sprint begins. They take the work items, carve them up into tasks, and begin doing these tasks.

The Team is the authority in the Daily Scrum. The SM facilitates this meeting. The Daily Scrum is a daily ritual. It is a meeting where the Team meets each day and discusses the work. Each Team member answers three questions: What did you do yesterday that contributed to achieving the sprint goal? What are you doing today? What obstacles are you facing? The Daily Scrum provides a way for everyone to know what everyone else is working on and what issues they are facing.

The Sprint Review has two parts:
- Product Demo
- Stakeholder feedback

The Sprint Review is followed by the:
- Sprint Retrospective

Both of these meetings occur at the end of the Sprint.

The PO is the authority in the Sprint Review. The SM facilitates this meeting. During the Demo portion, the Team displays the work completed. An important aspect of this is the Definition of Done. For each item of work in the Product Backlog, a description is inserted as well as a Definition of Done. This Definition of Done includes the Acceptance Criteria. If the Team completes the work so that the Definition of Done is satisfied, the work is declared Done. (The PO defines the Acceptance Criteria for each work item, and collaborates with the Team to create the Definition of Done.) When things go well, the Team gets to declare victory on the Sprint just passed. When things do not go as planned, we inspect why during the Sprint Retrospective.

The Scrum Team (the Product Owner, Development Team, and Scrum Master) attends the Sprint Retrospective. The Scrum

Team is the authority during this meeting. It is their meeting. This meeting occurs after the Sprint Review.

The SM facilitates this meeting. During this meeting, three questions are considered by everyone attending: What went well? What did not go so well? What do we want to change going forward?

Substantial group learning happens in the Sprint Retrospective.

Three Artifacts

Scrum has three artifacts:

- Product Backlog
- Sprint Backlog
- Increment

The Product Backlog contains the work descriptions, prioritized by business value. The topmost items are the highest priority. These are sized small enough to be digested by the team. The PO populates the Product Backlog with work items and prioritizes them. During Product Backlog Refinement the PO and the Development Team discuss the highest priority items to ensure that they all agree on what functionality the PO is requesting.

The Sprint Backlog is the list of work the team selects from the top of the Product Backlog during the Sprint Planning meeting. These are the items that the Team expects to complete during the Sprint. The team often carves the work items into tasks, and people on the Team sign up to do the tasks.

The Burndown Chart depicts the amount of work remaining in the Sprint Backlog. Although it is not a required element of Scrum, it is a useful way to show the progress the Development team is making toward completing the Sprint Backlog items. The horizontal axis represents time in days. The vertical axis represents work remaining. Each day, the work remaining is plotted at a point on the graph. The Team is responsible for updating this artifact daily and making it visible to anyone that might want to see it.

The Increment is all of the "done" backlog items that were completed in this sprint and all previous sprints.

Some Rules

1. The Product Owner is always a person, never a committee. Others may help the PO but the PO is always a single person. The Team interacts with this person around the work.
2. Only the PO is authorized to prioritize the Product Backlog.
3. The Product Owner and the Scrum Master should not be the same person.
4. Tasks are clearly defined and authorized by role.

The Scrum Guide specifies tasks and responsibilities for each role. As a group you should take the time to identify the nuances of each role and explicitly define the authority and boundaries of each:

Product Owner:

o Express Product Backlog items clearly
o Order the items in the Product Backlog to best achieve goals and missions
o Optimize the value of the work the Development Team performs
o Ensure that the Product Backlog is visible, transparent, and clear to all, and shows what the Scrum Team will work on next
o Ensure the Development Team understands items in the Product Backlog to the level needed
o Cancel a Sprint if the Sprint Goal becomes obsolete
o During Sprint Planning, discuss the objective that the Sprint should achieve and the Product Backlog items that will achieve the Sprint Goal
o Behave in conformance with Scrum rules at all Scrum ceremonies
o Accept or reject the increment based on whether its Acceptance Criteria are met

- o Develop Plans
- o Preside in authority at the Sprint Review
- o Participate in the Sprint Retrospective

Development Team:

- o Refine Product Backlog items to be small enough to finish during a single sprint, and provide the PO with estimates of the effort required to implement the requested functionality
- o Pull work (the ***what***) from the Product Backlog to the Sprint Backlog during Sprint Planning
- o Carve Sprint Backlog items into tasks (the ***how***) during Sprint
- o Execute Daily Scrum meeting per Scrum rules
- o Update the Burndown Chart daily
- o Demo increments at Sprint Review
- o Participate in Sprint Retrospective

Scrum Master:

- o Facilitate Sprint Planning meeting for the PO
- o Facilitate Sprint Review meeting for the PO
- o Facilitate Sprint Retrospective (retro) for the Scrum Team
- o Facilitate Daily Scrum (each day) for the Development Team
- o Protect Development Team from distractions and threats during the Sprint
- o Referee the rules of Scrum (keep the process)
- o Identify and remove impediments for the Development Team
- o Help the entire organization change its interactions with the teams to maximize the value created by the scrum team

Recap

Scrum's elegant set of roles, meetings, documents, and rules allow considerable latitude in how Scrum is implemented. Sprint by Sprint, the Scrum framework encourages the Product Owner, the Scrum Master, and the Development Team to engage in respectful interactions and continuous improvement as the customers discover what they want, the developers learn how to build it, and many things change along the way.

Appendix G – Kanban Introduction

The Kanban Method is defined in the book from David J Anderson entitled *KANBAN: Successful Evolutionary Change for Your Technology Business.* The method is explained further by Mike Burrows in *Kanban from the Inside: Understand the Kanban Method, connect it to what you already know, introduce it with impact.*

This method arranges and displays work items into a visible work flow. It then applies constraints on the introduction of new work to improve quality, predictability and overall throughput. Kanban reduces the variability of results and balances capacity with demand by applying Work in Process (WIP) limits. Kanban provides a way to visualize work flow, and then goes beyond that by applying constraints to greatly improve how the work is understood, managed and improved by the team actually doing it.

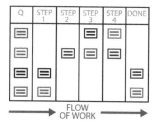

THE KANBAN METHOD

- WORK ITEM TYPES
- WORK IN PROGRESS LIMITS
- CLASSES OF SERVICE
- POLICIES
- CYCLE TIME
- A FOCUS ON FLOW
- INCREMENTAL CHANGE

THE KANBAN BOARD

Figure G.1: Basic Kanban Board

The Kanban Method starts with some basic principles:
- Start with what you do now:
  - There is no need for big upfront planning with Kanban. You can start with what you are doing now.

- Agree to pursue incremental, evolutionary change:
    - The idea here is to get good agreement from everyone on the team that we will change a little at a time, in the direction of improvement of the things we are managing and measuring, such as quality of deliveries, predictability of delivery dates, etc.
- Respect the current process, roles, responsibilities and titles:
    - Kanban does not require anyone to change their role. You simply start using it inside the current authority distribution schema (the hierarchy if that is what you are using).
- Encourage acts of leadership at all levels:
    - The idea here is to create the conditions for leadership to emerge. Kanban assumes the goal is continuous, incremental, and evolutionary change. Kanban encourages everyone to exercise leadership in pursuit of that goal.

Kanban uses these specific terms:

- Work Item Types:
    - Various kinds of work that are represented on a Kanban board. These may include bugs, issues, user stories, tasks, etc. Types may indicate severity, general size, and other attributes. The team must agree on the explicit definition of each type.
- Work in Progress Limits:
    - The maximum number of items that may be in a specific work step at once.
- Classes of Service:
    - Some work items have higher impact and/ or cost of delay, and thus need to be finished before normal work that is currently in progress.

- ○ Items that have higher than normal impact and/or cost of delay may need to be finished before work that is currently on the board. These items require a higher level of service. We represent each class of service as a separate row or "swim lane" on the Kanban board.
- Policies:
  - ○ Policies are the rules for an item entering or leaving a work state.
- Cycle Time:
  - ○ The amount of time that the team spends working on an item. It does not include the time spent waiting to move to the next step in the flow.
- Focus on Flow:
  - ○ Concentrating on completing work instead of having work in progress. In other words, "Stop starting and start finishing."
- Incremental Change
  - ○ Change one part of your process at a time, see how the system changes, and then identify the next most important change to try. Changing too much at once reduces the flow of work.

Kanban also has some core practices:

- Visualize the workflow
  - ○ Depicting work visually on a wall is a powerful way to understand that work as a group. Kanban has this feature.
- Limit Work In Progress (WIP)
  - ○ The flow of work needs to be regulated to increase quality of output and reduce variability overall. Limiting the WIP is the primary way to do this. Instead of allowing work to enter the flow without any qualifications, the Kanban Method applies

a set of rules for adding new work. WIP limits manage flow by managing WIP.

- Manage flow
  - An increase of the flow of quality deliveries is the primary goal of Kanban. By applying rules, Work Item Types, Classes of Service and WIP limits, the flow of work can be effectively managed.
- Make Process Policies Explicit
  - In Kanban, rules for managing flow are made explicit. In this manner "common knowledge" can be created. Creating common knowledge is a primary way of coordinating large groups of people.
- Improve Collaboratively (using models & the scientific method)
  - Desired outcomes are discussed and evidence-based management is utilized to create positive change and improvement in Kanban. The idea is for the whole group to use results-oriented, rational approaches to making changes with intent to improve.

The Kanban Method started as a way to manage the flow of software development work. However, it is extremely flexible and can be used to manage the flow of work in a variety of contexts. This makes Kanban a great business agility tool.[1]

With that flexibility comes great responsibility. Teams that diligently follow Agile fundamentals can be very successful with Kanban. It can be very tempting to adopt Kanban merely because of its low overhead. Teams that do so without Agile discipline and maturity will fail to reap the full benefits of the method.

---

[1] For more information about the Kanban Method, see www.invitingleadership.com/book/links/#kanban.

Appendix H – OpenSpace Agility Introduction

Employee engagement is absolutely essential for creating authentic and lasting organizational change. In 2015 Daniel, Mark, and co-authors published *The OpenSpace Agility Handbook*, defining an Engagement Model for digital and agile transformation for the first time.[1]

OpenSpace Agility (OSA) is a tool that Inviting Leaders can use to initiate and trigger positive change in their organizations. It leverages these well-understood patterns that support rapid and lasting organizational change:

- Iteration, inspection and adaptation
- Invitation
- Ritual and the generation of "Common Knowledge"
- Self-management and self-organization
- Bounded containment and Enabling Constraints
- Psychological Safety

OSA also provides a way to broadcast leadership communications and the emergence of a new and enabling cultural narrative that supports change and higher performance. OSA thus provides a platform and scaffolding for applying leadership semiotics as described in this book. It can be used for introducing agile and digital transformation programs into any level of any organization. You can experiment with OSA at the team level and eventually work your way up to using OSA for total enterprise transformation.

---

[1] For more information about invitational employee Engagement Models, see
www.invitingleadership.com/book/links/#engagement-models.

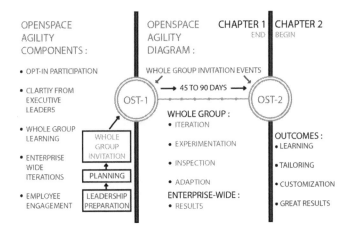

Figure H.1: OpenSpace Agility Overview

OpenSpace Agility (OSA) implements enterprise-wide iterations of improvement that have a clear beginning, middle, and end. It is a safe, pragmatic, and repeatable technique for encouraging and achieving rapid and lasting improvement.

OSA works with what you are currently doing. OSA can be added at any time. OSA is used to actively engage as many employees as possible in your enterprise change program.

For executive leaders, OSA is an Employee Engagement Model and A-B-C template that operationalizes the core values of Lean, namely: *respect for people, and continuous improvement.*

For executives who are truly committed to these values, OSA represents a simple, effective, and very efficient way forward.

With OpenSpace Agility, you can expect:

- A dramatic reduction in the coaching & training costs of implementing your Agile program
- A genuine, rapid and lasting Agile transformation
- A dramatic increase in employee engagement scores
- A dramatic increase in stakeholder satisfaction, and potentially genuine stakeholder delight
- Predictable, reliable, repeatable, *evidence-based* improvement in overall results

Here are some of the key features of OSA:

Invitation: OSA is an invitational approach to evolutionary and incremental enterprise change. No one is compelled to attend the enterprise-wide OSA events.

Open Space: A cycle or "chapter" of learning in OSA is a 45 to 90 day period that begins and ends with an invitational whole-group meeting event called Open Space. These opt-in events can elicit very high levels of employee engagement.

Iteration: The 45-day to 90-day period represents an iteration of whole-group learning. The whole group engages in new ways of working, with intent to inspect the new processes and improve them as the group gains experience.

Experimentation: OSA is a kind of template for implementing safe, pragmatic, inspectable, whole-group iterations of learning and change. The whole group learns to try new things for a reasonable period of time, followed by a careful inspection process when that period of experimentation is over.

Rapid Adaptation: The whole intent of OSA is to help the whole enterprise to learn to adapt. OSA achieves this by defining very clear time boundaries that create a clear story (an iteration) that has a beginning, a middle, and an end. OSA helps the whole organization learn how to adapt so that the next iteration can generate even more progress. Over time this adaptation and learning is cumulative and creates the conditions for authentic, rapid, and lasting improvements.

Authentic and Lasting Results, Enterprise Wide: Organizations that rapidly adapt to changing conditions outperform those that do not. Once an organization learns how to learn, it creates an unbeatable advantage over competitors who do not. OSA enables enterprise-wide organizational learning and real results.

OpenSpace Agility is being used worldwide in organizations of all sizes.[2]

Prime/OS, Open Source Licensing and Culture Technology

OpenSpace Agility (OSA) was formulated from 2010 to 2012 and introduced in 2013 during Daniel's keynote of the Global Scrum Gathering conference event in Paris, France. OSA is published under an 'open source' license, the "CC BY SA 4.0" license from Creative Commons. This license allows derivations to be constructed and even commercialized, provided the author of the derivation provides explicit attribution back to OSA, and also publishes the derived work under the exact same open and free license.

Shortly after OSA was introduced in 2013 in Paris, an organizational development consultant in France named Pablo Pernot contacted us. He explained that he was using the before/after Open Space procedure of OSA, but not for Agile transformation. He was using it to introduce the use of new software across a global multinational enterprise. Pernot used the OSA template and procedure to introduce a completely different kind of change, change that had nothing to do with Agile at all. He said "Daniel, this technique works well for introducing any kind of change in any kind of organization. You must generalize this."

As a result of Pernot's report and his suggestion, we decided to do the following:

---

[2] For more information about OpenSpace Agility, including case studies, see www.invitingleadership.com/book/links/#openspace-agility.

1. We created a "generalized OSA" that describes the before/after Open Space events and the experimental period in between. We did not define the content or focus of the experimental period, leaving that for the end user to define. We called the new and generalized thing "Prime/OS."
2. We published Prime/OS under the CC-BY-SA-40 open source license.
3. We rewrote the OSA licensing so it explicitly derived from the more general Prime/OS.
4. We encouraged others to do the same, and to use Prime/OS as a base or foundation to create specific and new derived works, much like OSA.

In 2018 Silke Hermann and Niels Pflaeging, organizational development consultants from Wiesbaden, Germany, became aware of Prime/OS and became aware of the fact it was published under an open source license. They created a derived work based upon Prime/OS that they call "OpenSpace Beta." It is a set of operating principles for designing, creating, and maintaining an adaptive and responsive organization.[3]

We expect many others will derive from Prime/OS in the same way in the years to come. The iterative nature of Prime/OS with before/after Open Space events provides a robust method and template for introducing organizational change.

Regarding Culture Technology

Prime/OS in general, and OSA in particular, are examples of "culture technology." Culture technology is any set of procedures, meeting designs, or frameworks that encourage a specific kind of intentional and designed culture. In general, we believe culture technology is essential to the progress of not just Organizational Development, but also to the progress and evolution of business,

---

[3] For more information about the details of OpenSpace Beta, see www.invitingleadership.com/book/links/#engagement-models.

communities, societies, and even civilization itself. Because of this stance, we are strong advocates of open source licensing for sociocultural technology designs including meeting designs, frameworks, and governance systems. If and when you design a new piece of culture technology, we encourage you to publish it free, under the open source CC-BY-SA-4.0 (or higher) license. Doing so encourages innovation and progress.

For more information about roles, rules, events, and artifacts of Prime/OS, open source licensing, and culture technology, see www.invitingleadership.com/book/links/#prime-os.

Appendix I – Additional Tools

These additional tools are also very useful:[1]
- The Debate
- Make A Meeting Optional
- The A1 Meeting
- Lean Coffee (also known as "Agile Coffee")
- The Core Commitments
- Leadership Scrum™
- OpenSpace Beta

The Debate
- A meeting format that invites participation in the debate of an item, issue or concern. This is a very versatile tool that can be used with leadership teams or product teams in either a public or private context
- Use for dialogue leading to group-level understanding of the issues and eventual alignment on plans

Make A Meeting Optional
- An invitational technique we developed for gaining direct experience in the dynamics of Invitation-Based Change and Inviting Leadership
- Used for dialogue and deciding

The A1 Meeting
- An invitational meeting we developed that focuses on socializing the core idea, related constraints, and rules of an organizational

---

[1] For more information about these tools, see www.invitingleadership.com/book/links/#tools.

change that is focused on agile change and business agility

- A meeting design used for dialogue
- Can be generalized to begin socializing any kind of change, starting with the leadership group

Lean Coffee (also known as "Agile Coffee")

- A meeting format that is versatile and applicable to a wide range of small-group scenarios. Lean Coffee is an invitational meeting format that is both a subset and a superset of Open Space Technology and is appropriate for smaller groups from about 2 to about 20 people
- Useful for dialogue and ideation, and also for the making of decisions

The Core Commitments

- Eleven specific invitation-based rules for interactions that are commitments to specific norms that support higher performance developed by Michele & Jim McCarthy
- A set of rules and norms used for generating dialogue and decisions

Leadership Scrum™

- A version of Scrum customized and tailored for improving the results of leadership teams and leadership teamwork
- A framework containing several supporting meeting events, used for discussing and making leadership decisions

OpenSpace Beta

- An Engagement Model similar to OpenSpace Agility and based on Prime/OS²
- Introduces a set of 12 principles for building a responsive and adaptive organization

---

² For more information about Prime/OS, see www.invitingleadership.com/book/links/#prime-os.

Glossary

Acceptance Criteria *n.*
> In agile software development, these are the characteristics that must be present for a work item to provide the desired business value. See also: Definition of Done.

adjacent possible *n.*
> The frontier or growing edge of what is possible after an action is taken. The adjacent possible is a term originating with Stuart Kauffman of the Santa Fe Institute.

agile software development *n.*
> Using a set of values, principles, and practices that support the Agile Manifesto and that allow software development teams to adapt to change and realize business value quickly. See also: www.invitingleadership.com/book/links/#agile.

agreement *n.*
> A binding of commitments and understanding between two agents in a social system.

authority *n.*
> 1. The right or permission to do a specific kind of work.
> 2. Status within a social system that confers one's right to do work. See also: power, right to do work.

authority distribution schema *n.*
> The map of authority and authorization relationships in a social system. Dimensions include formal/informal and networked/hierarchical.

authority engineering *n.*
> 1. An emerging discipline in the social sciences.
> 2. The act of designing and applying an authority distribution schema in a social system.

authority helping *n.*
> An authority orientation whose tendency is to identify who

has authority to lead, and then to help that individual. See also: Group Relations, valence.

authority map *n.*

A radar graph or "spider graph" diagram which depicts all of the authorized tasks for a role and the percent of coverage of that task for a specific individual occupying that role. See also: authorized task.

authority opposing *n.*

An authority orientation whose tendency is to identify who has authority to lead and then to oppose that individual. See also: Group Relations, valence.

authority seeking *n.*

An authority orientation whose tendency is to seek authority to lead and/or make decisions for the group. See also: Group Relations, valence.

authority studies *n.*

An emerging and interdisciplinary field of social science that investigates social systems primarily through studying the properties, methods, events, and other aspects of authority and authority distribution.

authority thinking *n.*

A pattern of thinking about social situations in terms of who is authorizing whom to do what and how the authorization is occurring. See also: authority studies, authority engineering.

authority valence *n.*

One's tendency regarding seeking, supporting, or opposing authority and authorization. See also: Group Relations.

authorization *n.*

The process of sending and receiving authority.

authorized task *n.*

A specific kind of work that a person has a right or permission to perform. Making decisions is one such kind of work.

BIAS *n.*

Boundary, Invitation, Authority, and Self-Management.

Inviting Leaders have a positive BIAS toward action and real, lasting change.

big data *n.*

Information that is gathered from a large percentage of sources and is analyzed to reveal patterns of human behavior.

biosemiotics *n.*

The study of signaling in living physical systems, especially at the cellular level.

bottom-up authorization *n.*

The flow of formal authority from senders who have less formal authority than the receivers. See also: top-down authorization.

boundary management *n.*

Ensuring that boundaries are clearly understood and agreed to, and that they are not being violated.

boundary violation *n.*

Any action that crosses a boundary or allows a boundary to be crossed without proper formal or informal authorization.

business agility *n.*

The capacity of a goal-seeking (business) organization to rapidly sense and respond to change, in service to continuous improvement in the delivery of genuine value as defined by paying customers.

C2 Journal *n.*

A publication of the Dept of Defense Command and Control Research Project which focuses on maximizing the effectiveness of the US military through the application of requisite agility in military structures, processes, and operations. See also: requisite agility.

Clean Language *n.*

An interviewing technique using a set of simple questions that reflect the interviewee's own words without introducing any content or judgment by the interviewer. Clean Language was developed by psychotherapist David Grove and applied to groups by Caitlin Walker. See also: www. invitingleadership.com/book/links/#clean-language.

closed space *n.*

A social situation that disrespects the freedom of participants to express what they want, think, and feel. Everyone in closed space is aware that certain topics of high interest to the members are not open to discussion. See also: open space.

commander's intent *n.*

A succinct description of what constitutes success for the operation. It includes the operation's purpose, key tasks, and the conditions that define the end state. It links the mission, concept of operations, and tasks to subordinate units. See also: Definition of Done, www.invitingleadership.com/book/links/#commanders-intent.

communitas *n.*

The "spirit of community" including membership and the sense of belonging.

complex adaptive system *n.*

A system of individual agents formed in order to adapt to the changing environment and increase survivability.

consent *n.*

Willing acceptance of an invitation or request based on one's understanding of what is being offered or asked.

credibility *n.*

Evidence that one is worthy of being recognized as an authority. See also: authority.

culture design *n.*

A discipline whose plans and activities result in a desired cultural state. Also known as social system design.

culture engineer *n.*

One who uses social system design to improve the culture of a group. See also: social system designer.

culture engineering *n.*

See also: social system design.

culture hacking *n.*

Using one's informal and formal authority to alter and improve the culture of the group.

culture technology *n.*

A direct application of culture design that includes events

and procedures for influencing organizational culture. Events include highly specialized processes for large and small meetings. Procedures include interaction protocols, work procedures, and frameworks. Designed frameworks such as Scrum and Kanban are cultural compositions of roles, rules, protocols, and meetings.

de-authorization *n.*

The withholding or withdrawing of the right to do work.

decision frequency *n.*

In self-managed, team-sourced decision-making, decision frequency is a measurement of the average period of time between decisions. In general, the higher the decision frequency the higher the probable levels of employee engagement. See also: self-management, requisite decision frequency.

decision impact (magnitude, or amplitude) *n.*

In self-managed, team-sourced decision-making, the impact is the level of change that the decision creates beyond the team, creating change for related teams and potentially the organization as a whole. In general, the higher the decision impact, the higher the probable levels of employee engagement. See also: self-management.

Definition of Done *n.*

In agile software development generally, the Definition of Done includes all the conditions of satisfaction and the defined end-state of a successful delivery of product. See also: Acceptance Criteria, commander's intent.

delegation *v.*

The formal assignment of responsibility and/or authority to someone in a lower-authority role.

Designing the Future

A significant essay on social system design by Jay Forrester, the originator of system dynamics modeling. See also www.invitingleadership.com/book/links/#system-dynamics.

devops *n.*

A combination of development and operations, leveraging

highly efficient systems and software to validate the quality of and then deploy production-grade software systems.

drafting *n.*

The act of nominating someone to occupy a role. May be expressed or implied. Pertains generally to informally authorized roles. See also: informal authorization.

dynamic authorization *n.*

The sending and receiving of authority in real time (the "here and now"). See also emergent leader.

ecotone *n.*

A narrow or wide, local or regional transition area between two communities where members of those communities meet and integrate. The boundary between the two communities may be blurred and fuzzy, containing some members from both communities or it might begin at a distinct, sharp boundary.

emergent leader *n.*

A member of a group who suddenly receives informal authority and the potential to exercise it inside the group.

emergent leadership *n.*

Informal authorization that arises as a person takes initiative and leads something they are passionate about. Informal authorization arises from colleagues, peers, and communities over time as the informal leader develops engagement, progress, accountability, and authorization within the organization.

empowerment *n.*

An imprecise term commonly used to describe the sending of formal or informal authority.

enabling constraints *n.*

Rules, regulations, or limits that bring order while allowing emergence and implementation of new ideas. These constraints provide clarity and allow for creative variation. For example, when top executives set direction and explain "why," they enable product leadership to determine "what." When product leadership determines "what" they enable teams to determine "how." For more information, see www. invitingleadership.com/book/links/#enabling-constraints.

engaged employees *n.*

Employees who are involved in, enthusiastic about, and committed to their work and workplace. (Source: The Gallup Organization.)

engagement model *n.*

Any pattern or set of patterns, reducible to practice, which result in more employee engagement, especially during the implementation of an organizational-change initiative.

experience design *n.*

The design of events, products, or environments with an emphasis on improving the participant or user's experience. See also: meeting design.

extraorganizational ecotone *n.*

A region of transition between two adjacent organizations that may or may not be cooperating or competing.

formal authorization *n.*

Authorization that is conferred from the formal organization to someone in a role defined and duly authorized by that organization.

FGS *n.*

Four-part game structure: clearly described goals, rules, progress tracking, and opt-in participation.

game *n.*

Any activity with goals, rules, a way to track progress, and opt-in participation. Game types include mutable, immutable, finite, and infinite.

game design *n.*

The discipline and act of creating a game. See also: social system design, experience design.

Group Relations *n.*

A worldwide community of practice focused on the study of leadership, authority, and unconscious processes in groups. This body of knowledge originated with the work of Wilfred Bion and was subsequently developed further and refined by the Tavistock Institute and other communities of practice.

holding space *n.*
The act of maintaining openness in a social situation such that the participants are free to express what they want, think, and feel.

hosting *n.*
The act of creating a social and/or physical space whose primary feature is the invitational nature of participation.

illegitimate authority *n.*
Authority that is exercised without having broad informal support from the group as a whole.

illocutionary acts *n.*
Spoken communications that are characterized as assertions, directives, commissives, expressives, or declarations. See also: speech acts.

inattentional blindness *n.*
A psychological lack of awareness due to focusing one's attention elsewhere. The concept is illustrated by the "invisible gorilla" research by Christopher Chabris and Daniel Simons. See www.invitingleadership.com/book/links/#IB.

inauthentic authority *n.*
Authority that is asserted or expressed without having broad informal support from the group as a whole. See also: illegitimate authority.

influence *n.*
One's ability to affect the decision-making of another without having formal authority over that person. See also: informal authority.

influentials *n.*
People who have received informal authority to exercise authority within the group. See also: informally authorized leaders.

informal authority *n.*
Authority that emerges from the group as a whole based on relationships and interactions with people in the organization, without respect to the formal hierarchy.

informal authorization *n.*

Receiving authority from peers and colleagues rather than formally from the organization.

informal de-authorization *n.*

De-authorization of an individual currently occupying an informally authorized role. See also: de-authorization.

intraorganizational ecotone *n.*

A region of transition between two communities inside an organization.

invitation *n.*

1. The act of offering someone the opportunity to go somewhere or do something.

2. A written or verbal offer for someone to go somewhere or to do something.

3. A situation or action that tempts someone to do something or that makes a particular outcome likely.

Note: A genuine invitation may be declined without any sanctions or other implied or expressed negative consequences.

invitation engineering *n.*

The process of creating a well-formed invitation. See also: well-formed invitation.

Invitation-Based Change™ *n.*

A change in policies, procedures, or plans in which participation is not entirely mandatory and may in fact be completely optional.

Inviting Leadership *n.*

1. A style of leadership that a) intentionally designs group experiences focused on tasks and decisions that affect the whole group, and then b) invites participation by the members of the group who are affected by the completion of the task or decision.

2. The leadership act of requesting participation in developing or making decisions that affect all of the members of a group.

inviting leadership *v.*

The act of exercising authority by issuing genuine invitations

to others to influence and/or make decisions that affect the
group as a whole.

leadership *n.*

1. Direct participation in making any decision that affects all
of the members of a group.

2. An individual or set of individuals who participate directly
in making any decision that affects all of the members of a
group.

3. Exercising authority with respect to making decisions that
affect all of the members of a group.

leadership invitation *n.*

An invitation issued by a formally authorized leader of the
organization. It's not necessarily an invitation to lead in any
way (although it could be).

leadership linguistics *n.*

The study of speech acts and illocutionary acts within the
context of exercising leadership and authority. See also:
illocutionary acts.

leadership semiotics *n.*

The study of the signs, signals and symbols used by leaders to
more effectively communicate, motivate, and lead.

leadership signaling *n.*

Written, verbal, and non-verbal communication that is
sent by leaders and received by others who interpret it
as guidance. See also www.invitingleadership.com/book/
links/#leadership-signaling.

leadership storytelling *n.*

A deliberate kind of signaling in which a formal authority
expresses a narrative intended to reduce anxieties, worries,
and liminality within the organization.

legitimate authority *n.*

Formal or informal authority that has broad informal support
from the group as a whole.

malicious compliance *n.*

Intentionally inflicting harm by strictly following the orders
of a superior, knowing that compliance with the orders will
not have the intended result. The term usually implies the

following of an order in such a way that ignores the order's intent but follows its letter. (Source: Wikipedia)

manipulate *v.*

To control or influence (a person or situation) cleverly, unfairly, or unscrupulously.

meeting design *n.*

The discipline and act of crafting a meeting or event as a good game with clear goals, rules, a way to track progress, and opt-in participation. See also: experience design, FGS.

micro-authorization *n.*

The passing of a small amount of authority from invitation sender to invitation receiver, especially when the sender is the formally authorized leader to whom the sender must report. This authority is permission from the sender to the receiver, who is expected to act on the invitation according to the personal preferences of the receiver. This includes the timing and content of the response (accepting or declining the invitation).

microcommunity *n.*

The small society that is created by a team and their stakeholders when both groups agree on purpose, goals, and aims.

microculture *n.*

The small culture created whenever a meeting takes place. Every well-designed meeting is a game with clear goals, rules, feedback/progress tracking mechanisms, and opt-in participation. Poorly designed meetings are poorly designed games and result in weak microculture.

microtransaction *n.*

The exchange of small units of authority between individuals. These transactions are achieved through written, verbal, and nonverbal communications of offers, requests, and invitations. See also: micro-authorization.

Open Space *n.*

A meeting format originally formulated by Harrison Owen as described in his book *Open Space Technology: A User's Guide*.

open space *n.*

A social situation that respects the freedom of participants to express what they want, think, and feel. Everyone in open space is aware that all topics of high interest to the members are open to discussion. See also: closed space.

Open Space Technology *n.*

A synonym for Open Space, often abbreviated as "OST."

organizational structure *n.*

An imprecise term for "authority distribution schema." Such schemas include hierarchies and networks which may be formal or informal.

overstep *v.*

To exceed the authority contained in a given role or defined by a boundary. Overstepping includes breaching the boundary around one's own authority from the inside out. It also includes breaching another person's authority from the outside in. See also: boundary violation, under-step.

passion *n.*

Enthusiasm expressed as an emotion and manifested in thoughts, words, and actions.

permission *n.*

An imprecise term commonly used as a synonym for formal or informal authority.

personal authority *n.*

The way a person in a formally authorized role takes up that role. See also: formal authorization.

persuade *v.*

1. To cause someone to do something, through reasoning or argument.

2. To cause someone to believe something, especially after a sustained effort; to convince.

3. To provide a sound reason for someone to do something.

plenipotentiary *n.*

A role with "full powers" (from the Latin plenus "full" and potens "powerful").

plenipotentiary adj.

Something that conveys full powers.

power *n.*

The exercise of authority.

requisite agility *n.*

A level of Agility that balances the costs of attaining it with the consequences of not having it, given the situation. See also: www.invitingleadership.com/book/links/#requisite-agility.

requisite authorization *n.*

The level of authority needed to complete a delegation of responsibility to complete a task.

requisite decision frequency *n.*

The average decision frequency that maximizes support for the highest levels of employee engagement.

responsibility *n.*

Accountability for intended and unintended outcomes, results, and consequences.

right to do work *n.*

A definition of authority that originated in the Group Relations (Tavistock) community. One important kind of work is influencing and making decisions that affect the group as a whole. See also: leadership.

self-authorization *n.*

The act of sending authority to yourself instead of receiving it from elsewhere. See also: authorization.

self-management *n.*

Taking responsibility for decisions that affect oneself and others. Self-management can be applied at the individual, team, and enterprise levels. A self-managed team makes most of the decisions that affect the work of that team as a whole.

self-organization *n.*

A process by which order arises in a social organization as a result of interactions between members of the group without being initiated or managed by a formal authority.

semiotics *n.*

The study of signals, symbols, and signs. See also: leadership signaling, biosemiotics.

servant leadership *n.*

A philosophy and set of non-authoritarian leadership practices that attends to the needs of others and helps those people reach their potential. It enriches the lives of individuals, builds better organizations, and ultimately creates a more just and caring world. See also: www. invitingleadership.com/book/links/#servant-leadership.

social neuroscience *n.*

The neuroscience of social behavior, especially in humans.

social system *n.*

A complex adaptive system that describes interrelationships of individuals and groups of people that includes goals, rules, values, principles, and norms, all of which form what is in fact a game, or collection of games.

social system design *n.*

An emerging discipline of the social sciences which applies system dynamics for determining policies in social systems. Components include authority distribution schemas and systems that serve the stated goals and objectives of the people who lead and participate in them. The term was first introduced by Jay Forrester in the "Designing the Future" speech he delivered in Sevilla, Spain in 1998. See www. invitingleadership.com/book/links/#social-system-design.

social system designer *n.*

A culture engineer who applies system dynamics to improve the structure of an organization or other social institution. See also: culture engineer.

speech acts *n.*

Spoken communications that are considered actions in relation to purpose, effect, or intention. See also: leadership linguistics.

stigmergy *n.*

An indirect coordination mechanism between independent agents in a biological or social system such as a mound of termites, a hive of bees, or a group of humans. Stigmergy relies on the unilateral broadcasting of signals by agents that do not require replies from the agents that receive the signal.

structure *n.*

An imprecise term for "authority distribution schema." Such schemas include hierarchies and networks which may be formal or informal. See also: authority distribution schema.

structurelessness *n.*

The absence of any formal and/or explicitly agreed-upon description of how authority is distributed in a group. See also: Tyranny of Structurelessness.

Tavistock Institute *n.*

An organization based in England that is dedicated to the application of social science to contemporary issues and problems. See also: Group Relations, www.invitingleadership. com/book/links/#group-relations.

Theory of Constraints *n.*

A theory of management that is focused on increasing the flow of value by first identifying the largest impediment or clog in the flow of value, removing it, and repeating this process. The Theory of Constraints when applied to organizational change will often identify the way decisions get made as the primary and largest impediment to the flow of value in a value stream. See also: value stream.

TINO *n.*

Transformation in name only.

top-down authorization *n.*

The flow of formal authority from senders who have more formal authority than the receivers. See also: bottom-up authorization.

Tyranny of Structurelessness

An essay about power relations that defined the term "structurelessness," written by feminist Jo Freeman. According to the article, tyranny arises when the actual structure of an organization is not made explicit. Reference link: www.invitingleadership.com/book/links/#the-tyranny-of-structurelessness

unambiguous yes *n.*

Solid agreement demonstrated by words and behavior.

under-step *v.*

To exercise less authority than is allowed by a given role or boundary. Under-stepping allows unauthorized people to breach the boundary around one's own role from the outside in. See also: boundary violation, overstep.

valence *n.*

A person's basic tendency about responding to authority. It is an innate and natural part of your personality. There are three types of authority valence: authority seeking, authority helping, and authority opposing.

value stream *n.*

The series of steps, activities, and decisions made to build and deliver a product or service to a paying customer.

well-formed invitation *n.*

An offer to go somewhere or do something that clearly expresses the goals, the limits, and the progress-tracking mechanisms of the genuinely invited activity. Goals, limits, and tracking mechanisms may be defined at the individual and/or group level. See also: invitation, FGS.

willingness *n.*

That aspect of a person's current state that allows them to agree, say yes to an invitation, or otherwise go somewhere or do something.

willingness test *n.*

An experiment that is designed to determine someone's readiness to go somewhere or do something. See also: invitation.

Bibliography

Alberts, D. S. "Agility, Focus, and Convergence: The Future of Command and Control." *The International C2 Journal*. Volume 1, Number 1, 2007, pp. 1-30. [Print].

Alberts, B., Johnson, A. D., Lewis, J., Morgan, D., Raff, M., Roberts, K., Walter, P. Molecular Biology of the Cell (Sixth Edition). W. W. Norton & Company. [Print].

Anderson, D. J. (2010). Kanban: Successful Evolutionary Change for Your Technology Business. Blue Hole Press. [Print].

Austin, J. L. (1970). How to Do Things with Words: Second Edition (The William James Lectures). USA: Harvard University Press. [Print].

Bion, W. R. (1991). Experiences in Groups: and Other Papers. Routledge. [Print].

Block, P. (2018). Community: The Structure of Belonging. (2nd ed.). Berrett-Koehler Publishers. [Print].

Bogost, I. (2010). Persuasive Games: The Expressive Power of Videogames. USA: The MIT Press. [Print].

Bogost, I. (2016). Play Anything: The Pleasure of Limits, the Uses of Boredom, and the Secret of Games. Basic Books. [Print].

Burgess, M. (2015). Thinking in Promises: Designing Systems for Cooperation. USA. O'Reilly Media, Inc. [Print].

Burrows, M. (2018). Agendashift: Outcome-oriented change and continuous transformation. New Generation Publishing. [Print].

Burrows, M. (2014). Kanban from the Inside: Understand the Kanban Method, connect it to what you already know, introduce it with impact. USA: Blue Hole Press. [Print].

Chwe, M. (2013). Rational Ritual: Culture, Coordination, and Common Knowledge. USA: Princeton University Press. [Print].

Coplien, J.O., Harrison, N. B. (2004). Organizational Patterns of Agile Software Development. Prentice Hall. [Print].

Elias, G. S., Garfield, R., Gutschera, K. R., Whitley, P. (2012). Characteristics of Games. USA: The MIT Press. [Print].

Flores, F. (2013). Conversations For Action and Collected Essays: Instilling a Culture of Commitment in Working Relationships. CreateSpace Independent Publishing Platform. [Print].

Freeman, J. "The Tyranny of Structurelessness." *The Second Wave*, Volume 2, Number 1, 1972. Also *Berkeley Journal of Sociology*, Volume 17, 1972-73, pp. 151-165, and *Ms. magazine*, July 1973, pp. 76-78, 86-89. [Print].

Gharajedaghi, J (2011). Systems Thinking: Managing Chaos and Complexity: A Platform for Designing Business Architecture (3rd ed.). Morgan Kaufmann. [Print].

Green, Z. G. and Molenkamp, R. (2005). The BART System of Group and Organizational Analysis: Boundary, Authority, Role and Task. Available at: www.invitingleadership.com/book/links/#BART. [Online].

Greenleaf, R. K. (1977). Servant Leadership: A Journey into the Nature of Legitimate Power and Greatness. Paulist Press. [Print].

Hermann, S., Pflaeging, N. (2018). OpenSpace Beta: A handbook for organizational transformation in just 90 days. Wiesbaden: BetaCodex Publishing. [Print].

Holliday, M. (2016). The Age of Thrivability: Vital Perspectives and Practices for a Better World. Cambium. [Print].

Kirkpatrick, D. (2017). Beyond Empowerment: The Age of the Self-Managed Organization. JETLAUNCH. [Print].

Kleiner, A. (2003). Who Really Matters: The Core Group Theory of Power, Privilege, and Success. Currency/Doubleday. [Print].

Kline, P., Saunders, B. (1998). Ten Steps to a Learning Organization. (2nd ed.). Arlington, VA: Great Ocean. [Print].

Maassen. O., Matts, C. , Geary, C. (2016). Commitment: Novel about Managing Project Risk. Hathaway te Brake Publications. [Print].

May, M. E. (2009). In Pursuit of Elegance: Why the Best Ideas Have Something Missing. New York: Broadway. [Print].

McGonigal, J. (2011). Reality Is Broken: Why Games Make Us Better and How They Can Change the World. New York: Penguin. [Print].

McKergow, M., Bailey, H. (2014). Host. Solutions Books. [Print].

Mezick, D. (2012). The Culture Game: Tool for the Agile Manager. USA. Freestanding Press. [Print].

Mezick, D., Pnotes, D., Shinsato, H., Kold-Taylor, L., Sheffield, M. (2015). The OpenSpace Agility Handbook (2nd ed.). USA. Freestanding Press. [Print].

Moffat, S. R., Atkinson, J. (2005). The Agile Organization: From Informal Networks to Complex Effects and Agility (Information Age Transformation). CCRB. [Print].

Moore, G. (2015). Zone to Win: Organizing to Compete in an Age of Disruption. Diversion Books. [Print].

Neal, C, Neal, P. (2011). The Art of Convening: Authentic Engagement in Meetings, Gatherings, and Conversations. Berrett-Koehler Publishers. [Print].

Owen, H. (1985). Spirit: Transformation and Development in Organizations. Potomac, MD: Abbott Publishing. [Print]. (free PDF available via www.invitingleadership.com/book/links/#spiritbook.)

Owen, H. (2000). The Power of Spirit: How Organizations Transform. San Francisco: Berrett-Koehler. [Print].

Owen, H. (1999). The Spirit of Leadership: Liberating the Leader in Each of Us. San Francisco, CA: Berrett-Koehler. [Print].

Owen, H. (2008). Wave Rider: Leadership for High Performance in a Self-organizing World. San Francisco: Berrett-Koehler. [Print].

Purser, R. E., Cabana, S. (1998) The Self-Managing Organization : How Leading Companies Are Transforming the Work of Teams for Real Impact. Free Press. [Print].

Schwaber, K., Sutherland, J. (2012) Software in 30 Days: How Agile Managers Beat the Odds, Delight Their Customers, and Leave Competitors in the Dust. Wiley. [Print].

Schwaber, K. and Sutherland, J. (2017). The Scrum Guide™ - The Definitive Guide to Scrum: The Rules of the Game. Available at www.invitingleadership.com/book/links/#scrumguides.

Surowiecki, J. (2005). The Wisdom of Crowds. Anchor. [Print].

Thomas, D., Brown, J. S. (2011). A New Culture of Learning: Cultivating the Imagination for a World of Constant Change. CreateSpace Independent Publishing Platform. [Print].

Trevisani, D. (2016). Semiotics for Leaders: The Exa-Leadership Model for Leadership and Human Potential Development. Medialab Research. [Print].

Turner, V., (2001). From Ritual to Theatre: The Human Seriousness of Play, PAJ Publications. [Print].

Walker, C. (2014). From Contempt to Curiosity: Creating the Conditions for Groups to Collaborate Using Clean Language and Systemic Modelling. Great Britain. Clean Publishing. [Print].

Weisbord, M. R. (2012). Productive Workplaces: Dignity, Meaning, and Community in the 21st Century (3rd ed.). Pfeiffer. [Print].

Index

43142186R10214

Made in the USA
Middletown, DE
24 April 2019